W9-BZW-328

BROTHER TARIQ
THE DOUBLESPEAK OF TARIQ RAMADAN

Brother Tariq

The Doublespeak of Tariq Ramadan

CAROLINE FOUREST

Translated into English by
Ioana Wieder and John Atherton

ENCOUNTER BOOKS
New York and London

First edition published in 2007 by Encounter Books, an activity of Encounter for Culture and Education, Inc., a nonprofit, tax exempt corporation.

Encounter Books website address: www.encounterbooks.com

Manufactured in the United States and printed on acid-free paper.

∞ The paper used in this publication meets the minimum requirements of ANSI/NISO Z39.48-1992 (R 1997)(*Permanence of Paper*).

FIRST EDITION

Library of Congress Cataloging-in-Publication Data

Fourest, Caroline.
[Frère Tariq. English]
Brother Tariq : the doublespeak of Tariq Ramadan / Caroline Fourest ; English translation, Ioana Wieder and John Atherton.
p. cm.
Includes bibliographical references and index.
ISBN-13: 978-1-59403-215-8 (hardcover : alk. paper)
ISBN-10: 1-59403-215-7 (hardcover : alk. paper)
1. Ramadan, Tariq. 2. Scholars, Muslim—Switzerland--Biography. 3. Theologians, Muslim—Switzerland—Biography. 4. Islam—20th century. I. Title.
BP80.R343F6813 2008
297.2092—dc22

2007044867

Contents

Foreword

Tariq Ramadan is a global phenomenon, speaking and writing as he does with such great fluency in French, Arabic, and English. Not for centuries has Switzerland had a native son who enjoyed such fame and impact as a communicator. In Europe, he is the most quoted and circulated writer on his religion, Islam, and on the issues related to the Muslim community in Europe and further afield.

Despite being an author with several books to his name, and a regular contributor to the opinion pages of the world's newspapers, it is at rallies in France, or at Muslim gatherings in Africa, the Middle East, and elsewhere that Tariq Ramadan makes many of the telling interventions that reveal his thinking and his ambitions. Most are recorded, to be played later to a wider audience, as guidance or as religious-political talks. Caroline Fourest has done us a great service by listening to, transcribing, and translating Ramadan's words, since the picture on offer to those who only read his books or columns in English, or who only hear him speak at conferences in Britain, is necessarily limited. Ramadan grew up in a Francophone culture and spoke Arabic from birth. His profile is very different in France and in Switzerland, and for anyone who seeks to understand him, this biography is essential reading.

In spite of having been born in Switzerland and educated in the French-speaking part of that country (the question of his higher academic qualifications and the reasons that led him to quit his job as a schoolteacher make interesting reading), Ramadan stresses his family background as the grandson of the founder of the Muslim Brotherhood and as the son of the main propagator and propagandist of Muslim Brotherhood ideas beyond Egypt after 1950.

For most of the twentieth century, the different currents of religious politics in the Muslim world were little known beyond a narrow circle of specialists in Europe's universities and research institutes. The politics of the Arab world, particularly in the second half of the last century, saw a confusing mixture of regimes—some cast in a nationalist, socialist, fascistic, or authoritarian European mold, others based on absolute monarchies blessed with unlimited oil wealth.

The interstices of ideology and religious belief are difficult to trace. The abolition of the Caliphate and the rise of a proto-modern state, Turkey, with its largely Muslim population, further complicate the picture—as indeed do the quarrels between different branches of Islam, notably the Sunni–Shia conflict.

A further twist of the kaleidoscope of political and religious identity in the Arab world came from the issue of the Jewish right to create a state called Israel in a part of the world that Jews had inhabited continuously for much longer than Christians or Muslims had lived in lands that they claimed as their own. Add to this the various struggles for national identity, as French and British colonialisms were dismantled . . .

The great movements of people and ideas over the past half century have resulted in the development of major Muslim communities in Europe: in Britain, with links to Pakistan, India, and Bangladesh; in France, with links to the Mahgreb; and in Germany, with links to Turkey. The Islam of these new communities has varied, but, as there turned out to be no easy solution to the problems of social equality, acceptance in political and civil society, or economic opportunity, the issue of religion/ideology and identity became more pressing.

The development of Muslim communities in Europe coincided with the last quarter of the twentieth century, when it seemed that the best values of Europe—those associated with the Renaissance and the rationality of Galileo, with the Enlightenment appeal of Voltaire to drive out superstition, with the welcome liberation of women and gays, and with freedom of expression—were starting to gain the upper hand over conservative religiosity and the dominance of women by men. Under the umbrella of the European Union, nations turned their backs on conflict, decided that disputes should be resolved by secular and democratic rule of law, and that the right of people to speak, travel, and live their sexuality free from religious constraints should be upheld.

I first came across Tariq Ramadan when I was working in Geneva before my election to the House of Commons in 1994. It was the early 1990s, and he was involved in an attempt by Muslim activists in Geneva to stop the production of a play by Voltaire. It is certainly true that Voltaire managed to insult all religions, and he was odious about Christians, Jews, and Muslims alike. But he is also commonly held to have coined the immortal phrase about disagreeing with what a person has to say but defending that person's right to say it—a concept that makes the difference between life worth living and life lived under the orders of authority from on high.

John Stuart Mill described "the necessity to the mental well-being of mankind (on which all their other well-being depends) of freedom of opinion, and freedom of the expression of opinion." I was deeply disturbed when the city of Geneva (near which Voltaire lived, so that he could, if necessary, escape the heavy hand of the religious and absolutist *ancien régime* of eighteenth-century France) refused to support freedom of expression, and instead allowed religious ideology to impose censorship. Ramadan argued that it was a question of decency, or good manners, not to insult Muslim identity by staging the Voltaire play. Mill also deals with this objection in his famous essay on freedom of thought and discussion, pointing out the "impossibility of fixing" where the "bounds of fair discussion" should be placed. To place religious belief beyond the bounds of polemic and intellectual assault is to deny all of Europe's heritage and values.

I was further shocked a decade later, when Ramadan identified as "Jews" those left-wing writers and intellectuals in France who took positions different from his own on international politics. For many on the Left—and for most in the democratic socialist parties of France and Switzerland—Ramadan's remarks about Jews were unacceptable, and he lost much of the audience he had had in those countries.

Ramadan is a supreme finder of words that elide and hide meaning, that glide away sinuously from confrontation. The great service of Caroline Fourest's book is that we can read here much of what Ramadan has said in many different settings and in various languages.

This book was first published as *Frère Tariq* by the mainstream French publisher Grasset in 2004. It is a disgrace that British and American publishing houses did not bring out a translation sooner, and this American edition by Encounter Books is most welcome (an English edition has been published by the London-based Social Affairs Unit). Ramadan has been the subject of half a dozen other books in French, and it is high time that readers of English had a fuller understanding of his beliefs and words.

The Tariq Ramadan of today may, of course, be a different man from the Tariq Ramadan of five, ten, or fifteen years ago as described by Caroline Fourest. (I said and believed in things earlier on in my political life that I would not say and do not believe in now.) Unlike Caroline Fourest, who is a devoutly militant atheist, I respect religious belief. But I cannot accept the supremacy of religion over democracy, and I am dismayed at any arguments that appear to subjugate women to men or to religion.

I was recently in Pakistan. In the north of the country, three people were stoned to death after accusations of adultery. The mosque used its loudspeakers to call the faithful to witness the lapidation. On his website, Ramadan calls merely for a "moratorium" on lapidation, and he elides the religious-sanctioned stoning to death of people with state-authorized capital punishment. He has refused to call for the immediate abolition of stoning. I have read his justifications many times, and the words fall into neat, eloquent patterns. But they do not use his high authority to call without equivocation—now and worldwide—for an immediate end to this barbaric practice. The loudspeakers of mosques will call people to witness this inhuman act again and again, until such time as every shaper of Muslim opinion says it must stop, and until the people organizing such evil are put in prison. And the same goes for so-called "honor killings," where men murder their daughters or wives in the name of a perverted interpretation of Islam.

There are other problems to do with the "double discourse" that rightly condemns the perpetrators of the 7/7 attacks in London, but does not condemn those who prepare suicide-bomb terrorists to kill Jewish children and women in the Middle East. As Jason Burke and other investigators of terrorism linked to fundamentalist religiosity have shown, it is the same ideas, the same passions—often the same men—who have developed the suicide-bomb killer of the innocent and harmless in both the Middle East and Europe. To say the murder of a Christian woman or child on the London Tube is to be deplored, but the murder of a Jewish child or a mother on a Tel Aviv bus is not to be condemned with equal vigor is to enter a moral universe that all decent people should shun.

Readers must make up their own minds. This book is rigorous in quoting from sources, and no one has challenged its accuracy, even if Ramadan and his supporters dislike its tone and content.

Ramadan is clearly one of the most gifted communicators of our times. His brilliant talents could help shape a new life for Europe's twenty million Muslims, so that they could live in peace and respect with and for their faith—but do so in a manner that does not challenge the right of every European to live a full, secular, rule-of-law life, in which women and gays face no discrimination, and where electoral democracy decides the common laws we live under.

In Egypt, the country of Ramadan's grandfather, there is a need for renewal and reform that will allow true democracy to put down roots and avoid both of the twin fundamentalisms—the nationalist statism and anti-Semitism of Nasser, and the subordination of the Egyptian people to religious rule, expressed most notably in the denial of the rights of women.

Though for a short time a schoolteacher in Geneva, Ramadan has spent most of his life as an activist writer-preacher. It is perhaps too much to ask him to carry the burden of history by appealing for an end to the Islamism that is causing so many problems, in so many different ways, in so many different parts of the world.

Born in 1962, Ramadan has had to act as the link between so many different worlds. Perhaps he is simply asked to do too much, or to say and do things he simply cannot say or do.

But as we search for answers to questions both about the meaning of

Islam for our society and for British Muslims, and about the meaning of Islamism as a powerful ideology in the modern world, we should strive to understand the words and ambitions of this important man. We are at the beginning of a long process of comprehension, and it is important that researchers, policy makers, and the general public have as much access as possible—in English—to the key texts and statements of the key players in this new area of concern to democracy. It is for all of us to make judgments, based on what we believe and understand. But to make a judgment, we need evidence. And this book provides important evidence on one of the most significant phenomena of our times.

Denis MacShane
June 2007

Preface

I would really have preferred Tariq Ramadan to remain true to his promise: the promise of a proud and dynamic Islam, but one that was enlightened and modern. I can well understand that a number of Muslims in the West see in him a model, or even a hero—especially now that he has been demonized and can play the martyr's role. Will devoting a whole book to him succeed only in further demonizing him and so providing him with yet another platform? When challenged by demagogues, democrats have only one weapon: education—an education that is difficult even to begin in the course of a single article or in a TV program, when one is pressed for time and forced to improvise, allowing the demagogue to escape with a flippant remark, an evasive answer, or a lie that is soon forgotten. The best of programs can serve to alert people, sow doubt in their minds and wake them up, but it can be only a brief spark, a snapshot. Tariq Ramadan is one of those people who perform admirably on the spur of the moment. In a few seconds he has anyone who suspects him of "doublespeak" backed into a corner. The accusations have been around now for more than ten years without really harming him. Again and again the question arises but is never resolved: is he an intellectual who advocates a modern, liberal Islam; or is he a smooth, astute, well-mannered Islamist preacher?

People are divided on the matter. In Europe, the United States and North Africa—wherever he goes—his public statements and growing celebrity spark off endless debates between adherents to "the sincerity theory" and proponents of the "duplicity theory." The former are often irritated when the media persist in mentioning his family ties with Hassan al-Banna, the founder of the Muslim Brotherhood. As if that was proof of something. Are we responsible for our grandparents? They fail to understand the intransigence of his critics, which they attribute at best to a misunderstanding of his message, at worst to "Islamophobia"—even when these critics are themselves Muslim and almost always Arab.

Those who are somewhat skeptical but well intentioned have read other articles that speak of Tariq Ramadan in favorable terms, as someone holding out the promise of "a modernized Islam," an expression that he himself never uses but that some journalists have attributed to him. Pushed by curiosity they decide to make up their minds on their own by attending one of his lectures for the general public that are organized by left-leaning bodies such as the Human Rights League (Ligue des droits de l'homme), the European Social Forum, or UNESCO. On such occasions, nothing is said that shocks them; on the contrary, it is a "reformer's" speech, the speech of someone who claims to be attached to secularism, even if he wants to see it evolve. To confirm their impression, the most dedicated leaf through one of his books (often too boring to be gone over carefully). A few may even go so far as to stop by an Islamist bookshop and buy one of his audio cassettes (in most cases, it will never subsequently be taken out of its plastic wrapping). Others have made an effort to listen to what he has to say. But listening doesn't bring understanding. They remain convinced that accusations of "double-speak" are not justified. Doesn't he always speak of reform, of education, of appealing for dialogue? Is he not hard on the traditionalism of certain Muslims? Does he not invite Muslims to "speak in clear terms"? Here and there certain statements may rub them up the wrong way, leaving them a bit uncertain, with the impression of not having understood everything, but nothing bears the slightest resemblance to Hassan al-Banna's line or to the rhetoric of the Muslim Brotherhood. The problem is: none of them have read Hassan al-Banna. They constitute the perfect public for Tariq Ramadan, who excels at producing speeches that raise no hackles—unless, that is, one actually takes the time to fit all the pieces together: his language, his allusions, his points of reference and the evolution of his discourse. Unless, finally, one sets aside fleeting impressions to take a look at what is hidden behind. And that takes a whole book.

I dedicate this book to all those who have been impressed by Tariq Ramadan and yet are willing to listen, learn, and understand the sterile ideology that lies behind his rhetorical dexterity. In writing this book I have followed the advice that Ramadan gives his followers (and which I myself have always heeded without making a big issue of it): never caricature an enemy, but carefully study his words and deeds, the better to do battle with him and confront him with dignity.

Nevertheless, I did hesitate before embarking on this undertaking—not through fear of retaliation, but through dread of what such a dissection implied: months spent in reading, analyzing, checking, and double-checking, so as not to become a prisoner of first impressions, so as to omit nothing and exaggerate nothing. The process is particularly exhausting when it is a question of tracking a rhetorician as skilful and verbose as Tariq Ramadan: a hundred or so cassettes, fifteen books, 1,500 pages of interviews and articles on him published in the English, French, German, and Spanish press, never mind the historical studies of the Muslim Brotherhood and of Hassan al-Banna, the brochures published by the Ramadan family, and the countless investigations and interviews necessary to unscramble pieces of the puzzle. For even though the contrast between Tariq Ramadan's language on the cassettes and the language he uses in talking to journalists is in itself instructive, it is not sufficient. Ramadan's rhetoric is so complex that it cannot be decoded without supplying the context and filling in the allusions, which are often fleeting. Once this work was accomplished, it was necessary, for the sake of clarity, to measure the impact that he has had on his followers. It is understandable that others have got lost in this process or have given up midway. I am relieved not to have done so. While it is true that even non-mystics can sometimes feel they are entrusted with a mission, I must admit that I fulfilled this one with the unpleasant sense that it was both urgent and necessary.

PART ONE

TARIQ RAMADAN:
HIS RECORD AND BACKGROUND

Chapter 1

"Islam's Future" or the Future of the Muslim Brotherhood?

Tariq Ramadan was born in 1962, in Geneva, into a family of Egyptian origin that had been exiled to Switzerland on account of their Islamist activities. He makes no secret of it: his parents were the first to have given him a taste for a political Islam. His father, Saïd Ramadan, was, up to his death, in charge of propagating the Muslim Brotherhood's brand of Islam throughout Europe. His mother, Wafa al-Banna, was none other than the favorite daughter of the founder of the Muslim Brotherhood, Hassan al-Banna, whom all Islamists, including the most extreme, consider a seminal figure. Tariq Ramadan dislikes it when his family origins are held against him, considering it a form of persecution. "I am exasperated to have to reply to these accusations!"[1] Yet he himself boasts of his descent. In the course of the TV program *Noms de Dieu* [*In the Names of God*] that was devoted to him, he was proud to exhibit the photograph of his grandfather to illustrate his background.[2] In an interview for *Journal du Mardi,* he objected to those who had the temerity to accuse him of a "genetic offense," while at the same time stating: "I lay claim to this heritage since, if today I am a thinker, it is because this heritage has inspired me."[3]

What are we to make of this? Is he a faithful heir to the Muslim Brotherhood or a man who has kept aloof from al-Banna's ideology? "Angel or Demon?" was the title of an article on him that appeared recently in a Moroccan magazine.[4] The *Boston Globe,* the New England daily, preferred not to take sides: "The reformer to his admirers, Tariq Ramadan is Europe's leading advocate of liberal Islam. To his detractors, he's a dangerous theocrat in disguise."[5] Where does the truth lie? Until recently, when he became more provocative, the press was inclined to grant him the benefit of the doubt. He was even presented as one of the most promising Muslim leaders of his generation. In December 2000, *Time* magazine named him as one of the six religious figures that could contribute to the renovation and revival of the Muslim religion in the coming century. Yet, in the mid-1990s, Hassan al-Tourabi, the high priest of Sudanese Islamism, whose regime had at one point offered Osama bin Laden asylum, thought fit to declare: "Tariq Ramadan? Why, he's Islam's future!" Can one individual simultaneously embody the hopes of an Islamist high priest and the promise of *Time* magazine? Is the American press better equipped than Hassan al-Tourabi to understand Islam and to situate Tariq Ramadan—to know what sort of Muslims he will be turning out? The only way to get a clear picture is to examine the ways in which Tariq Ramadan has transmitted the philosophy and the methods of his grandfather.

Hassan al-Banna as a model

Hassan al-Banna is a figure revered by Islamists the world over. In the early years of the twentieth century, this Egyptian preacher developed a program for reasserting social and political control that has served as a model for all those engaged in the fight to extend the reign of a form of political Islam that is both archaic and reactionary. He oversaw the birth of a diabolical machine—the Muslim Brotherhood—that to this day grinds out its fundamentalist message, spreading it to the four corners of the world. Even Al-Qaeda is no competitor in terms of the scope of this negative force. Al-Qaeda militants were often fascinated by al-Banna before they crossed the line into bin Laden-type terrorism. Given the nature of al-Banna's influence, which remains a constant threat, citizens of Muslim origin are often uneasy when they see Tariq Ramadan continue his grandfather's work in the very heart of the West.

In a collection of interviews with Alain Gresh, editor-in-chief of *Le Monde diplomatique*, Tariq Ramadan made no secret of the fact that he had taken Hassan al-Banna as a model: "I have studied Hassan al-Banna's ideas with great care and there is nothing in this heritage that I reject. His relation to God, his spirituality, his mysticism, his personality, as well as his critical reflections on law, politics, society and pluralism, testify for me to his qualities of heart and mind." And he added: "His commitment also is a continuing reason for my respect and admiration."[6] This admission is in itself terrifying. Every word was chosen to play down the fanaticism and totalitarianism advocated by al-Banna, a man for whom "the Islamic banner must wave supreme over the human race."[7] His name still fills any Muslim who is modern and liberal—or simply healthy-minded—with rage over the crimes that have been committed in the name of Islam. Yet his grandson finds nothing wrong in all this. On the contrary, in a book written for a popular audience, he fully accepted his role as one whose mission it was to continue in the footsteps of his grandfather, whom he presented as a model of "spirituality" and of "critical appreciation of society." By extolling his grandfather's "critical reflections on pluralism," essentially he was praising the virtues of al-Banna's totalitarian outlook.

Well aware of the negative effects that an admission of this kind could have, al-Banna's grandson took the precaution of adding: "I put Hassan al-Banna in the context of his period and his society, and I take that context into account in analyzing his objectives and the means he used to achieve them."[8] In effect, Tariq Ramadan does not repudiate al-Banna's objectives and methods as such; he only says that he is prepared to adapt them to a changed environment: not Egypt in the early years of the twentieth century, but the West at the beginning of the twenty-first. In other words, what is involved is a strategic adaptation, designed to be more efficacious in this new "field"—and not a true rejection. One could, however, be tempted to think otherwise when reading the rest of the interview in *L'Islam en questions* [*Questioning Islam*]: "I don't consider anything in al-Banna's way of thinking to be sacred: my approach is to make a selection, keeping what remains interesting and well advised for today, leaving aside what is dictated by the context and the strategy of his time, and leaving aside all sorts of judgments that I don't agree with."[9] Even if this does not amount to an outright condemnation of al-Banna's philosophy—one may well wonder what is to be considered "interesting" about it—such statements have sufficed to convince a good number of people that Tariq

Ramadan is capable of taking a critical view of his heritage. At any rate, that's what he claims. However, if one listens carefully to his lectures and reads his writings attentively, it becomes evident that exactly the opposite is true.

If he had really wanted to adopt a critical perspective in regard to his heritage, and not simply transmit it, Tariq Ramadan would not have been content to simply sift through al-Banna's program, but would have clearly denounced what he found to be negative in it and in that of the Muslim Brotherhood. But he has never done so. When speaking to a Muslim audience, in particular young Muslims under his guidance, Tariq Ramadan never criticizes Hassan al-Banna or the Muslim Brotherhood in any way. He does, of course, emphasize certain aspects, but he remains true to the doctrine of the Brotherhood, and the Brotherhood's leader is clearly identified as a model to be imitated.

He has converted a whole generation of French-speaking Muslims to Hassan al-Banna's brand of political Islam, thanks to a series of cassettes, of which tens of thousands have been sold by Tawhid, an Islamist publishing house with close ties to the Muslim Brotherhood. In these cassettes—which are, in effect, taped lectures—Tariq Ramadan begins by introducing the Brotherhood's ideology and its theoreticians. Two of the first three cassettes—which are intended as training material for Tawhid's audience—are entirely devoted to Hassan al-Banna's philosophy, presented as the culmination of "contemporary Muslim thought," and as a turning point in the "Muslim renaissance." Far from expressing any reservations regarding the fanaticism that is an integral part of al-Banna's ideology, he accuses those who would point to the unsavory aspects of his political and family heritage of conspiracy or post-colonial racism. He then invites his audience to disregard such caricatures and witch hunts; on the contrary, they should take inspiration from al-Banna's message—which he describes as "a step-by-step philosophy," "a profound philosophy," "a philosophy without violence," but "a demanding philosophy."[10] This unquestioning acceptance sometimes even finds its way into articles written for the general public. In a glossary that figures as an annex to the French edition of *Etre musulman européen* [*To Be a European Muslim*]—which was originally intended as part of a special issue of the weekly magazine *Le Nouvel Observateur*—his grandfather is presented in these terms: "Hassan al-Banna: founder of the Muslim Brotherhood, often cited but seldom read. In the West he is known by what his political enemies have to say about him, in particular English colonialists and Zionist militants."[11] This description merits a closer look.

The greatest reformer of the century?

Al-Banna was born in 1906 in a small Egyptian village and grew up in a family with strong political and religious beliefs. His father, a clockmaker in the town of Mahmudiyya, was a fervent imam of the Hanbalite school, the most rigorous of Islam's four legal schools. At an early age, his eldest son left home to begin his studies in a Koranic school, where the principal activity was learning to recite the Koran by heart. The young al-Banna was a zealous student. At the age of twelve, he became the leader of a Society for Correct Moral Behavior, an association whose aim was to enforce discipline and ensure that within the school strict moral standards were maintained. His zealousness in this respect was to be a permanent feature of his character. A few years later he founded a "group for the prevention of illicit acts," proposing that Egyptians denounce in writing any immoral behavior that they witnessed. The struggle to establish moral order seemed literally to haunt the young boy, influenced as he was by his father's fundamentalist propaganda. Gamal al-Banna, Hassan's younger brother, recalls: "He was the oldest of us, which meant he was his parents' favorite. More than any of us, he soaked up the religious atmosphere in which the family lived. My parents used to tell me that, when he played hide-and-seek, he played according to his own rules. He was the leader of the Muslim army combating the enemies of God."[12]

This Manichean outlook was to be a lasting trait. As an adolescent, he continued his training as a mystic in a particularly orthodox Sufi fraternity, where he developed a taste for secrecy and for brotherhood in the service of Islam. Unlike other fraternities, his fraternity rejected any kind of innovation in religious matters. Many of their meetings consisted simply of chanting extracts from the Koran and from the Sunna for hours on end. But al-Banna would not have stayed for long if the fraternity was simply a separatist mystic movement. He wanted to act; he dreamt of "fighting against evil" by preaching. And the opportunity was close at hand. He and his comrades preached unendingly against the Christian missions, which they accused of corrupting morals "by charity work, by healthcare initiatives and by their teaching in the schools." His rejection of colonialism was based not on a commitment to independence but on his fundamentalism. In his eyes, the worst feature of colonization was not the occupation itself, but the fact that the occupation went hand in hand with an acceptance of Christianity and, above all, with the liberalization of moral standards. If Egypt had not been a colony, Hassan al-Banna would no doubt have had the same sort of career as William Jennings Bryan, the American fundamentalist Protestant who crusaded against Darwinism and the moral decadence of his fellow countrymen in the 1920s. But al-Banna was born into a quite different context, at a time when the war against modernity could easily be taken for a war against colonialism. Thus al-Banna's combat against liberalizing moral standards led him to take part in the popular demonstrations against British occupation in 1919 and 1922.

He was already more of a political than a religious figure. Instead of becoming a theologian at Al-Azhar, the prestigious Islamic university of Cairo, he chose to enrol in the Science House in order to become a schoolteacher. Not that he intended to give up preaching—on the contrary. A teaching job would bring him into close contact with the people and thus provide an opportunity for a far more effective kind of political proselytizing: "I will serve as a counselor and a teacher. Even if I have to spend most of my time instructing children, I will also instruct their fathers about Islam, at times by writing, at other times by giving talks and engaging them in conversation, and by travelling as well."[13] These were the terms in which he was later to explain to his companions his reasons for choosing teaching as a profession. But al-Banna always considered pedagogy as a means of propaganda. His vocation was strengthened after he was assigned to a school close to the Suez Canal, where he could observe with disgust the Westerners' style of life. His revolt intensified when he settled in Cairo, where city life horrified this puritan villager. Everywhere around him he saw decadence, and this he attributed to Western influence. Adopting the style of the Protestant preachers, quick to imagine new methods for "awakening" faith, he took to preaching in the streets and cafés against the "creeping modernism" that was contrary to the spirit of Islam. Tariq Ramadan has provided us with an impassioned description of his grandfather's gift for seducing his listeners and adapting his message to fit the audience in question—a description that tells us as much about Ramadan himself as it does about al-Banna: "His personality, his way of speaking, his charisma and his erudition won over those who heard him speak. Gifted with a prodigious memory, capable of adjusting the level of his discourse so as to reach not only the academics and the city ulemas but the village peasants as well . . . he was simple, accessible, and affectionate, as well as intellectually rigorous and demanding. His personal qualities contributed greatly to the spread of his ideas."[14]

The Cairo intelligentsia was then in a state of constant upheaval, torn between conflicting political and religious options. In 1923, Mustafa Kemal Atatürk—who ascribed the decline of the Ottoman Empire to a mixing of politics and religion that had paralyzed the Muslim world—abolished the caliphate that was the symbol of this fusion and founded Turkey as a secular state. This was a traumatic event for an ultra-religious person such as al-Banna, all the more so since Egypt was itself caught up in the debate. In 1925, Ali Abd al-Raziq published an audacious book, *Islam et les fondements du pouvoir* [*Islam and the Origins of Power*], which argued that Mohammed had never taken steps to provide for a government that would succeed him. On the contrary, the Koran, in a sura known as the "consultation" sura, clearly encouraged men to "conduct their affairs by mutual consultation."[15] The author then encouraged his compatriots to set foot once again on the road to progress via a secular Islam and by instituting a system that would separate religion and politics. The book created a scandal comparable to the reception of Darwin's theories that split the Protestants into two camps: one arguing that the Bible should be updated to take account of the new scientific discoveries; the other arguing for a return to fundamentalist Protestantism that rejected the theory of evolution. Abd al-Raziq's book had exactly the same effect: on one side were the Muslims who favored an *aggiornamento* of Islam; on the other, the purists who wanted to return to Islam's initial precepts. But once again, the Egyptian context and the fact of colonization make interpretation of these debates more complex. In the United States, the fundamentalist movement was immediately identified as a reactionary movement, to which progressive Protestants were firmly opposed. On the other hand, Muslim fundamentalism (which includes literalist Salafism and reformist Salafism)[16] claimed to be an alternative to colonization, which gave it a far more ambiguous status. Afghani (1838–97), the founder of the Salafist school, was also an anti-colonial militant. At one point, he advocated a rationalist secular reform as a way to breathe new life into the Arab world, but he subsequently initiated a brand of reformism that consisted essentially of a return to basic religious principles; in so doing he was following in the footsteps of Ibn Taymiyya (1236–1328), a medieval Hanbalite jurist who, in opposition to the rationalist Muslims of his era, argued for a purification of Islam. To this day, a number of Arab nationalists and progressive Muslims admire Afghani, even if, in referring to him as a source of inspiration, they find themselves in the company of a religious generation that is more fundamentalist than anti-colonial. The difference between the two is, however, considerable. An anti-colonial militant resists colonization because he believes in the people's right to self-determination and refuses all forms of domination, whereas a fundamentalist opposes colonialism because he believes Islam is superior to the West. Moreover it is in order to re-establish this superiority that he wants to purify Islam and return it to its founding precepts—in order to recover the power that had fuelled Muslim expansion. In other words, he wants to return to a form of colonialism of which he is the beneficiary and not the victim.

Hassan al-Banna was all the more inclined to agree with the latter outlook, in that he was a student of one of the most rigorous proponents of the Salafist school, Rashid Rida. Unlike Afghani or Mohammed Abduh, who had studied in France and was relatively open to modernizing influences, Rida, motivated by intense anti-Western sentiment, did all in his power to make the reformist impulse more rigid and steer the Salafist school towards an archaic fundamentalism. It is thus not without interest that al-Banna should have attended courses in the reformist Salafist school during this period, nor that he should subsequently have given birth to a movement that was to turn reformism into a version of Islamism violently opposed to any form of rationalism that bore the slightest resemblance to Western ways—blocking the *aggiornamento* of Islam for generations to come.

For this achievement, Tariq Ramadan considers his grandfather as "the most influential of the reformist Muslims of the century"[17]—an opinion that he developed at length in his thesis, defended in 1998 at the University of Geneva, "Hassan al-Banna and the reformist tradition since al-Afghani." This was a masterpiece of propaganda in praise of Hassan al-Banna. His argument runs as follows: reformists such as Afghani, Abduh, or Rida were brilliant intellectuals, but they were not effective enough. As intellectuals, they remained on the fringes of a true dynamic and true social and political drive. Providentially, Hassan al-Banna appeared and provided the political movement with the reformism it needed. In other words, Tariq Ramadan considers al-Banna's philosophy and the Muslim Brotherhood as the high point of Salafist reformist thought and of the Salafist reformist initiative. In addition to boasting of his grandfather's success in combating atheism and permissiveness, he situated all the reformist intellectuals in the same tradition, despite the differences that existed between men such as Abduh or Rida. His aim was to make Hassan al-Banna appear as the successor to all of them, the most fundamentalist as well as the most open-minded. Yet there existed significant differences between them, as Ali Mérad, a specialist on Muslim reform movements, has reminded us: "Mohammed Abduh is the father of rationalist reform. He tried to open up Muslim thinking to rationalist influences. But one of his disciples, Rashid Rida, was determined to rigidify this aspect of his thought and to rid it of all rationalism. He passed himself off as Abduh's heir, so as to be in a better position to minimize the new perspectives proposed by Abduh."[18] But it was Rida's lectures that al-Banna attended, and not those of Abduh, at a time when everyone was free to attend them and to become a supporter, thanks also to the influence of his review, *Al-Manar*. Ramadan does not deny that this is true, but insists nonetheless on presenting al-Banna as the disciple of Abduh, whereas in reality he was obviously the heir to Rida's uncompromising fundamentalist reformism. It serves his purpose to skip over his apprenticeship to Rida, so as to convince those who are not going to bother to check the facts that his grandfather was committed to modern reformism. This does not prevent him, page after page, from disparaging the rationalist reformers who followed in the footsteps of Abd al-Raziq. In the course of a footnote, Tariq Ramadan clearly implies that Abd al-Raziq's ideas were the result of Western scheming: the translation of Ali Abd al-Raziq's book was "sponsored by the French mission for research and cooperation in Egypt." "We know how eager the Western governments are to publish and distribute texts that are in harmony with their system of values and their view of the world . . . . It was no accident."[19] This biased view, nakedly propagandist, might have gone unnoticed by novices in the field, but it did not escape the University of Fribourg's thesis jury, to whom he had initially submitted his manuscript. Presided over by Charles Genequand, a specialist on the Arab world, and made up of scholars of Muslim reformism, the jury was simply dumbfounded by the exceedingly partisan nature of the thesis. According to the jury's president, it "was intended as an apologetic" for Hassan al-Banna[20]—an opinion shared by the other members of the jury. They unanimously refused to accept it as scientific in character. Tariq Ramadan was furious; he threatened to bring the jury and the university to trial, but without success, since a jury has a perfect right to refuse to accept work that it does not consider to be scholarly. Ramadan was obliged to convoke *in extremis* a second jury, which included Bruno Etienne,[21] to have his diploma granted—without honors—by the Faculty of Arts of the University of Geneva. The important thing for him was to have a scientific imprimatur before publishing his thesis in book form. The jury gave him permission, adding that it "authorized the publication of the thesis without expressing any opinion regarding its contents."[22] They could not have been more explicitly critical. In spite of everything, this handbook in praise of Hassan al-Banna was published under the title *Aux sources du renouveau musulman* [*On the Origins of the Muslim Renaissance*], by Tawhid, but also by Bayard, a far more mainstream publishing house. The two editions are prefaced by Alain Gresh, editor-in-chief of *Le Monde diplomatique*. Since then it has not been uncommon to hear non-Islamist militants—even secular militants—tell you, with the most naive candor, that al-Banna was "a great reformer" and that the Muslim Brotherhood was "a liberation movement . . . "

The Muslim Brotherhood portrayed as a "liberation movement"

The Muslim Brotherhood began organizing when, in March 1928, six companions, fired with enthusiasm by al-Banna's preaching, sought him out to ask him to launch a political campaign in the name of Islam: "We have listened to your message, we are aware of where we stand, we are committed, but we do not know what practical steps to take to reinforce Islam and bring betterment to Muslims."[23] The Guide was at last to have the opportunity to demonstrate his gift for organization. He began with a piece of advice that would provide the Muslim Brotherhood with the means to survive the obstacles that repression was to bring—and to counter its critics: the cult of the informal. "One of his companions asked: 'By what name shall we be called?' And al-Banna replied: 'None of that; leave aside appearances and officialdom. Let the principle and priority of our union be thought, morality, and action. We are brothers in the service of Islam, so we are the Muslim Brotherhood.'"[24] A judicious piece of advice. Al-Banna had understood that a movement that could not be pinned down would be indestructible. In giving his movement a name that was both a title and an expression currently employed in Arabic, in which believers often address each other as "brother," he created a means of identification that was discreet. From its birth on, the Brotherhood was both an official movement and a school of thought that one could claim to belong to, or deny being part of, according to circumstances. On the other hand, the watchword was clear and unambiguous: "Our motto will forever be: God is our objective. God's messenger is our guide. The Koran is our constitution. Struggle is our path. Death on the road that leads to God is our ultimate desire."[25]

In other words, it was never al-Banna's intention to advocate a rationalist, secular Islam; on the contrary, he wanted to organize a movement capable of putting pressure on Egypt, and then on the rest of the world, to adopt a fundamentalist social order destructive of freedom. As proof, one has only to read the political and social program drawn up by al-Banna in 1936, a program entitled "Fifty Demands," which was the Muslim Brotherhood's manifesto for "concrete reform." The manifesto spelt out in detail the steps to be taken to establish legislation, and subsequently a social, political and economic system based on the sharia. Throughout the manifesto, it is said that individual liberties must yield to dictatorship by divine right. As to method, the Brotherhood intended to "go beyond political differences and direct the energies of the "umma" [the worldwide community of Muslims] towards one sole aim": the attainment of a political Islam. The organization defined its objectives as "reforming the laws in conformity with Islamic legislation, particularly as regards the definition of offenses and the punishments for crimes,"[26] and spreading "the spirit of Islam throughout all the branches of government so that all citizens consider it their duty to put Islamic precepts into effect." In the meantime, in their everyday dealings, the Brothers intended "to initiate respect for morality among the people and make everyone aware of the regulations set down by the law," which meant that "the punishments for violations of the code of morality should be strictly applied." This objective, which was central to the program, involved several provisions, namely "eradicating prostitution," "treating fornication, whatever the circumstances, as a serious crime punishable by law," but also "forbidding co-education," "considering all private contact between members of the different sexes as a punishable crime," "closing down dance halls and other centers of debauch, as well as outlawing dancing and any form of physical contact between a man and a woman." And that is only a brief résumé of the contents.

The manifesto was, for many years, available only in Arabic, until the journal *Islam de France* decided to publish it in French, so as to enlighten all those who, misled by the angelic presentation of the text given by Tariq Ramadan, were ignorant of the basically fundamentalist and reactionary nature of the Muslim Brotherhood. The publication of this program, which proved to be quite different from the version that Ramadan had spread among the anti-globalization leftists, was by no means welcomed by al-Banna's grandson. Michel Renard (born a Christian, but a convert to Islam), one of the founders of *Islam de France*, recalls having been the target of the latter's anger: "It's then that I realized that he practiced doublespeak: you can't believe in a secular society and in Hassan al-Banna at the same time."[27] This affront to the founder's dignity resulted in the closure of the journal. Al-Bouraq, the house that published the journal, but that also publishes Tariq Ramadan, all of a sudden canceled its contract after the publication of the issue in question, bringing to a close one of the most stimulating editorial initiatives devoted to Islam in France.

For Tariq Ramadan, it is essential that the movement that inspired him be seen in terms of his own particular perspective. For someone who is aware of the harm done by the Muslim Brotherhood's fundamentalism—and I am referring not only to the violence but also to the fanaticism that Tariq Ramadan considers to be wholly legitimate—it is frightening to hear him explain to European Muslims that the "extremely critical remarks" made concerning his grandfather are to be accounted for by the fact that his "national liberation movement" was a thorn in the side of Westerners.[28] He points to the fact that the Anglo-Saxon press presented the movement in 1936 in favorable terms, until the day when the Muslim Brotherhood stood up against "the Zionist presence in Palestine": "It is quite clear that once it became evident that there was popular support for the Brotherhood's stance, they began to cast suspicions on Hassan al-Banna's activities, to spread rumors about him, and disparage the movement as a whole."[29] This was a way of implying that all the criticisms made of al-Banna and the Brotherhood were the result of a campaign of lies designed to protect the Zionist interests. In fact, what we can conclude from all of this is that *Time* magazine—which was to designate Ramadan as one of the "innovators" in the year 2000—was not particularly perspicacious . . .

It is true that, during al-Banna's time, the British government and King Farouk thought they could make use of the Muslim Brotherhood as a counterweight to the Egyptian Left and the Wafd Party. According to Olivier Carré and Michel Seurat, they even received a formal grant of 500 Egyptian pounds from the Suez Canal Company, a building permit for a first meeting place, as well as a mosque under their control. These findings emerged in the course of research into the first bulletins published by the Brotherhood, in which al-Banna attempted to explain things to his companions. According to Carré and Seurat: "Banna, who would subsequently deny the gifts from the Canal

Company, began by trying to justify what he had done in the eyes of his companions, who expressed their indignation, and took leave of him."[30] Subsequently, al-Banna would simply state that he had never received any such gifts. A Muslim Brother, then, is free to lie or change what he has said, if it serves his purpose. At any rate, that's one aspect of the Muslim Brotherhood's past that Tariq Ramadan is by no means eager to remember when he speaks to an anti-globalist audience—or even to an audience of Islamists that he wants to convince of the fact that the Muslim Brotherhood has always, right from the very beginning, been a movement of resistance to colonialism. The Muslim Brotherhood did, in fact, take part in the putsch organized by the army officers that liberated Egypt from the yoke of colonialism, but this liberation was only a phase dictated by the immediate context. Egyptian independence was never, for the Brotherhood, an end in itself, but rather a prelude to the setting up of an Islamic dictatorship.

The Brotherhood's participation in the struggle for independence has, in addition, been considerably exaggerated by the movement's propaganda. But even in the course of their attempts to falsify history, certain partisans of the Brotherhood revealed the extent to which al-Banna was, above all, obsessed by the idea of re-instituting Islamic values. To that end, he was prepared to negotiate with any government whatsoever. In 1946, for instance, he was in the thick of negotiations to obtain the right to publish a daily, and to acquire land on which to construct his propaganda centers, when the communists sparked off a massive wave of strikes in the Cairo textile industry in order to force the British to leave the country. The communist "Committee to Liberate the Nation" asked al-Banna to send his troops to join in the general strike scheduled for February 21, but al-Banna refused, partly because he did not want to jeopardize the ongoing negotiations, but also out of deep-rooted suspicion of the communists. On the appointed day, a number of Brothers disregarded instructions, and joined up anyway with the strikers. Bypassed by the rank and file, al-Banna finally consented to call for a strike on the following days, but refused to join in the collective movement, which then fell apart.[31] It was not until 1948 that al-Banna decided in earnest to organize joint demonstrations with the communists against the British occupying forces. It was an alliance dictated by the circumstances—and one that did not last for long. In the same year (1948), al-Banna still included the communists in the lengthy list of enemies who were conspiring against the Brothers: "Worldwide Judaism, and international Communism, the colonial powers, and the advocates of atheism and moral degeneracy—they all, from the very first day, considered the Brothers and their message as major obstacles."[32]

A step-by-step strategy of conquest

Tariq Ramadan has always made a point of presenting the Brotherhood as a "social movement."[33] If you listen to him, you can end up thinking that political power was never really of interest to the organization. It must be said that it was in terms of actual practice that the Brothers were awesomely effective. Their unrelenting day-by-day fundamentalism succeeded in damaging, little by little, the social and cultural fabric of the country chosen as its target; but this did not mean they had given up the idea of one day taking power, once conditions were ripe. The fact that they concentrated first of all on "grassroots Islamization," to quote Gilles Kepel, did not mean that al-Banna had abandoned his offensive in the higher spheres. Olivier Carré and Michel Seurat have amply demonstrated that he was ready to negotiate with practically all of Egypt's political components—including the Wafd (the nationalist populist party), the throne, and even the British themselves—in order to gain political influence. He was even a candidate for election to the legislature in December 1941, an initiative that took some of his companions by surprise. He was to explain why, three years later, in the Brotherhood's journal: "I have been asked: Did this taking part in elections not mean that the Brotherhood was abandoning the field of religion to engage in politics, and thereby transforming what had, up to then, been a religious movement into a political organization? Our reply is that Islam recognizes no such distinction concerning the affairs of the nation: an Islamic religious institution is duty bound to give the Islamic viewpoint in every area of life, and the parliament is the shortest and the best road to this end."[34]

At this time, al-Banna, encouraged by the rapid success of his movement, really did think it possible to institute an Islamic regime by means of the ballot box. But lobbying and political representation were only one aspect of commitment to the Islamization of society. Tariq Ramadan is perfectly explicit in this regard: the pursuit of political power through elections was only one step—a step that should not be taken in haste: "In such matters, any nation that attempts to go against the rules of nature will inevitably fail," al-Banna would say. This is a piece of advice for today's Islamists to meditate on—especially those who may have made the mistake of forcing the pace in Algeria, running the risk of a counteroffensive. On the strength of this experience, Tariq Ramadan has called on European Islamists to be astute in the way they apply his grandfather's "methodology," in particular his strategy of graduated conquest. One section of his lecture on "contemporary Muslim thought," edited as a cassette by Tawhid, stresses the importance of respecting the rhythm that his grandfather had insisted on:

> The Muslim Brotherhood's program is made up of a series of stages that are closely controlled and clearly defined. We know perfectly well what we want and the means we should use to attain our objectives. Consider the three stages; they are well known and solidly anchored in a methodology that takes social issues as a point of departure:
>
> 1. We want first of all human beings that are Muslim, that is to say individual human beings who are Muslim in their thoughts, in their faith, their morality, their feelings, their activities and their initiatives. That is our program for individuals.
> 2. Then we want Muslim families, that is to say families that are Muslim in their thoughts and beliefs, in their morality and feelings, in their activities and initiatives; and here we are thinking of women as well as men. That is our program for the family.
> 3. And then we want there to be a Muslim people, formed in the same manner; and that is why we want our message to reach inside all homes, our voice to be heard everywhere, and our way of thinking to pervade every region, every village, every town, city, capital and metropolis.[35]

This first part of the program (three sections out of a total of seven) is enough to send shivers up and down one's spine. However, for Tariq Ramadan, the fact that Hassan al-Banna intended people to be indoctrinated before an Islamic regime is established is enough for him to claim that the program is a model of open-mindedness and democracy. In the same lecture that served as an introduction to Hassan al-Banna's philosophy, he specifies: "Note that it is only after these first three stages that al-Banna mentions an 'Islamic government,' which, according to the reform program proposed by his organization, represents the logical outcome of the process of renewal initiated on the individual level. A government is not, then, simply a superstructure that is foisted on society; it is the end product of a reform process which, at a certain stage in its evolution, takes shape as a political model that harnesses its basic drive. Here we are a long way from any formalism."[36] So we needn't be worried . . . . It is not a question of "formalism," but of "drive." But where is this drive to lead us? Ramadan is sufficiently prudent to keep from rushing his audience through the later stages; he alludes only briefly to what remains in store for us, namely the setting up of an Islamic empire. Here are the following four points of al-Banna's program that Tariq Ramadan takes pains not to discuss:[37]

4. Subsequently we want a Muslim government whose members will lead the people under Islamic guidance, as, in the past, did Abou Bakr and Omar, disciples of the Prophet, may he rest in peace. That is also why we will not accept any form of government not based on Islamic foundations and not true to Islamic principles. That is also our reason for refusing to recognize political parties and the traditional authorities with whom the deniers and the enemies of Islam have forced us to govern, thus contributing to their growth. We will strive for the renaissance of a totally Islamic government, a government based on Islamic foundations . . . .

5. We want next to reassemble all those who are part of Islam and that Western policies have made a point of keeping separate and which European cupidity has misled and sealed off within national borders. Thus we reject all international agreements that have transformed the nation of Islam into a collection of powerless entities, weak and riven by internal conflicts, that can easily be taken over by those who would rob them of their rights. And we will not remain silent when their liberties are denied

and unjustly confiscated by outsiders. Thus Egypt, Syria, Hidjaz, Yemen, Tripoli, Tunisia, Algeria, Marrakech, and wherever there lives a Muslim who recites the words "There is no God but God himself"—all of these territories belong to our great nation; we will liberate them, free them from domination, deliver them from tyranny, and bring them together as one whole. If the German Reich makes it a principle to protect all those with German blood in their veins, well then Muslim faith makes it a principle for every Muslim who has the opportunity to act as the protector of all those who have taken to heart the teachings of the Koran. It is thus forbidden, in accordance with Islamic tradition, to treat the ethnic factor as more important than the ties that bind by faith. And belief is the heart and soul of Islam. Moreover, is not faith basically a question of love and hate?

6. We want the Islamic flag to be hoisted once again on high, fluttering in the wind, in all those lands that have had the good fortune to harbor Islam for a certain period of time and where the muezzin's call has sounded in the *takbirs* and the *tahlis*. Then fate decreed that the light of Islam be extinguished in these lands that returned to unbelief. Thus Andalusia, Sicily, the Balkans, the Italian coast, as well as the islands of the Mediterranean, are all of them Muslim Mediterranean colonies and they must return to the Islamic fold. The Mediterranean Sea and the Red Sea must once again become Muslim seas, as they once were, even if Mussolini has usurped the right to rebuild the Roman Empire. This so-called empire of ancient times was founded on cupidity and lust. It is thus our duty to rebuild the Islamic Empire, that was founded on justice and equality and that spread the light of the true way among the people.

7. We want, after that and with that, to disseminate our Islamic message to the entire world, to reach people wherever they may be, to spread our message to the four corners of the globe, and overcome the tyrants until the day when agitation ceases and religion is entirely devoted to God. When that day comes, the believers will rejoice in God's help. He saves those whom he wishes to save; He is the source of all Power and all Mercy.

It is notable that this *Epître aux jeunes* [*Letter to the Young*], in which Hassan al-Banna proposes Nazism as a model, advocates extending Islamic imperialism to include all those nations in which a single Muslim is to be found.

All means are justified

In this same set of lectures on Hassan al-Banna, Tariq Ramadan adopted as his own the maxim by which his grandfather urged the Brotherhood to use all means at their disposal in order to impose their vision on society. "To that end we shall spare no effort; we shall not stop at any means."[38] That Ramadan should adopt this maxim is in itself frightening, even if he is a past master in the art of presenting the Muslim Brotherhood's tactics in a favorable light.

With this same idea of respect for the rhythms imposed by the West, and so as not to give the impression that the Brotherhood is a movement hungry for power, the preacher emphasized his grandfather's "phenomenal contribution in social and political matters." He pointed to the creation of "two thousand schools" and the "social measures for the promotion of women."[39] He is quite right to remind us that al-Banna was obsessed by the creation of schools, including schools for young girls. But this obsession was in no way a disinterested commitment to reducing illiteracy! Al-Banna wanted to "reform instruction . . . so as to establish a model society in terms of Islamic law."[40] As is the case with leaders who want to create a faithful following, he was convinced that the only way to change people was to change the children. The schools that he founded throughout Egypt were not intended to foster independence of thought and intellectual freedom. They were Islamic schools, designed to indoctrinate as many young Egyptian boys and girls as possible, from the earliest age. The Muslim sisters, the women's section of the Brotherhood, were encouraged primarily to combat women's emancipation. And the movement campaigned against co-education in the state schools. From 1937 on, the Brotherhood frequently addressed letters to the university administration demanding that there be separate instruction for men and women. To claim that Hassan al-Banna was a great figure on the basis of his contribution to public instruction—while omitting to say that it consisted of a means of indoctrination in the service of a totalitarian ideology—is pure propaganda. Like all authoritarian movements, the Brotherhood was also obsessively concerned with training the young boys in sports. Are we to conclude that their primary mission was to combat obesity? All of the Islamic movements active in the field function in this same way: they systematically fill the smallest gaps left by the state by proposing courses in Arabic, remedial instruction or humanitarian aid—not out of the goodness of their hearts, but in order to recruit.

The Brotherhood's totalitarianism does not appear to have come as much of a shock to Tariq Ramadan. In the same lectures on "contemporary Muslim thought," he explains that his grandfather was right to advocate a single-party system, for the Egyptian people of his time did not possess a sufficiently solid political culture to make the right choice—i.e. to choose an Islamic regime. As al-Banna put it: "Given the situation, elections were pointless; they served no purpose, since, if the majority of the population was ignorant, how could they know what they really wanted?"[41] Ramadan quotes his grandfather to prove how right he was to encourage Islamic education, while at the same time refusing pluralism and democracy for as long as it took for this education to take effect. That is what Ramadan refers to as his grandfather's "critical attitude in regard to pluralism."

However hard al-Banna's heirs attempt to portray themselves as a political alternative to the authoritarian and paternalistic governments of the Maghreb and the Middle East, they are themselves hardly any better. A regime issuing from the ranks of the Muslim Brotherhood would be the first to flout democratic principles once in power. For proof, one has only to observe the way in which their own movement has functioned over the years. As Supreme Guide, al-Banna had a very singular notion of what consultation consisted of. He accepted the principle of consultation as stipulated in the Koran, but without ever taking the risk of making it democratic in practice. Within the official structure of the Brotherhood, the power to take decisions rested, during his lifetime, with the Bureau of Orientation, composed of twenty members chosen by the Guide. As a pure formality, his choice was ratified by an Assembly of 150 members, who had the right to comment on the decisions before voting by a two-thirds majority. But their countervailing power was strictly limited, since it was the Bureau of Orientation that had the last word .... But then the Guide could dismiss any one of its members if he so chose! This does not mean that there were no differing ideological tendencies within the movement, or relatively diverse subgroups. Yet, as Olivier Carré has explained: "All serious rifts ended in blind submission, in secession or exclusion."[42] These procedures made it possible for the Guide to exclude systematically those who reproached him for having made deals with the regime in power or who accused him of nepotism. What a splendid organizational model for a "liberation movement!"

And that was only the official organizational structure. Tariq Ramadan fails to mention—and thus to criticize—the other method to which the Brothers have had recourse as they strive to put their program into effect: infiltration. They have been remarkably adept at taking control of an organization without its being aware of it, often through one of its members who kept silent on the fact that he belonged to the Brotherhood. It is a technique that is difficult to expose, especially while it is happening. Luckily, there exists a number of first-hand accounts that show that this practice existed from the very outset. One of these accounts is provided by Zaynab al-Ghazali, a woman activist in the service of the Brotherhood, whose memoirs were prefaced by Tariq Ramadan.[43] Thanks to her, we can get an inside view of the Brotherhood's tactics of infiltration. We learn that the members have no scruples about talking with two voices or even resorting to lies when it can serve their cause. In 1936, Zaynab al-Ghazali was president of the Association of Muslim Women, the aim of which was to propagate "the Muslim religion and the resurrection of the *umma*, which will provide Islam with the power, the force and the glory that it once enjoyed." The association was by no means a progressive organization; however, its members refused to join the Muslim Brotherhood, despite Hassan al-Banna's insistence—which infuriated the Guide and embarrassed al-Ghazali. She came up with another solution: "On the occasion of our last meeting at the Muslim Sisters' headquarters I had tried to calm the late al-Banna's anger by promising, as a gesture of support for the imam, to have the Association of Muslim Women figure among the Muslim Brotherhood organizations, without, however, abandoning its identity, its name or its autonomy."[44] The imam accepted this form of allegiance in a letter: "I have accepted your oath of allegiance and agree that the Muslim Women will, for the moment, keep the same status."[45] The phrase "for the moment" serves to remind us that the Guide always proceeded in stages. Thus al-Ghazali decided to ignore the refusal expressed by her followers and underhandedly pledged allegiance to the Guide without their knowing of it. While denying that she was in any way linked to the Brotherhood, she became its agent and oriented her association's policies in line with its strategy. This taste for dissimulation was not unusual for the Brotherhood; it was a reflex inherent in their way of functioning.

Built-in doublespeak

From the very start, the Muslim Brotherhood has been based on an ambiguity: that of being at one and the same time an organized movement and a way of thinking. The movement's founding law, which dates from 1945, defines an "active member" as someone who has pledged allegiance to the Guide, but the great majority of those committed to serve the Brotherhood's ideology do so on an informal basis. These agents spread al-Banna's message and his methods, without being an integral part of the organization.

The movement had, to be sure, an official structure that represented it in political dealings with institutions. The Brotherhood even had a flag: two crossed swords with the Koran as a background. The organization's officers introduced themselves as members of the Muslim Brotherhood if, in so doing, negotiations with the Egyptian government or other administrations were facilitated. But the Brotherhood consisted of much more than this official façade. Some sections were engaged in infiltration operations that were of necessity undercover. Other sections organized terrorist attacks that had to be publicly condemned so as not to discredit the official line taken by the head office. Steps were taken to separate, as far as possible, the sections that were in the public eye from the undercover cells, either because the latter were more radical or because their mission had to remain confidential. This led to the creation of an unofficial branch, known as the Secret Organization, in charge of the most sensitive operations. As well as this division into official and secret branches, the informal nature of the movement's organization meant that it was always possible to prevent its active supporters from being identified. If a member of the Brotherhood was caught engaged in a mission prejudicial to the movement's public image, the official branch could deny having any connection with him. And conversely, if the fact of being exposed as a Muslim Brother threatened the success of a mission, the latter could always deny belonging to the organization. You could say it was the movement's golden rule. Many fraternities resort to lies and dissimulation in their dealings with the outside world if that serves to protect them and help them achieve their objectives—the Muslim Brotherhood more so than any other. Trained in the Sufi fraternity, al-Banna admitted that he had been marked for life by the advice given him by his sheikh, who taught him the advantages of speaking with two voices: "I remember that, among his wise teachings, one was to prevent the Brothers who were his disciples from expressing themselves too freely in debates on judicial issues or on obscure questions, or to repeat in front of ordinary people what atheists, strangers, or missionaries might have said. He advised them: 'Discuss these questions among yourselves and study them in the company of those who are well informed; but as for ordinary people, speak to them in such a way as to have an immediate influence and render them more obedient to God.'"[46] This sentence, quoted by Tariq Ramadan in *On the Origins of the Muslim Renaissance*, shows us—better than any analysis could—where his habit comes from of speaking with one voice to people outside his community and with another to people within it.

Islamists in general have learned how to lie in order to avoid exposure. This principle even bears a name: *taqiyya*. The Shiites applied this prerogative when lying or even when swearing that they were not Shiite in order to survive when they were persecuted by the Sunnis for their religious beliefs. The reflex has remained with them. It spread to the Sunni Islamists intent on furthering their cause despite the strict surveillance they were under in Arab countries. Today, it is used by Islamists living in the Western democracies, not in order to avoid arrest, but simply as a means of pursuing their ends while remaining disguised.

Students of Islamism, who have heard militants say one thing in public and another when with their brothers, have become accustomed to this kind of doublespeak. Many have been disconcerted by the doublespeak until they have come to understand that this behavior forms an integral part of Islamist rhetoric. For Jean-Yves Chaperon, a reporter for Luxembourg's radio and television (RTL) who has been covering the subject for many years, it no longer comes as a surprise: "With the Islamists you'll always find this kind of duality: sweetness on the outside, and fire within."[47] Nonetheless, it is always a bit disconcerting when somebody lies to you, often with a broad smile. Another Islamist speciality is to make totally unacceptable remarks in the most angelic manner. Hassan al-Tourabi is a prime example of what the Muslim Brotherhood is capable of producing (although he has since denied any connection with the Brotherhood). He often astounds his listeners by his habit of stirring up hatred in a good-natured, almost likeable, manner. This friendly host studied in Paris, where he founded the Association of Islamic Students of France. He enjoys receiving French journalists in order to explain to them, in the most cheerful of tones, how his social model will, in the end, destabilize the entire planet.[48] This trait is even more crude in the case of Omar Bakri, for many years the London leader of the now banned Al-Muhajiroun, a man who makes no secret of the fact that he has organized trips to Afghanistan and served as an agent of Al-Qaeda propaganda. He delights in summoning journalists and proclaiming, a broad smile on his face, that he is a fervent supporter of bin Laden, and that non-Muslims will soon be defeated or will burn in hell. To utter such anathemas in the very heart of the West, without taking the slightest risk thanks to the right of free speech, is, for him, an additional source of pleasure. It should be mentioned that such statements would, in his native country of Syria, result in his immediate imprisonment, and probably in his torture. The situation is a bit more complex for activists whose objective is strategic. They are obliged to tone down their rhetoric, even to learn how to lie—with a smile that expresses their disdain for the naiveté of non-Muslims. And who can blame them? It is typical Western naiveté to think that one can form an opinion of determined, anti-democratic militants by relying on good impressions and to believe that fanatics don't lie. The result is that Western journalists, when confronted by Islamists who are even a little cunning, are constantly thrown off the track.

A Brother or not a Brother?

"I have no functional connection with the Muslim Brotherhood," Tariq Ramadan made a point of declaring for the benefit of the press. As if the Brotherhood was a party that issued membership cards. As if the lack of a formal tie vindicated the rehabilitation of his grandfather and the teaching of the latter's thought to European Muslims—without any attempt to adopt a critical perspective. "It's time to put a stop to these fantasies," he declared to the *Nouvel Observateur.* "I am independent; there are differences of opinion between me and the Brotherhood in regard to matters of doctrine, even if one of my uncles, Al-Islam al-Banna, is a member of the movement's governing body. But you know, the Brotherhood is not a homogeneous organization. There are differing groups and subgroups . . . "[49] There are, in effect, different tendencies within the Brotherhood. But it is important to understand that these differences concern questions of method—never the objectives to be attained. It is quite likely that certain Muslim Brothers do find the heir's methods a bit too modern for their taste. But that does not make of Tariq Ramadan a modern Muslim! You can be communist without having the party card and you can disagree with other communists; but that doesn't turn you into an anarchist. Wherever he goes, Ramadan spreads the form of Islamism that he inherited. An ambassador for Islamism who is all the more dangerous and difficult to pin down since he claims to be autonomous. Antoine Sfeir, founder of the *Cahiers de l'Orient* [*The Orient Review*], who has written several books on Islamism and who was one of the first to have exposed Tariq Ramadan's doublespeak, is certainly not mistaken in saying: "As far as I'm concerned, he is no doubt one of the key figures of the Brotherhood."[50] Richard Labévière, a Radio France International (RFI) reporter and author of several books on Islamist terrorism, backs him up. In April 1998, in the course of a trip to Cairo, he had occasion to interview the head of the Brotherhood, Guide Machour. The latter confirmed the fact that belonging to the Brotherhood was not a question of "being a member" or "not being a member," but a question of adhering to a certain way of thinking; he added: "The work carried out by Hani and Tariq is totally in keeping with the purest traditions of the Muslim Brotherhood."[51]

Violence? What violence?

Tariq Ramadan vehemently denies that his grandfather had anything to do with the ever-increasing recourse to violence in the name of Islam. In his eyes, Hassan al-Banna is "by no means the 'father' of that 'modern Islamism' characterized by violent demonstrations and simplistic, obtuse anti-Western prejudice."[52] Listening to him, one tends to forget that al-Banna founded a movement that intended to raise high the flag of Islam by whatever means, even if this meant "death on the road to God": "Despite the portrait given of him by the British colonizers (who, in Egypt and elsewhere, have always accused their opponents of the worst violence and the most horrible crimes) al-Banna never killed anyone or arranged for a political assassination," declared Ramadan in *Questioning Islam*[53]—even at the cost of escalating from revisionism to negationism.

Hassan al-Banna was quite explicit in his praise for the armed jihad that he considered to be the highest form of courage. In 1940, he described, for the benefit of the Muslim Brotherhood, what holy war entailed: "What I mean by holy war (jihad) is the duty that must be obeyed until the day of resurrection and which God's messenger sets down in these words . . . . The first stage in the sacred war is to expel evil from one's own heart; the highest stage is armed combat in the service of God. The intermediate stages are waging war with one's voice, one's pen, and one's hand, and by words of truth addressed to unjust authorities."[54] This glorification of armed combat as the supreme degree of the jihad was not a vain formula. In the months that followed, the Brotherhood decided to create a secret armed section, the Special Organization. Its mission was to prepare a selected number of militants for armed resistance. Tariq Ramadan does not deny the fact, but he describes it as a way of preparing for self-defense, an understandable concern when they were up against the British, who might well decide "to physically eliminate their opponents"—or in case "they refused, after repeated urgings, to leave the country."[55] The truth of the matter is that the Special Organization was primarily engaged in sending militants to fight in Palestine. Even before the creation of Israel in 1947, the Brotherhood sent armed squads to track down the Jewish immigrants. Tariq Ramadan takes pride in recounting these events: "Al-Banna provided assistance to the Palestinians by sending them an advisor and a specialist in military training, raising funds to buy weapons, and setting up training camps that he ran jointly with members of the Special Organization. Volunteers came to Palestine in groups to support the resistance."[56] Later on, another armed group in Palestine was to claim close links to the Brotherhood—Hamas. Its very existence suffices to refute the idea that the Brotherhood's ideology has nothing violent or fanatic about it. But Ramadan takes pains to explain that, in Palestine, violence has nothing violent about it, since it is legitimate: "Hassan al-Banna was opposed to violence and approved of the use of arms only in Palestine as a way of resisting Zionist colonialism."[57]

Tariq Ramadan was well aware of the fact that his grandfather had called for a jihad, but he vindicated him by explaining that the call was strictly limited to situations of "legitimate defense" or "resistance in the face of injustice"[58]—two criteria that are highly subjective. On this basis, violence was legitimate when it was a question of facing up to Nasser, just as it was in opposing British occupation. Or just as it will be every time that any obstacle threatens to block the Muslim Brotherhood's quest for domination. Ramadan is brazen enough to claim that the association has never been responsible for acts of violence. Yet in March 1948, for example, a judge was assassinated for having condemned a Muslim Brother. And on December 28 of the same year, before al-Banna's death, the Brotherhood claimed responsibility for the assassination of Prime Minister Nuqrashi Pasha.[59] These deaths could not have occurred without the Guide's knowledge.

Hassan al-Banna had, on occasion, barred activists who were in too much of a hurry to go into action, as he did in 1938–39, not because he repudiated the idea of an armed jihad, but because he felt the time was not ripe. During this period, his movement was gaining ground among the people. He was intent on consolidating his political influence, and therefore sought legitimacy. If the Brotherhood were to be condemned for illegal acts, for assassinations or for setting off riots, it would disrupt the evolution of his campaign. In 1948, the Brotherhood went too far; another assassination tipped the scales and the organization was dissolved by military decree. On November 15, a demonstration organized by the Brotherhood to honor their "martyrs" degenerated into a riot, in which two British officers were killed in their jeep. Those in charge often lost control of the young activists that they had fanaticized. Despite what Tariq Ramadan has said, the organization that his grandfather created was bound to produce fundamentalists who—when it appeared that indoctrination alone would not suffice—would be tempted, sooner or later, to take up arms in order to achieve their objectives. However, the fact that violence was a last resort is considered by Hassan al-Banna's grandson to be proof of great moderation in their choice of tactics. He turns the cool and calculated radicalism of his grandfather into something more spiritual. By way of example, he cites one of al-Banna's speeches, in which the latter tells his followers to weigh the pros and cons of using force carefully, but to take responsibility for whatever course is deemed necessary. "The Muslim Brotherhood will use force only as a last resort, when there is no other choice, and when they are convinced that they have achieved total faith and union. And if they must employ force, they will be dignified and sincere, they will give advance notice and wait for a reply; only then will they advance with nobility and pride, prepared to bear the consequences of their decision with confidence and calm."[60] In other words, the Muslim Brotherhood has no intention of calling for an armed revolution, but they will be forced to do so if they don't get their own way. This it what Tariq Ramadan, fascinated by the rhetoric, calls the Muslim Brotherhood's "clear perception."

An army of martyrs

It scarcely comes as a surprise, then, that, armed with such "clear perception," certain Brothers should have called for an armed jihad once they realized that victory by propaganda alone was not to be theirs. The death of al-Banna served to make them even more radical. He was shot dead on February

12, 1949, coming out of the headquarters of the Association of Young Muslims, where he had just taken part in a "reconciliation meeting" with the government in power—that is to say, the throne. The Brothers immediately denounced it as a political murder. Tariq Ramadan even takes it a step further: "The assassination of Hassan al-Banna was planned jointly by the British, the French, and the Americans."[61] It is hard to imagine the three powers reaching a common agreement on this assassination at a time when the independence movements and the communists were of far greater concern to the Americans and the British than the Islamic movements, but Ramadan's version has the advantage of making al-Banna a martyr not only in the struggle against the colonizers, but in the struggle against all Western powers. In Egypt, the death of al-Banna was taken as proof of the fact that coming to power via the institutional route was impossible. It was therefore necessary to advance to the next stage. Shortly before death put an end to his career, al-Banna himself had predicted that the Brothers were going to have to enter this second, far more radical phase. Every time Tariq Ramadan evokes al-Banna's speech, which his father had heard with his own ears, his voice cracks. He quotes al-Banna almost word for word in his lecture: "I want to read this passage to you, it will take up some of our time, but you must listen to it because he [al-Banna] has a clear premonition of what will happen after his death." In his speech, the Guide warns his companions: once their true objectives are revealed, they must be prepared to withstand the counterattack. "I want to be honest with you; your message is not widely known, but once it becomes known, once they realize what your objectives and your aims are, then you will encounter determined opposition and they will be relentless in their efforts to stop you." The rest is incredible. Hassan al-Banna gives a list of the misfortunes that await the Muslim Brotherhood—a list that amounts to a litany of the injustices and slanders to come:

> Governments will rise up against you and attempt to confine your sphere of action by blocking you in any way they can. Usurpers will stop at nothing to keep you from growing stronger and will seek to extinguish the light that your call sends out. To do so they will utilize ineffectual governments and will promote immorality; they will

> put these impotent governments under intense pressure and submit you to humiliation and hardship. They will contaminate your message by spreading infamous rumors and unjust suspicions, and make use of your slightest failing to portray you in despicable terms, relying on their superior power, their money, and their influence. No doubt you will then be caught up in the cycle of experience and adversity. You will be arrested, imprisoned, deported, and tortured.[62]

The most surprising thing is not that Hassan al-Banna was able to predict that his plan to subjugate the world under Islamist totalitarianism was going to provoke adverse reactions, but that his grandson should consider these reactions to be profoundly unjust! Tariq Ramadan, who claims to be non-violent and who denies having any connection with the Brotherhood, makes use of al-Banna's speech in the courses he gives for his followers as if it were an arcane last will and testament, proving that his grandfather knew, through divine intuition, of all the misfortunes that were—most unjustly—to strike him and his brothers.

> Those close to him, and in particular my father, were in the habit of saying: "But what was wrong with what we were doing? I didn't understand what he [al-Banna] was getting at—we were calling for reform, we were doing social work and he was talking to us about the gallows" .... In fact, he knew that his non-violence and his pursuit of deep-rooted reform were more dangerous than any kind of radicalism or revolution.[63]

One thing is certain: al-Banna could continue with his deadly, fundamentalist liberty-denying work without having to call openly for a jihad. On the other hand, one is left speechless when Tariq Ramadan asserts that the Muslim Brotherhood did nothing to provoke a crackdown. In his eyes, the Brotherhood's turn to radicalism was not the consequence of their ideology, but was due solely to the fact that they encountered resistance: "The radicalization of segments of the Muslim Brotherhood was the consequence and not the cause of Nasser's repression," he explained to the press.[64] It is time to take a closer look at the historical record.

Al-Banna's death left the Muslim Brotherhood disorganized and divided.

Some were in favor of continuing at the same pace, others wanted to speed things up. The Secret Organization was supposed to have been dissolved. In actual fact, it continued to exist and even served as a back-up force for the military putsch launched on July 23, 1952 by army officers headed by General Neguib and Gamal Abdel Nasser. One of the officers' emissaries, Anwar Sadat, met frequently with al-Banna to try to reach an agreement on a joint program, but without success. The officers were mistrustful, and suspected that the Muslim Brotherhood was playing a double game with the king.[65] Contact was re-established only after al-Banna's death. From then on, Sadat and other members of the Revolutionary Command Committee (RCC) developed close links with the Brotherhood. It was even rumored that Nasser himself had been one of their militants. One thing is certain: both Nasser and the officers sought the support of all the mass movements—be they communist or the Muslim Brotherhood—that could help in organizing a popular uprising that would legitimate their seizure of power. The Islamists, therefore, joined in with the growing number of Cairo students who were staging demonstrations in support of the general's *coup d'état*. But straight away things broke down. The Brothers wanted to be rewarded for their contribution: they asked the officers to set up a judicial system based entirely on the sharia, intimating, with their habitual rhetorical skill, that this would be the sole means of creating a fair balance between the benefits and penalties promised by Islam. Nasser was disconcerted by their demands. For a while, he tried to go along with them by appointing a number of their leaders to key posts; but they were never satisfied. Sayyid Qutb, in charge of the Brotherhood's propaganda, refused, in particular, to back the "Rally," the alliance that was to serve as Nasser's single party. Not that Qutb objected to a single-party system, which al-Banna himself had approved of; simply, he accepted the idea of a single party if—and only if—it served an Islamist government. Nasser thus found himself in the very same position as the Arab governments which, years later, were unsure how to stem the rise of the Islamists. After having made a good number of concessions, he concluded that it was not possible to negotiate with the fundamentalists. As early as 1954, he explained: "I have met several times with the Supreme Guide of the Brotherhood, who overwhelmed me with his demands. The thing he first asked for was for the government to ordain that women be veiled. Subsequently he made other demands, such as closing the cinemas and the theaters and other things as well that would make life gloomy and sinister. It was, of course, impossible to do such things."[66] Other evidence, emanating from the Brothers themselves, points to the same conclusion: the Brothers wanted to establish an Islamist regime. Nothing else would do. Nasser was prepared to make use of Islam in order to consolidate his power base, but his social project was nonetheless far more modern. On the other hand, he can hardly be described as an outstanding democrat. After having survived a period of intense colonialism, Egypt saw its future played out in an aggressive confrontation between nationalist dictators and fanatics. The nationalists were to win the first battle. Eight days after the signing of the Anglo-Egyptian treaty that the Muslim Brotherhood's Guide had denounced, a Brother fired eight shots at Nasser, who survived unscathed. The Brotherhood claimed that it was a set-up. At any rate, the failed assassination attempt resulted in the dissolution of the movement on October 29, 1954. From then on, Nasser embarked on a policy of bloody repression that made of the Brothers "an army of martyrs" in Olivier Carré's terms. Between 1954 and 1970, several thousand Muslim Brothers were arrested, imprisoned, tortured and, in certain cases, executed. They were not the only ones. Nasser's repression was also to take a heavy toll of the communists, the socialists, and the Wafdists, but the Brothers were the only ones to make use of their martyrdom as *a posteriori* justification of their own violence. Among them, Sayyid Qutb, the second prominent leader of the movement after al-Banna, called openly for an armed jihad and for the assassination of the "apostate tyrants."

Sayyid Qutb "initiates a perceptible shift . . . "

Sayyid Qutb is the theoretician that most Islamists engaged in terrorist acts consider their mentor. His career parallels that of al-Banna: he was born in the same year and also studied to be a schoolteacher. His hatred of what was modern stemmed not from experience with city life, but from an encounter with American society: he spent two and a half years in the United States as a trainee teacher. Before that, he published several books in which he tried to reconcile socialism and Islam, books such as *La justice en Islam* [*Islamic Justice*]. On his return, he published a book that was decidedly more Islamist and anti-capitalist than his previous works: *Le Combat entre l'Islam et le capitalisme* [*The Struggle between Islam and Capitalism*]: "Let us not be dupes of the struggle between the East and the West, which gives every appearance of being hard-fought and bitter. Both of them have in common a materialistic philosophy of life . . . . The real struggle is between Islam on the one hand, and the East plus the West on the other."[67]

Qutb joined the Brotherhood movement in 1951, and quickly rose in the hierarchy until he was put in charge of propaganda. He became one of the most prominent leaders after al-Banna's death, and therefore one of the first to be imprisoned when Nasser unleashed his repressive campaign against the Brothers. It was from prison that his influence was to spread more than ever. He was released and re-imprisoned several times. Each time, despite being tortured, he vehemently denied intending to conspire against Nasser. Once back in his cell, however, he set to work on another book, *Signes de pistes* [*Trail Markers*], in which he called in no uncertain terms for Nasser—whom he called an apostate—to be overthrown: "The present governments of the Muslims are in a state of apostasy. They feed at the table set out for them by the imperialists, be they Crusaders, Communists or Zionists . . . . Apostasy must be eliminated even if it is not strong enough to wage war."[68] Qutb described Egyptian society as living in a state of *jahiliyya*, the term used in the Koran to describe polytheist and pre-Islamic barbarity. The cult of Nasser was, according to him, but a new form of idolatry. He incited the Brothers to resort to any means in order to put an end to such decadence: "The establishment of an Islamic state is a categorical obligation." And he added: "If such a state can only be established by means of war, then war becomes our duty."[69]

Qutb was hanged on August 26, 1966, thus becoming the second martyr of the Brotherhood. His political testament spread like wildfire. A series of murders followed. The two most important, those that have changed the course of history and for which we are still paying the price today, were the assassination of the Algerian President Boudiaf on June 29, 1992 and the assassination of Anwar Sadat in October 1981. In both cases, the killers claimed to have been inspired by Qutb. Sadat had, however, established a truce with the Muslim Brotherhood and released most of them from prison, but he made the mistake of establishing diplomatic relations with Israel. One of the members of the group that had plotted Sadat's execution, an Islamist engineer, had brought out a book in which he called for the execution of "the apostates of Islam, who have fed at the table set out by the Zionists and the imperialists."[70]

It is evident, then, that bringing up Qutb's name today is a delicate matter, even for the Muslim Brothers, among whom the more moderate consider that "he went too far"—without, however, questioning their own views. At first sight, Ramadan would appear to belong to this group. In *On the Origins of the Muslim Renaissance*, he explained that Qutb initiated "a perceptible shift, but one that was particularly important in relation to Hassan al-Banna," without coming out clearly against this "shift."[71] He is content to preserve intact his grandfather's philosophy by describing Qutb's interpretation as "perceptibly" different. A shift that he accounts for by pointing to the fact that Qutb had lived in the West and had developed a form of thought that was "reactive" and "strained," and motivated by hatred of the West. As if al-Banna himself had never developed a "reactive" and rigid view of the West! It is typical of Ramadan's approach that he refuses to admit that the intent to return to an Islam "purified" of all outside influences is itself "reactive," preferring to think of it as an attempt to recover the purely positive aspects of the past. This can only be a form of blindness or else simply propaganda.

He also attributes the "shift" initiated by Qutb to the influence of thinkers such as Mawdudi, the famous theoretician of the Islamic state and founder of the Jama'at-i-Islami, a Pakistani movement similar to the Muslim Brotherhood. As if Qutb could not have found in al-Banna's philosophy reason enough to found an Islamic state. It is clear that he borrowed from Mawdudi the contemporary use of the term *jahiliyya*, but the idea of a defensive jihad that could be revived in case of adversity was already foreseen by al-Banna and was there, ready to be reactivated.

The other factor that, according to Tariq Ramadan, explains the shift initiated by Qutb has to do with Nasser's repression. Here, he is in agreement with the view expressed by many historians. It is certain that Qutb would not have called for the assassination of Nasser if the latter had agreed to establish the type of Islamist regime demanded by the Brotherhood. But does this make of Qutb a Brother different from the others? Would not al-Banna himself, in the same circumstances, have written a book similar to *Trail Markers*? Al-Banna died before it became clear that his plans for the future would be brutally cut short by Nasser. If he had been faced with such an insurmountable obstacle, thrown into prison and tortured, he, too, would most probably have called for a holy war. Did he not assert that the resort to armed combat was the highest degree of jihad and that the resort to force was justified if other means failed?

Tariq Ramadan prefers not to indulge in such conjectures, obsessed as he is by the rehabilitation of al-Banna's model—which does not mean that he rejects Sayyid Qutb. On occasion he refers to him by name in his lectures, as if he were a thinker of no particular importance, but for the most part references to him remain allusive, as if Ramadan wanted to avoid revealing his true thoughts. But Ramadan is a fervent admirer of one of Qutb's female disciples, who was imprisoned and tortured during the same period: Zaynab al-Ghazali, for whose memoirs Ramadan wrote a preface in 1996. Entitled *Des jours de ma vie* [*Some Days from My Life*], the book is a raging firestorm that recounts in detail the tortures and humiliations suffered at the hands of Nasser's jailers. One would expect that reading this book would be a moving experience. But one finds instead a woman who was an ultra-fundamentalist before the first arrests even took place. At a time when Nasser was making numerous conciliatory gestures to this woman, whose association advocated the Islamization of women and who served as one of the Brotherhood's agents, she refused, for example, to join a public meeting organized by the Socialist Union in support of Nasser—not in order to maintain her independence, but out of respect for "decency": "I have made it clear: members of the governing board of the Muslim Women and members of the General Assembly live in conformity with the Muslim rites and cannot, consequently, take part in the sort of activities where many people congregate and where members of both sexes commingle freely with no respect for decency."[72] That's the sort of person who, Tariq Ramadan tells us in his preface, should be "a model for all Muslim women."[73] The rest of the book is even more enlightening. After having refused to negotiate in any way, al-Ghazali took part in the Brotherhood's speculations on how to overthrow Nasser. When the latter threatened to dissolve her organization for disturbing the public peace, she declared: "Thanks be to God for having filled Nasser with hatred and fear of me. I, too, hate him for the love of God. His cruelty and his tyranny will only reinforce our resolve as combatants to listen solely to the dictates of our conscience and to live for our cause, for our unique way and for monotheism, and by the grace of God we will triumph."[74]

Al-Ghazali was thrown into prison and left without food and water for six days. On arrival, she was locked in a room with dogs that snapped at her. At any rate, she was terrified by what she thought was happening to her, but when they released her, she realized that she had not bled at all. The dogs must have been toothless, or had perhaps been trained to simulate biting. She interpreted this as a miracle. Despite torture, she refused to admit that the Brotherhood was intent on overthrowing Nasser. But she did this in her own particular way:

> The Muslim Brotherhood has no intention of assassinating Nasser or anyone else. Neither do they intend to lay waste the country or stir up trouble. If anyone has ruined the country, it's Nasser himself. Our objective is far more important and far more noble. Our objective is to reveal the pure truth, the supreme truth, the presence of a sole God on earth, monotheism, the veneration of the unique God, respect for the commandments of the Koran and the Sunna and their application. Our cause is to govern in the name of God and in accord with his commandments. The day when this comes about, their institutions will vanish and their legends disappear. Our objective is to reform, to make better, to seek perfection and not to destroy, devastate or stir up trouble.[75]

One can well imagine that the police officer who was interrogating her did not find her reply all that reassuring. Al-Ghazali herself saw no reason for him to be skeptical.[76] She denied taking part in a conspiracy, but at the same time indicated that she agreed with Qutb when he called for the murder of representatives of apostate governments. In the same book she recounts how the author of *Trail Markers* had given her the manuscript of his book before she was taken to prison, where she spent part of her time in the company of Qutb's two sisters. Even several decades later, when she was writing her memoirs, she never expressed the slightest criticism of the man who had served as theoretician for the Islamists that killed in the name of Islam. On the contrary, throughout the book she expresses her admiration for his courage and his perspicacity. The fact that Tariq Ramadan wrote the preface for this book is thus not without significance, all the more so since he endorsed the book in the following terms: "Zaynab al-Ghazali never went too far . . . "[77]

Trained by the Islamic Foundation

Because Ramadan has taken pains to protect al-Banna from the criticism to which Sayyid Qutb was subjected does not mean that he disapproves of Qutb. In 1998, the very year in which he defended his doctoral thesis on reformist thinking and the "perceptible" shift initiated by Qutb, he left for a year of study at the Leicester Islamic Foundation, an Islamist institute whose mission was to use England as a base for spreading the doctrines of Mawdudi and Qutb!

Founded in 1973, the institute accommodates an Islamic training center known as the Markfield Institute of Higher Education, a most pompous title for what is neither more nor less than a university of propaganda. Conceived at first as a means of ensuring that Muslim students in England had a refuge that would protect them from contamination and keep them from forgetting Islam, the foundation, little by little, became a base camp for promoting "an Islamic social order in Great Britain."[78] The British environment seemed congenial to the most radical of Islamists. Adopting a strategy that many find incomprehensible, Britain gladly welcomed jihadists intent on organizing their projects far from the oppressive surveillance of Arab Muslim dictatorships. Prince Charles himself even provided the Leicester Institute with a certain degree of legitimacy by granting it a prize in recognition of its service in the spread of a religious culture. Apparently searching for any means to demonstrate his morality, the future sovereign—who is also the head of the Anglican Church—decided to support any religious movement, however marginal or extreme, that enabled him to present himself as the defender of religious liberty—even if it meant lending an aura of legitimacy to the most controversial Islamic training center in Europe. Thanks to this official recognition, Tariq Ramadan no longer had reason to conceal the fact that he had been trained there. At the age of 36, he lived with all his family on the Leicester campus, where the alleyways are named after Qutb and Mawdudi. In the introduction to his book *To Be a European Muslim*, he thanked the institute for the instruction received there: "If this book has been possible, I owe it first of all to the excellent working conditions offered by the Islamic Foundation. I owe particular thanks to the president, Professor Khurshid Ahmad, for the trust he placed in me, and the institute's director, Dr Manazir Ahsan, for his warm welcome."[79] He had every reason to express his thanks. For the entire year that he passed at the institute, he received a scholarship of £1,000 a month, in addition to free lodgings.

The Pakistani Islamists who offered him this opportunity have, for a long time, worked hand in hand with the Muslim Brotherhood network, in particular with Tawhid, the bookshop in Lyon that serves as Tariq Ramadan's headquarters. Until recently, the Islamic Foundation supplied the bookshop with books by Qutb or Mawdudi. But now it is a two-way exchange. The most radical Islamic foundation in Europe so appreciated Tariq Ramadan's works that they have undertaken to translate them and distribute them in England. Mohammed Seddiqi, one of the leaders, confirmed that Ramadan's writings fitted perfectly into the institute's tradition, as represented by Mawdudi and Qutb: "In the beginning, the foundation was inspired by the Islamic movement to translate Mawdudi's works and also those of Qutb. Today we publish more contemporary authors, such as Tariq Ramadan."[80] The Swiss preacher's books are popular with British Islamists; 20,000 copies have been sold and they are to be found on the shelves of the foundation's library. One book will never have a place there, except as an object of abhorrence: *The Satanic*

Verses by Salman Rushdie. The Islamic Foundation spearheaded the campaign against him. It is the foundation that served as the intermediary in the campaign launched by the Mawdudi network in Pakistan with which the institute is linked. In obedience to orders sent out by the Islamic Foundation of Madras, the Leicester foundation distributed to all the Muslim organizations a condemnation of the "blasphemous" book. According to Gilles Kepel, this campaign gave Mawdudi's followers a dominant influence within the English Islamic circles that have a reputation for extremism (often known as Londonistan)—a world in which the name of Tariq Ramadan strikes a harmonious note.

Chapter 2

The Heir

Tariq Ramadan admits that he is descended from a dynasty that is both religious and political: "Even before I had been formed intellectually, my education had given me the idea that we were entrusted with the inheritance of certain values."[1] He not only teaches about Hassan al-Banna, but he also imitates him down to the last detail—starting with the firm intention of employing his pedagogical talents in the service of Islamism. Many newspaper articles refer to him as a theologian, others as an imam. In fact, he has no degree from Al-Azhar University. His religious learning comes from his family, an education in an exceptionally political Islam, completed by a rapid-fire apprenticeship in Cairo and, above all, by a year's study at the Leicester Islamic Foundation. His thesis, granted without honors by the Faculty of Arts of Geneva, is nothing more than an opus in praise of Hassan al-Banna. He wrote a Master's thesis on "The concept of suffering in Nietzsche's philosophy," but his knowledge of philosophy has served principally to assail Voltaire's and Dostoevsky's permissiveness in conferences often organized by the Muslim Brotherhood. In lectures to students, he takes a more prudent stand. Ramadan has often been introduced as a university professor, but in truth, up to the time when an American Catholic university decided to appoint him to a chair in the autumn of 2004, he was simply a modest schoolteacher in Saussure (Switzerland). Before being invited, in 2006, to be Senior Research Fellow at the European Studies and Middle East Center of St. Antony's College, Oxford, he did teach once a week at Fribourg University, but as an outside collaborator and only for courses on the Islamic religion.

Tariq Ramadan owes his fame and his reputation as an intellectual to his status as a Muslim leader. But what can legitimize this status, since he is in no way a theological scholar? First and foremost, he is a preacher—whose aura for Muslims had long been due to his direct descent from the mentor of modern Islamism. That is, up to the day when he made a name for himself not as a scholar but as a political leader with a considerable following thanks to the tapes of his lectures, as edited and distributed by the Muslim Brotherhood network. He was first presented as a religious leader, but was subsequently conceded the status of an "intellectual" on the basis of his many books on Muslims and the West—books that go over and over the same ground, but that have been published and republished with additions and rewordings first by Islamist publishing houses, and then by mainstream publishing houses impressed by the sales posted by his first publishers. His charisma, his undeniable pedagogical talent, and his perfect mastery in adapting the level of his discourse to the audience in question, Muslim or otherwise, have taken care of the rest. Always on the go, he sets off heated arguments in whatever country he visits, monopolizing public debate and defending his grandfather's Islam in veiled terms. Despite this subversive reputation, or perhaps on account of it, he has become a media idol in many European and North African countries. One imagines him to be somebody exceptional. In fact, the heir apparent has done nothing but follow in the footsteps of his grandfather and his father, along a path determined from the moment of his birth.

The influence of his father, Saïd Ramadan

Not only is Tariq Ramadan the grandson of Hassan al-Banna, but he is also the son of Saïd Ramadan, the Guide's favorite disciple, who spread the Muslim Brotherhood's Islam beyond Egypt's frontiers. Tariq was brought up in the cult that his father devoted to Hassan. "He [Saïd] had learned all that he knew from this man that had given him so much and provided him with so much, and who had, from his earliest age, formed and protected him," wrote Tariq Ramadan in the preface to his book *Le face-à-face des civilisations* [*The Confrontation of Civilizations*]. "He never stopped talking about him . . . . For hours on end he recounted from memory the events and the occasions that had left their mark on him, his spiritual son, whom they called Hassan al-Banna junior."[2]

"Banna junior" was born on April 12, 1926 in Shibin el-Kom, seventy kilometres north of Cairo. He was only fourteen years old when he first heard the name of the great al-Banna mentioned in a lecture given in Tanta. He was still at secondary school when he joined the Brotherhood. After obtaining a law degree from Cairo University in 1946, he was chosen by the Guide as his personal secretary, as well as editor of his review, *Al-Shihâb*. Of all his faithful disciples, Saïd Ramadan was undoubtedly the one he preferred, to the extent that he gave him his cherished daughter, Wafa al-Banna, in marriage. A woman of whom Tariq Ramadan tells us: "My mother was fully imbued with this heritage: she was the eldest of Hassan al-Banna's children, but in addition, until the age of fifteen and a half, she was very close to him and greatly influenced by his spiritual appeal. Through her I have come to know my grandfather's unique qualities, as a man and as a father."[3]

Tariq Ramadan's parents grew up in the cult devoted to al-Banna, and they transmitted this cult to their children. Tariq Ramadan remembers how hard his father fought to rehabilitate Hassan al-Banna's reputation. "Hassan al-Banna, through his total devotion to God and God's teachings, had let light into his [Saïd's] heart and laid out the path of his commitment. To those who criticized him, who spoke of him without even having met him or listened to him, or had only read him, he would recall how he had learned spirituality, love, fraternity, and humility at his side."[4] This is a tradition taken up today by Tariq Ramadan, brought up in the same atmosphere of idolatry. The heir apparent admires his grandfather as much as he does his own father. He speaks unendingly about Saïd Ramadan's military prowess when, at the age of twenty-one, he set off for Palestine to fight the Zionists. Tariq Ramadan claims that he "took part in the defense of Jerusalem." It was in 1947 and the state of Israel did not yet exist; the territory was divided between Egypt and Jordan under British mandate. It was not thus a question of helping the Palestinians recover the occupied territories, but of training anti-Jewish resistance units. The contact in the field, the person who helped the movement conduct its operations, was no novice as regards fighting the Jews: he was none other than Haj al-Husseini, the man who had asked the Muslims to fight alongside Nazi Germany in the Second World War. He had even trained two Bosnian army divisions—both of them in SS uniforms—assigned to massacre the Serbian population. He counted on Adolf Hitler to rid the world of the Jews. Hitler's downfall left him an orphan in a particularly awkward predicament. Providentially, Hassan al-Banna—another friend whom he had known since 1935—arranged for his political exile. Thanks to him, he rapidly found employment, becoming the mufti of Jerusalem, a position that meant organizing the arrival of fighters drawn from the ranks of the Muslim Brotherhood's Special Organization, come to combat the Jewish immigrants, some of whom had only just been released from concentration camps. The latter saw in Israel a place of refuge where they would no longer have to suffer from anti-Semitism. And they landed up face to face with al-Husseini, busy raising new legions of combatants. The head of these legions was named Saïd Ramadan.

From 1945 on, Tariq Ramadan's father was in charge of establishing a branch of the Muslim Brotherhood in Palestine. Al-Banna's special envoy kept his promise. He carried out his mission as both war leader and diplomat, and became the indispensable ally of King Abdullah of Jordan, who, at that time, would stop at nothing to prevent Jerusalem from becoming a majority Jewish town. It was he who proposed that the king send tanks into the old quarters of Jerusalem to evict the Jews, a feat of military prowess that is recounted on the website of the Geneva Islamic Center: "One night he [Saïd Ramadan] woke King Abdullah of Jordan to announce that Jerusalem was about to be taken over by the Haganah and Irgun gangs, and to ask him to send the Jordanian army to help defend the holy city. Which Abdullah did, and Jerusalem remained free until June of 1967, the year in which it fell with almost no resistance. This time, there was no one on hand to wake King Hussein."

King Abdullah named Saïd Ramadan head of the military court of Jerusalem, but he resigned after two months. He was not there to pursue a career. The movement needed him to set up cells in Muslim countries that would pledge allegiance to the Guide. He would be al-Banna's ambassador, as well as his secretary. Everywhere he went, he served as the Brotherhood's envoy in key posts. In 1948, shortly after the creation of Israel, he left for Pakistan on a particularly important mission: to represent the Muslim Brotherhood at the World Islamic Congress in Karachi. His name was put forward for the post of general secretary of the Congress, but his extremism alarmed Congress members, who themselves were far from being moderate Muslims, and a less controversial candidate was chosen. With his characteristic gift for euphemism, Tariq Ramadan came retrospectively to the defense of his father: "his determination frightened the 'diplomats.'"[5] When he was not busy denying the fanaticism of his grandfather, he was occupied defending the reputation of his father. All forms of criticism are but calumny. But no matter. Polemics have never prevented the Ramadans from pursuing their program.

Even though he was not elected secretary of the Muslim Congress, Saïd Ramadan was to have a decisive influence on the debate in Pakistan during the 1950s. This new nation, bringing together Muslims of the Indian subcontinent, had just been born and was in search of an identity based on pride in being Muslim. Saïd Ramadan had no trouble convincing the elite to choose an Islamic republic. No one knew better how to monopolize a national debate (a technique that he passed on to his son). He soon became very popular with young Pakistani intellectuals, thanks to his weekly radio program on Muslim world affairs. He also published booklets that were easy to read and therefore reached a wide public. The prime minister of the time, Ali Khan, even wrote a preface for one of them. In his *jinah*, the traditional Pakistani headdress, this chameleon-like person made people forget he was Egyptian. At the heart of the debate on what direction the constitution was to take, he was omnipresent in the media—arguing, on every occasion, for legislation based on the sharia. In 1956, a few years after his stay in Pakistan, the country ended up becoming an Islamic republic. It was at this point that he met Mawdudi, the true theoretician of the Pakistani Islamic state. In an article written as a funeral eulogy in memory of his father, Tariq Ramadan wrote in somewhat mysterious terms: "Mawdudi had thanked him for having saved him from his recklessness."[6] Which would imply that Saïd had a moderating influence on Mawdudi, but this remains to be proved. At any rate, the two men were acquainted.

In 1949, al-Banna's emissary was on tour for the Muslim Brotherhood, with, as pretext, a cultural mission for Pakistan, when he learned that his master had died. Tariq Ramadan tries to have us relive his suffering when faced by the death of the man who had taught him to "bow his head to the ground" when praying, as a sign of humility. He fails to remind us that his master had taught him above all to lift his head up and fight in the name of the jihad. In his usual euphemistic style, Tariq Ramadan recounts: "After the assassination of his master in 1949, he had learned his lesson and sacrificed everything to spread the liberating message of Islam." Saïd Ramadan, who had by then become one of the masterminds of the organization, returned to Egypt in 1950, the year in which the decree banning the movement was lifted. The regime in power had made a gesture of conciliation, in the hope that the organization would become less aggressive once deprived of its leader. But that was leaving "Banna junior" out of account. On his return, Saïd Ramadan took up the fight where al-Banna had left off. "Once back in Egypt, he became involved in the mobilization for social and political reform. He travelled round the country giving lectures and organizing meetings,"[7] his son tells us. For two years, 1950 to 1952, the Brotherhood movement became more fanatical and better mobilized than ever. It was the eve of the generals' putsch. But Saïd Ramadan continued to be obsessed by the idea of spreading Islamist ideology beyond Egypt's frontiers. He edited a monthly review, *Al-Muslimoon*, published in Arabic and English, that served as the principal vehicle for the influence of the Brotherhood's ideology and spread its message everywhere it could establish a foothold: from Morocco to Indonesia via Palestine, Sudan, Jordan, Lebanon, Algeria . . .

It was his international perspective that was to provide him with a way out before and after independence. When Nasser's repression struck, he was imprisoned—as were all the other officers of the movement who had demanded that the sharia be applied. But he was not held for long. He was released after four months, thanks to General Neguib, who apparently remained convinced that the Brotherhood could serve as an ally. Once freed, in 1954, he left for Jerusalem accompanied by Sayyid Qutb, who had also been released. They attended the first meeting of the World Islamic Congress of Jerusalem as representatives of the Brotherhood. This time he was elected general secretary of the Congress. But not for long. To borrow his son's words, Saïd Ramadan's "determination" once again frightened the "diplomats," this time Glubb Pasha, whose real name was Sir John Bagot Glubb. This local "Lawrence of Arabia" was a general who had joined up with the Arabs. It was he who commanded the legendary Arab Legion of King Abdullah of Jordan, the legion that had reduced the Jewish section of the old city of Jerusalem to ashes during the 1948 war. And yet, Saïd Ramadan frightened him to the extent that he banished him from Jerusalem.

"Banna junior" could have returned to Egypt and suffered martyrdom, like Qutb, but he escaped adversity by journeying from one sponsor to the next, always obsessed by the idea of spreading the Brotherhood's philosophy on an international scale. He landed up in Damascus in Syria for a brief spell, from where he launched a new version of *Al-Muslimoon* with the help of a Syrian publisher. He also spent time in Jordan. But it was in Saudi Arabia that he found his true place of refuge.

A Saudi/American agent versus Nasser

Saïd Ramadan was warmly welcomed by the Wahhabite monarchy, which lacked both administrators and intellectuals. Saudi society had rapidly evolved from a primitive Bedouin state to all-out modernism thanks to the intake of petrodollars. The only bond that welded the country together was Wahhabism, an Islamic fundamentalism close to the Muslim Brotherhood's Salafism, although markedly more traditional in outlook.

Wahhabism was the result of a politico-religious pact negotiated in 1774 between Ibn Saud, a tribal chief, and Muhammad Ibn Abdul Wahhab, a Salafist preacher faithful to the teachings of Ibn Taymiyya, the father of Islamic fundamentalism. During the period when some Muslim Brothers in Egypt were planning to go into exile, Saudi Arabia was undergoing a radical transformation; it was attempting to maintain the teaching of Salafist Islamism that served as an ideological straitjacket, but it was hampered by the lack of an educated elite. Thus, the Brothers, who were familiar with Ibn Taymiyya and had studied Ibn Abdul Wahhab, were enthusiastically welcomed. During the time he spent in Saudi Arabia, Saïd Ramadan served as tutor to the royal family, teaching them Wahhabism and becoming one of their most trusted advisors. In 1962, he even oversaw the creation of the Muslim World League (Al Rabita al Islamiya Al Alamiya), a conduit for financing the spread of the Islamic faith (the Saudi version of the Islamic faith) worldwide, even if this meant serving as a trust fund for Islamist terrorism on account of the obligation to give alms (*zakat*). The Rabita (another name for the League) was supported by the Americans, who counted on Saudi Arabia in the struggle against Arab nationalism and communism. Pakistan, in which Saïd Ramadan had placed his hopes, seemed reluctant to assume this role. It was thus necessary to find another country ready to promulgate Islamism as an antidote to communism and Arab nationalism. The Saudis were more than ready to play the game. Fulfilling the obligation to give alms would atone for their incredible financial windfall; moreover, the funds would be used in the struggle against Arab socialism, which was highly offensive to these ultra-religious representatives, firm believers in private property. Saïd Ramadan was to be one of the architects of this alliance between the Saudis and the Americans against Nasser. He himself drew up sections of the constitutive charter of the Muslim World League—of which section 2 criticizes by implication the Bandung Conference and the Non-Aligned Movement. It called for combating "dangerous conferences in which the enemies of Islam intend to encourage Muslims to rebel against religion and destroy their unity and fraternity."[8]

This historical background is particularly significant. Tariq Ramadan claims today that there is a fundamental difference between the Brothers' ideology and that of the Wahhabis. Ever since Saudi Arabia gave the Americans permission to establish military bases on the ground on which Mecca stands—ever since, in particular, the world has become aware of the havoc produced by Wahhabism—the Swiss preacher has never missed an occasion to castigate "the traditionalist reactionary Islamism" of the Saudis, not only out of anti-Americanism, but also in order to appear more modern in the eyes of the anti-globalist and communist militants that he is intent on attracting. He forgets to mention that his model father helped the Saudis to become the sponsors of this Wahhabism, second to none in the virulence of its reactionary policies and anti-communism.

The creation of the Geneva Islamic Center

In the late 1950s, even before the founding of the Muslim World League, Saïd Ramadan persuaded Prince Faisal to help him found a network of Islamic centers in the main European capitals. The objective: to re-Islamize the Old World, that is to say, to facilitate the export of an ultra-reactionary, ultra-rigid Islam, spilling over into the sole region in the world that had succeeded in establishing a balance between politics and religion in a secular context.

After some two years of commuting between Jordan, Syria, Lebanon, and Saudi Arabia, Saïd Ramadan took up the question of what city would provide the best home base. He arrived in Geneva in 1958, but then travelled to Germany, where he earned a doctorate in law from the University of Cologne with a thesis, a very concise thesis, on the "sharia."[9] In terms of scientific contribution, it consisted mostly of advocating a return to the founding precepts and Salafist reformist doctrine of the Muslim Brotherhood. Tariq Ramadan speaks of "a synthesis of the basic views of Hassan al-Banna regarding the sharia, legal power, political organization and religious pluralism."[10] He was well advised to specify that his father insisted on "religious pluralism" and not political pluralism. In fact, Saïd Ramadan—as Hassan al-Banna had before him—dreamed of a political system that would be not democratic but theocratic, while allowing for pluralism, which meant that a diversity of opinions and interpretations was, of course, possible . . . But diversity only between Islamic scholars regarding interpretations of the sharia! In his thesis, Saïd Ramadan defended a clearly "totalitarian" concept of religion: "All religious ideas that shape the imaginative outlook and content of human mind and that determine the action of the human will are potentially or in principle totalitarian." Which would not be that bad, had Saïd not to add in the next sentence: "They must seek to impose their own standards and rules on all social activities and institutions from elementary schools to law and government."[11]

Published under the title *Islamic Law: Its Scope and Equity,* Saïd Ramadan's thesis comes with a preface written by Gerhard Kegel, a professor of international law at Cologne University. He hailed Dr. Saïd Ramadan as a "well-known active supporter of the Islamic Movement" who knows Islam from the inside and is thus likely to avoid the hidden pitfalls that await the "foreign student." He congratulated him on his "remarkable contribution to our knowledge of the Islamic people and, perhaps, to peace between all peoples." The "perhaps" takes on full significance when one reads a second preface that appeared in the French edition of the book—by M. A. K. Brohi, the former Pakistani Minister of Justice. He enlightens us regarding the pertinence of a thesis that redeems the sharia from the colonial version spread by "foreign researchers": "The problem is that it is impossible for Europeans, even the most enlightened, who have been brought up in a secular culture . . . to truly understand that a Muslim gives himself over entirely to the divine will as expressed in divine law, and that he is called upon to situate every one of his acts in a divine framework that is all-encompassing."[12] This double perspective points up the naiveté of some Western scholars, all too ready, as an anti-colonial reflex, to let Muslims who know Islam "from the inside" have their way. Saïd Ramadan already knew, well before his son, how to exploit this reflex when, in 1961, he chose to establish an Islamic Center in the heart of Geneva.

"Here the family will live in peace," reads the introduction to the Center. And it was indeed in an atmosphere of calm that Saïd Ramadan, accompanied by his wife and children, inaugurated the Islamic Center of Geneva, just a stone's throw from the seat of the United Nations, with the aim of persuading all believers to join in "the struggle against all forms of materialistic atheism,"[13] a creed that the Center has never ceased to invoke. "Dedicated to the service of God," the Center serves as headquarters for Muslim Brothers in exile. There you could run into famous Islamists, such as Malcolm X or Yusuf Islam (Cat Stevens), or less illustrious figures, such as members of the Islamic Salvation Front (FIS) of Algeria or Afghan veterans on their way through Geneva. In the beginning, the governing board consisted of well-known figures of radical Islam from Asia, India and Malaysia.[14]

It might come as a surprise to see an association founded by Islamists who made no secret of their sponsors, their contacts, and their objectives so respectably and publicly established. It is just that the Center chose the right country for exile. Switzerland is a haven of peace, a paradise for freedom of expression. Furthermore, during the period they were settling in, the Muslim Brotherhood was on excellent terms with the European and American secret services, in that they, too, were fighting "atheist materialism," that is to say communism, the top priority at the time. In a brochure published by the Center, Saïd Ramadan urged Muslims to fight Communism, which he considered a new form of idolatry: "Without an ideology that can counter theirs, that can face up to communist agents that are to be found everywhere . . . disaster is imminent." And he added: "Muslims are increasingly aware that it is for them a choice between communism and Islam."[15] Thus in Geneva, as elsewhere, the Muslim Brotherhood was considered a valuable American asset in the Cold War. Jacques Pitteloud, a former coordinator of the Swiss secret service, admitted as much: "At the time Saïd Ramadan was pretty much on the side of the allies."[16] Even when the Center was no longer clearly on the side of the allies, its Saudi sponsorship—in a country of banks—was enough to protect it. So it was from its Geneva base that the Muslim Brotherhood was to sow the seeds from which the enemies of the West were to grow. The Swiss authorities, whose initial welcome had cooled, were powerless to stop them.

In August of 1995, the fraternity's Supreme Guide, Mustapha Machour, officially acknowledged the existence of a coordinated international network: "We have branches abroad, in London, Germany and elsewhere in Europe. Every Muslim Brotherhood activist who left Egypt has set up a branch in the host country and remains in touch with the central organization."[17] Among them, Saïd Ramadan was the most militant. After Geneva, he opened an Islamic Center in Munich and then one in London in 1964.[18] His view of things was simple: the West was to be the place of refuge for them to have a free hand in planning revenge. He insisted on the need for lecturing and producing newspapers and journals that would transmit the Brotherhood's ideology, in particular via the Al-Muslimoon publishing house that he transferred from Egypt to Geneva. Located on Rue des Eaux-Vives, the Center is laid out along the same lines as the headquarters that Hassan al-Banna had built in Cairo. Gamal al-Banna, who was eight years old when his brother Hassan founded the Brotherhood, recalls the way the family home, which was also a political center, was organized: "We had acquired a spacious three-floor house; the first floor was reserved for the Brothers' meetings, the second for the family, and the third for Imam Hassan and his family." The Geneva Islamic Center is more or less a replica. The ground floor serves as a reception room and conference hall, whereas the space upstairs is reserved for more confidential meetings. Once a militant is sufficiently advanced in his religious apprenticeship, he can go upstairs, where the rhetoric is far more radical. Several former fellow travelers, interrogated in the course of investigations into terrorism in Europe, have confirmed the change of tone that they observed. Unlike the language of the public lectures, which has to be read between the lines, the preaching upstairs was apparently far more outspoken. No need to rush things. Whatever happens, demography is on the side of the Muslims; a thousand years from now and Europe will be Muslim.

Tariq the conqueror

It is in this Center, on Rue des Eaux-Vives, that Tariq Ramadan was born and grew up, surrounded by the choicest samplings of Islamic activism. In his book written with Alain Gresh, he fully accepts the fact: "He [Saïd Ramadan] had been put in charge of the Muslim Brothers in exile. So, from my birth in 1962, I was surrounded by the sayings and thoughts of Muslims who, while living in Europe, were totally immersed in the realities of the Muslim world, Arab but also Indo-Pakistani."[19] Tariq Ramadan was born barely one year after the creation of the Geneva Islamic Center. The family consisted already of four boys (Aymen, Bilal, Yasser, and Hani) and one girl (Arwa). Tariq was, then, the last—born in the heart of Europe. It was to seal his fate. His parents did not pick a name for him at random: "Tariq" echoes the name Tariq Ibn Zyad, the first Muslim conqueror to have set foot on the Christian soil of Spain. The name Gibraltar, which means "rock of Tariq" in Arabic, is a reminder. Tariq Ramadan is quick to explain to the press that this is a mere coincidence. According to him, "Tariq" had no belligerent connotation for his parents. Are we really supposed to believe that Saïd Ramadan and Wafa al-Banna, who had just created a center in the heart of Europe in order to Islamize the Old World, chose their son's first name at random? It appears unlikely, especially when we know the extent to which the career of each of the children was planned in advance. When he grew to manhood, Tariq, the aptly named, was to marry Isabelle, the Catholic. It is not a play on words: his wife is, in fact, called Isabelle, and she was Catholic up to the day she converted, donned the headscarf, and took the name of Iman in order to marry Tariq Ramadan.[20]

The sense of being responsible, from birth on, for continuing his heritage was not limited to Saïd Ramadan's youngest son alone. Despite their quite different careers and professions, his brothers all serve as administrators of the Geneva Islamic Center. His oldest brother, Aymen, is a brilliant neurosurgeon, but he is no less of an Islamist and presides over the governing board of the center. In a preface written for a re-edition of his father's book on the sharia, Aymen paid homage to the man whose aura still surrounds each of his children and grandchildren: "May God see to it that he remains the example of the true path we are to follow."[21] Saïd Ramadan, in charge of the Muslim Brothers in exile, is an example for everyone to follow—and in particular for Tariq, in whose eyes the greatest sin is to fail to honor one's father and one's mother: "Tell me how you behave with your parents, and I will tell you who you are," he insisted in a lecture devoted to the major sins.[22] In a eulogy after the death of his father, published as a preamble to his book on the confrontation of civilizations, he wrote: "Thanks be to God for having given me such a father."[23] Has Tariq really attempted to break free from the custody of such an imposing father? No doubt he did try, as do all adolescents, but with a fear of this patriarch and a respect for him that emerge even today when he speaks as an adult:

> I have an intense remembrance of his presence, his words, his silences. Long silences sometimes lost in memories, in thought, in bitterness .... It was often so. His eyes were bright, his expression penetrating and intense, conveying at one moment his warmth, his gentleness, his tears; at other times fortifying his determi-

> nation, his commitment, his anger. It was a difficult thing for me when I caught the expression in his eyes—wide-open, powerful, suggestive—questioning eyes that went with his words straight to my heart that was woken, aroused and shaken by them.[24]

From his earliest years Tariq Ramadan felt he was different from other children. When he was eight, he used to kick a soccer ball with all his might, dreaming of becoming a sports star, but his coach was obliged to explain to his team mates that, as required by his religion, Tariq took his shower fully dressed so as not to show himself naked.[25] At school, he was a fairly bright student—diligent even. He asked one of his teachers for his opinion of a play that he had written. When older, he offered to give remedial instruction courses for younger students who were having trouble, a family reflex. His grandfather had two obsessions: train minds and train athletes (he encouraged militants to be physically fit). His grandson chose teaching as a vocation and amassed exploits in sports: ski instructor, soccer coach, a ranked tennis player. His hyperactivity was less a proof of integration of some kind than an expression of the malaise and suffering that haunted all the members of his family.

Haunted by exile

The Ramadan family probably never fully appreciated the charm of Lake Geneva. All is drab when one's eyes are fixed on the Nile. For them, Switzerland was never a land of refuge, but a land of exile. A golden prison, where the essential thing was to organize for revenge, organize for the day when the Muslim Brotherhood, deprived of their nation, would return in triumph to Egypt to join in an Islamic government. Tariq Ramadan was brought up with the myth of this return, continually postponed. In this context, becoming integrated or "dissolved"—an expression that he uses frequently—in the West was out of the question. His brothers and his sisters learned to grow up in a family welded together by the promise of return. From his earliest years, he suffered to see his father endure exile. "His life was not life," he wrote when his father died, as a way of describing his forty-one years spent away from Egypt, haunted by the fear of being kidnapped or liquidated by the Egyptian secret service.

Before being banished from Egypt, Saïd Ramadan had already chosen to be the roving ambassador of the Brotherhood. But it is a different matter when the choice is not a free one. In addition to holding secret meetings and fomenting conspiracies in the name of the cause, Tariq Ramadan's father had to struggle to find funds. His son has bitter memories of the day when money from the Saudi benefactors stopped pouring in. For years, the Rabita sponsors had supported the family without protest and had subsidized all of Saïd Ramadan's projects. But after thirteen years of financial infusions, he could no longer tolerate the Saudi authorities' right to supervise his activities, and he wanted to have greater leeway, even if that meant refusing the hand that had nourished him in exile. According to the Center, Saudi contributions came to an end in 1971, but this remains to be proved. At any rate, Tariq Ramadan recounts that his father was in pitiful straits: "We were totally without financial support; we had no money left. I remember that I couldn't leave the country, we had no means, and no papers."[26] Saïd Ramadan had been stripped of his Egyptian nationality by Nasser, after having been condemned *in absentia* to three twenty-five-year prison sentences for high treason, in particular for having organized the World Islamic Congress in Jerusalem and damaging relations between Syria and Egypt. Years later, the Egyptians were to try to mend relations with the Brotherhood by proposing that Saïd Ramadan request that his nationality be reinstated; but he refused the opportunity, because—according to the Geneva Islamic Center—"he considered that he had never stopped being Egyptian." He could have asked for Swiss nationality, but had always scorned the idea. As a result, his children had a total of six different nationalities acquired in the course of his various political negotiations, but which he considered borrowed identities, and which, for a long time, kept them from making a place for themselves as real Swiss citizens. Tariq Ramadan readily admits that "this remained with me as something terribly disturbing and painful."[27]

For years, he felt himself to be a foreigner living in Switzerland. As a youngster, he had but one obsession: to return to Egypt—not that he had been born there, but he always considered it as his real homeland: "I always dreamed of returning to Egypt; it meant returning to my roots. Egypt was the land I most cherished and that deep down was 'my' country. Nothing in my political or religious concerns made me feel Swiss." In 1978, the opportunity arose. At a time when the relations between the Egyptian authorities and the Brotherhood were on the mend, Sadat was ready to try out a policy of appeasement. Hassan al-Banna's grandson took advantage of the chance to return to his native land. At the age of sixteen, he imagined Egypt to be a hotbed of radicalism, where all the politico-religious passions that he had known since childhood were to be found concentrated. The encounter with this mythical land was a real letdown. Suddenly he realized that the heroes of Muslim fundamentalism that he had dreamed of meeting in Egypt were not in Egypt, but in Switzerland. And he had grown up surrounded by them. The Egypt he discovered was a peaceful country, totally unlike the image of radicalism that he had fashioned for himself: "I must say that what I found there came as a great surprise. Basically, it was a great disappointment. In Switzerland I lived in a dynamic world intellectually, one that was activist . . . . For me, Egypt stood for the myth of the encounter with the concrete realities of a world that other militants had devoted their lives to. When I got there in 1978, I found a quite different political reality . . . . I did, to be sure, find the roots of a past with which I immediately felt in harmony, but I understood, despite my young age, how timid and insipid the political convictions were—far less developed than my family's."[28] Ramadan is quite clear. Disappointed not to have found in Egypt ideologists as fundamentalist as his parents, he decided to return to Europe and learn to take advantage of his Swiss citizenship, the better to advance the cause of political Islam, and one day—why not?—take the revenge so longed for by his father. He even envisaged asking for French citizenship, which he could have obtained, thanks to his wife. But, for the time being, he could not keep still. Since nowhere did he feel at home, why not be at home everywhere? The sense of total rootlessness drove him to want to travel the world—but not any old way. At eighteen, he joined an Islamic relief organization.

From Islamism to pro-Third World Islamism

When journalists ask him about his personal evolution, Tariq Ramadan prefers to describe himself as a "Third-World Muslim" who graduated from relief work to being a militant alongside trade unions and leftist organizations. He is apt to talk of Coup de Main (A Helping Hand), an association he set up with fellow teachers when he was assigned to a secondary school in Coudrier (Switzerland) in the 1980s. The laudable objective of the organization was to encourage young students to act responsibly and develop a sense of solidarity, in particular regarding cultures other than their own. The association, which was financed by the Geneva school district, offered the students—and Tariq Ramadan—the opportunity to travel to Mali, Senegal, Tibet, India, Burkina Faso, and Brazil. As a secondary schoolteacher participating in this program, the preacher was to encounter Sister Emmanuelle, Mother Teresa, the Dalai Lama, Edmond Kaiser, Hubert Reeves, Albert Jacquard, Guy Gilbert, René Dumont, l'Abbé Pierre, and Dom Helder Camara, one of the leading figures of liberation theology. The meetings were on occasion brief, but they were to stand him in good stead. Tariq Ramadan never missed an opportunity to speak of these encounters, however fleeting, so adding the right touch to the image of a perfect third-world globetrotter of the socially minded Christian kind. He dwells in particular on the encounter with Dom Helder Camara as a way of suggesting a comparison between the Muslim Brotherhood's Islam and liberation theology.

Liberation theology took root in the late 1960s in a very special context, as a means of resistance against the fascist and communist military dictatorships of Latin America. It drew on Christ's message to defend liberty and social justice, before being submerged in a broader radical left movement based no longer on a political system but on ethics. The Muslim Brotherhood movement can, indeed, appear similar—if you leave out the fact that its aim has been to replace a military dictatorship with a theocratic dictatorship, in the meantime fighting to establish a society in which individual liberties are denied, co-education despised, women dominated and forced to wear the veil, and sexual minorities persecuted—all in the name of the sharia.

Comparing the Muslim Brotherhood with liberation theology is as absurd as believing that Tariq Ramadan is a Marxist because he is pro-Third World. In his case, support for the Third World is always linked to his Islamist commitment. He claims to have worked alongside associations such as ATD Fourth World or Médecins sans Frontières, but fails to mention that, for the most part, he was involved with the Islamist solidarity network, Secours Islamique, otherwise known as Islamic Relief. It is no ordinary relief association, but rather an organization that spreads Islamism via relief aid.[29] The association was presided over by a certain Hany al-Banna. The name sounds familiar, but Tariq Ramadan insists that it was just a coincidence, that he was not a relative. Above all, Tariq Ramadan would have us believe that, since he is no relation of Hany al-Banna, he was never active in Islamic Relief. He exploits this error in order to discredit any investigation into his connection with the organization. At times, his denial is even more adamant. When Serge Raffy was preparing an article that appeared in the January 29, 2004 issue of the *Nouvel Observateur*, he was astonished to receive a letter from Hany al-Banna's lawyer stating that his client had never known Tariq Ramadan. A surprising claim, given that the *Daily Trust*, dated November 27, 2003, reported on a conference organized by the Muslim Council of Britain, during which Hany al-Banna and Tariq Ramadan shared the platform! They had occasion to meet once again during the annual conference of the FOSIS (Federation of Student Islamic Societies) held at Nottingham University between June 17 and 20, 2004. Moreover, in the course of a lecture given to a Muslim audience that was taped in 1999, Tariq Ramadan claimed that collaboration between the Geneva Islamic Center and Islamic Relief was of his doing! "I was personally involved, since I was on the executive board of the Islamic solidarity organization with which you are familiar and which did a terrific job here in Réunion under the name Islamic Relief. We worked with them in Geneva when I was on the board."[30] Furthermore, he urged his Muslim audience to pay no attention to the rumors spread by "the Western media" intent on "discrediting the association." In another conference on the media, returning again to the issue, he asserted that, despite the questionable reputation of the humanitarian organization, there are still journalists "honest" enough to speak well of the organization if things are properly explained to them . . . . In fact, Islamic Relief has long been remarkably successful in having people forget its Islamist features by referring to itself as an equivalent to the Red Cross. But the Red Cross does not have similar ulterior political motives. Thanks to its numerous sponsors in the Gulf states, Islamic Relief has dispatched militants to all the war zones where traumatized people might well turn to political Islam for consolation. They have turned up in Chechnya, Bosnia, Yemen, Iran, and, of course, Algeria, where every earthquake serves as a pretext for spreading their influence, as they distribute blankets and hot meals. Their charitable work is real enough, as is that of the Christian organizations in Iraq, but their true intention is undeniably to demonstrate that solidarity comes from Islam and not from the West. Similarly, the associations linked to the American religious Right that distribute food to the Iraqis make no secret of their attempts to convince them of the advantages of made-in-USA Christianity. Baptist organizations spent $250,000 sending blankets and powdered baby milk to Iraq in order to get close to the population, for motives of their own. Mark Kelly, the Baptist spokesman, explained quite clearly that they hoped to turn unbelievers into believers: "Conversations quickly get around to our faith."[31]

That's exactly the approach taken by Islamic Relief. It is also in this spirit of Islamic evangelization that Tariq Ramadan joined the African Cooperation Fund. The name suggests a charity organization that collects funds to help Africa. In fact, funds are collected above all to Islamize Africa. Ramadan presides over the governing committee and determines the goals for the bureau, which was created in August 2000 on the occasion of the first symposium of French-speaking Muslims. The resolutions of this symposium devote considerable space to the role of the *dawa* and the appropriate strategies for spreading the Islamic message, and then report on the creation of a fund destined "to provide African countries with books, cassettes, pedagogical material, and any other equipment designed to promote the transmission of knowledge."[32] Needless to say, it is Islamic knowledge that we are talking of.

There is one African country that Tariq Ramadan knows particularly well: Sudan. Islamic Relief was one of the very few humanitarian organizations authorized to open an office there in the 1990s, the very time when Hassan al-Tourabi issued his statement in praise of Tariq Ramadan. "The high priest of Islamism," the leading figure of the Sudanese regime, then in the midst of reinstating the sharia, was at the height of his power. In 1994, he was forced by international pressure to allow the French secret service to kidnap the terrorist Carlos. In 1996, he agreed to expel Osama bin Laden. In the meantime, Khartoum was a haven for terrorists. Every year, al-Tourabi staged a Popular Arab and Islamic Conference (PAIC), a sort of high mass intended to bring together nationalists and Islamists. A few pro-Palestinian radicals used to attend, but above all it was a meeting place for Muslim extremists, numerous delegates from the FIS, and notorious hostage takers. It was not uncommon for the closing ceremony to feature a splendid parade of kamikazes or youngsters armed with Kalashnikovs shouting "Death to Israel." Tariq Ramadan took part in the celebration in 1993. As he did when he travelled to Yemen (where another Muslim Brotherhood branch was seeking recognition), he contacted the journalists. One journalist recalled seeing a most likeable young man, obviously respected by the Islamists thanks to his relationship to al-Banna. Tariq Ramadan had been preaching for two years in the Muslim Brotherhood network and was earning a reputation inside the closed world of Islamism. Al-Tourabi took him seriously enough to consider him "the future of Islam."

First steps as a preacher

In the early 1990s, after having travelled the world in search of his true vocation, Tariq Ramadan decided at last to make Europe his home base. He is quite open about it: "Up to the age of 23 or 24 I felt more Egyptian than Swiss. I thought again of leaving. Then I decided I was European and Swiss and should accept the fact."[33] This decision was a strategic, thought-out political choice, rather than a heartfelt impulse. Tariq Ramadan was to remain marked for life by what was the very backbone of his identity: not Egypt, which was to remain a source of cultural enrichment, but the Islam of the Muslim Brotherhood that he was now determined to spread to the very heart of Europe. The Creil Affair of 1989, the first controversy in France concerning the wearing of the Islamic headscarf at school, seems to have sparked things off. It encouraged him to take a stand as a European Muslim. But to preach he needed a title, even if it fell short of the minimum course of religious training. In 1991, he decided to return to Egypt to study Islamic sciences in an accelerated program. He was then thirty years of age. Like his grandfather, he did not choose the long and complex apprenticeship offered by Al-Azhar University. He was not out to cultivate his mind, but to learn how to produce coherent arguments on the basis of a limited number of Islamic references. He settled down with his family in his mother's apartment near the airport, and in a few months went through "an intensive training program" in the form of private tutoring given by a friend of the family's, Sheikh Aqwabi.

On his return, Ramadan could at last give lectures on Islam. He was not yet quite sure of himself, and he lacked familiarity with certain verses of the Koran—which he was later to acquire, thanks to a year of study at the Leicester Islamic Foundation—but he had made enough of a start for his natural verve to do the rest. It is one of the advantages of waging political war in the name of Islam: no need to work one's way up through a rigorous hierarchy to become a preacher. He began taking over the role, in particular in the Geneva Islamic Center, where he sometimes presided over prayer meetings. After his second visit to Egypt, Hassan al-Banna's grandson was convinced of one thing: Europe was to be his land of *dawa,* his preaching land. The French intelligence services claim that, between 1992 and 1993, Tariq Ramadan was chosen by the Brotherhood to continue the Islamization project begun by Saïd Ramadan. Indeed, the heir presumptive stepped up the rhythm of his meetings, not only in Switzerland, but wherever the European branch of the Brotherhood could provide him with an occasion.

Propelled by the Union of Islamic Organizations of France

In 1992, shortly after his return from Egypt, he suddenly emerged as the star speaker at the annual congress of the Union of Islamic Organizations of France (UOIF), a French organization close to the Muslim Brotherhood.

When Fouad Alaoui of the UOIF was asked about his links with the Brotherhood, he replied: "It's one movement among others. We have respect for it, in that it advocates a renewal and a modern interpretation of Islam. But our job is elsewhere." And he added: "We have no functional connection with the Muslim Brotherhood." Obviously, as is the case for Tariq Ramadan, the French branch of the Brotherhood enjoys sufficient autonomy to be able to deny having any "functional connection" with the Egyptian head office. But despite this, the UOIF is indeed an organization modeled on the Brotherhood's philosophy and methods, working hand in hand with other Brotherhood organizations, in particular with the Geneva Islamic Center. The UOIF's ideology clearly belongs in this tradition, and its fundamental principles are almost entirely drawn from its Egyptian predecessor. One of the pamphlets published by the organization—*Critères pour une organisation musulmane en France* [*Criteria for Muslim Organizations in France*]—pays tribute to Hassan al-Banna in particular: "What distinguishes Imam Hassan al-Banna, who is rightly considered—and clearly merits—to belong to the tradition of great thinkers and reformers . . . is that he provided an organizational capacity for the spiritual and intellectual aspects of the movement." Not only does the UOIF refuse to repudiate any of the theoreticians that paved the way for Muslim fundamentalism, but it treats those who dare to criticize them as heretics: "Today you can find people who take pleasure in talking down Ibn Taymiyya, Ibn Abdul Wahhab, Sayyid Qutb, Yusuf al-Qaradawi, or Faisal Mawlawi. But what is to be gained by destroying Muslim memory? What is to be gained by destroying these Muslim founding figures? Unless it be the scorched-earth policy of people who are inspired by hatred, ignorance, or heresy?"[34] The UOIF, it should be said, belongs to the most radical school within the Brotherhood and has never dissociated itself from Sayyid Qutb, even if it does practice doublespeak: moderate on the outside and radical within.

Founded in 1983 by Abdallah Ben Mansour (a Tunisian student) and Mahmoud Zouheir (an Iraqi engineer), the UOIF was conceived as a means of radicalizing the young Arabs who had come to France as students. It has been remarkably successful in expanding, having established more than 200 associations throughout France.[35] The organization attracts a growing number of students of Muslim faith. From 1995 on, the UOIF took steps to accommodate the new influx, readjusting the make-up of its governing body. Two French citizens of Moroccan origin took over the leadership of the organization: Thami Breze and Fouad Alaoui. Despite this evolution, the UOIF continues to serve as an organization where French Muslim students become more radical through contact with Islamist theoreticians belonging to the Brotherhood: Yusuf al-Qaradawi, Faisal Mawlawi, Hani Ramadan, and, of course, Tariq Ramadan.

Tariq Ramadan wrote the preface for the first compilation issued by the European Council for Fatwa set up by the UOIF.[36] This body was officially introduced to the press as a highly promising initiative, capable of providing theological guidance adapted to the needs of European Muslims. Some journalists and university professors wrote laudatory articles in celebration of the founding of an institution that would issue *fatwas* (religious opinions) from Europe and no longer from Egypt or the Middle East. In fact, the very first *fatwas* to be published were adroitly chosen for their deceptively modern look. Two opinions attracted a lot of attention: one authorizing bank loans, the other suggesting that mixed marriages might be authorized. Unfortunately, alongside these two progressive *fatwas* (that the media made much of), the European Council for Fatwa quietly issued dozens of markedly less modern ones. Without going further than the compilation prefaced by Tariq Ramadan, one can read that the council authorizes a husband to forbid his wife from associating with certain persons and declares abortion illegal. In his introduction, moreover, Tariq Ramadan issues a warning: "Muslims who are always on the lookout for what is the easiest, the simplest and most 'moderate' will not find here what they are after, for each individual must be committed to avoiding the creation of a second-rate Islam, an Islam . . . without Islam." In fact it is a hardline Islam that the European Council for Fatwa advocates. How could it be otherwise? Its president is not a European Muslim, but the most virulent of theologians, and someone that the Muslim Brotherhood considers its Guide: none other than Yusuf al-Qaradawi, the man who issued the *fatwa* authorizing Hamas to engage in kamikaze operations.[37]

Qaradawi, who commutes between Egypt and Qatar, where he hosts a religious television program on Al-Jazeera, is one of the Brotherhood's legendary figures. He was even considered for the post of Supreme Guide. It seems that he declined the offer on the basis that he would be more useful in Europe. And, as president of the European Council for Fatwa, based in London, he has never been more effective at radicalizing Muslims. On the occasion of its eleventh meeting in Stockholm in July 2003, the council over which he presides issued, almost unnoticed, a *fatwa* justifying suicide attacks as martyrdom operations in perfect keeping with the Koran.[38] It is enough to make your blood run cold when you learn that Faisal Mawlawi is the council's second-in-command. A Muslim Brother, he put theory into practice as director of the Lebanese Jamaat Islamiyya, an organization involved in several terrorist attacks.

This aspect of the UOIF has been glossed over by the media ever since Nicolas Sarkozy, the French Minister of the Interior, decided, whatever the cost, to include the organization as part of the French Council of the Muslim Faith, adopting a strategy that specialists of Islamism have yet to fathom. In 2002, moreover, this integration was the subject of a violent quarrel between Tariq Ramadan and the UOIF. It was not simply a difference of opinion as to strategy, but a disagreement on fundamentals. Qaradawi was to remain the theological mentor for Ramadan and for all members of the Brotherhood. In London on July 12, 2004, the two of them, surrounded by the leading lights of the European Brotherhood, took part together in the launching of a vast campaign in support of the *hijab* (the Islamic headscarf). The presence of Qaradawi, who is barred from entering the United States, created a scandal, especially when he declared: "There is no dialogue between the Jew and us except by the sword and the rifle."[39] And this is not Tariq Ramadan's only brush with scandal. He also refers to Mawlawi as a theoretician worth consulting.

Despite the recent falling-out between the preacher and a number of UOIF officials, Saïd Ramadan's son is still a star in the eyes of the organization's activists. It is thanks to the French branch of the Muslim Brotherhood that Hani Ramadan, Tariq's older brother, organized his first series of conferences in France, becoming one of the accredited lecturers for the many clubs on the UOIF circuit. His writings serve as reference works for the institute that trains imams in Château-Chinon. Tariq Ramadan had only to follow in his footsteps to become the next guru of all the young Muslim associations connected to the UOIF, such as the French Muslim Students, an organization created for the purpose of Islamizing the campuses, or the Young Muslims of France, founded by the UOIF to attract a wider audience of the young interested in discovering or rediscovering radical Islam. All these young people were already under the influence of Hani Ramadan, an austere figure, when they succumbed to the charm of his brother, whose every lecture was a major event. But the organization that was to serve as Tariq Ramadan's true stronghold is the Lyon-based Union of Young Muslims. Abdelaziz Chaambi, its president, recalls: "It was like love at first sight. We were looking for a spokesman. And he was looking for a base."[40]

Tawhid, the Lyon bastion

An hour by train from Geneva, Lyon and the surrounding suburbs constitute the ideal stronghold for a young Islamist preacher. In the 1980s, the city was the driving force behind the Parade of the *Beurs* (people born in France of North African parents) and the anti-racist movement. Ten years later, the situation had not changed. Fed up with the political patronage, disappointed by the associations that had sprung up in the wake of the Parade of the *Beurs*, such as SOS Racisme, the youth of the city suburbs and of Vénissieux, on the outskirts of Lyon, tuned in to other voices that promised fulfilment of their dreams—the voices of Islamism. Associations such as Divercités (Diversity), created to offer an alternative that was more radical than the anti-racist associations, found a new source of self-assertion in proclaiming their pride in being Muslim rather than Arab, even if it meant no longer appealing for open-mindedness, but rather shutting others out. A Lyon Islamist activist put it this way: "You didn't want anything to do with me because I was Arab; so as a Muslim I'll turn my back on you."[41] This return to Islam was a reaction born of exasperation, but it quickly became a headlong rush into radical intolerant Islamism. The late 1980s were a propitious time in this respect.

In 1989, three young girls were expelled from a French lycée because they refused to take off their Islamic headscarves on the school premises.

The headmaster succeeded in arbitrating the matter, but the UOIF intervened, urging the young girls to take a more radical stand and refuse any form of compromise. As a result, the affair boiled over, and their expulsion strengthened the conviction that France was contaminated by anti-Muslim racism. The Gulf War did nothing to change matters. A good number of French youth of North African origin considered the American intervention as aggression vis-à-vis Arabs and Muslims in general, even if officially it was a question of defending a country that was itself Arab, and even if the dictator in question was a secular nationalist that the Islamists had execrated up to then. These events contributed to the success of Islamist associations—clearly inspired by the Muslim Brotherhood—associations such as the Union of Young Muslims, co-founded by Abdelaziz Chaambi and Yamin Makri some two years earlier.

The association has both money and ideas. It owns a big building located on Rue Notre-Dame in Lyon's sixth district. One entry hall gives onto a conference room; the other onto the bookstore, which displays the works of its publishing house, Tawhid ("divine unity" in Arabic)—the Muslim Brotherhood's favorite term, and the name given to their chain of bookstores. Created and financed by the Muslim Brotherhood, the Lyon bookstore is a showcase for radical Muslim thinkers. Some of its funds come directly from the Leicester Islamic Foundation, the propaganda center for Qutb and Mawdudi, where Tariq Ramadan received his training. It thus distributes the works of the most disreputable Islamist theoreticians, such as Qutb, Mawdudi, and Ibn Taymiyya. It resembles an Islamic version of a Pentecostal or fundamentalist Christian bookshop, in that it features anti-abortion and anti-euthanasia literature as well. But the publishing house's leading light, whose books are always on display, is, of course, Tariq Ramadan. The sales receipts of his works would suffice to finance the association, which claims to have sold several thousand copies of his books and audiocassettes. The figures cannot be verified, but they suggest the degree of influence exerted by the preacher over the Islamists of the region for the last fifteen years or so. It is no mean achievement if we are to judge by the increasingly fundamentalist positions taken by the young people who spend time there and visit the Tawhid bookstore, where one can always find the latest bulletin of the Geneva Islamic Center. Aware that his followers' radical opinions could spoil the image of respectability that he is at pains to construct on the exterior, Ramadan would have us believe that he has tried to exercise a moderating influence. He recounts how he had to prove he was bona fide before they were willing to accept him: "They were suspicious. I had the reputation of being too modern. The first time, they took me aside to one of the smaller rooms, not the large hall. They wanted to test me before presenting me to their audience."[42] It is a fact that the Union of Young Muslims makes a point of inviting speakers such as Rashid Benaissa, an Islamist militant close to the FIS. They might well have been on their guard having read newspaper articles that referred to Tariq Ramadan as a Muslim who wanted to modernize Islam, but on hearing him speak they were quickly reassured. Saïd Ramadan's son was perhaps modern in style, but in regard to essentials he was indeed the heir to al-Banna, their Guide. And he adopted the same line as their model speaker, Hani Ramadan. The same Islam, the same radicalism, but more charismatic, and, in addition, better suited to the media—the ideal synthesis. "Tariq was the combination of all the qualities we were looking for," Chaambi recounted. "He had the theological background, and a social and political vision, a Westerner who had succeeded in coalescing identities. He only lacked one thing: he was a well-established bourgeois from Geneva who knew nothing about our neighborhoods. We fed on his religious learning, and he soaked up our knowledge of the suburbs."[43]

This Swiss bourgeois of Egyptian origin was thus taken up and adopted, to the extent that he became the spokesman of the suburbs and of the French North African community. Ramadan had found his true audience, for whom he could play in earnest the role of political leader that was his destiny. As time goes by, the number of his followers only increases. Today he delivers several speeches a week all over the globe, sometimes for audiences numbering in the thousands. Often he arrives late, so as to increase the anticipation. However, his first try at politics was a resounding disaster.

Failure in Switzerland

Tariq Ramadan founded his first Muslim association in 1994, the Muslim Men and Women of Switzerland (MMS). Officially, its purpose was "to contribute to a more favorable reception of Muslims in Switzerland." The program appeared inviting, and the prestige that Tariq Ramadan enjoyed with the press ever since the publication of his book *Les musulmans dans la laïcité* [*Muslims in a Secular Society*] provided him with the opportunity to advertise the association's first congress, to be held from December 16 to 18 of the same year. He himself expected a lot of this first large-scale meeting, organized entirely by the networks that he had set up. Taken in by the preacher's charm, and persuaded that his influence on the Muslim community was beneficial, the journalists expected to find the hall crammed with the faithful, eager for a modern and dynamic Islam. The disappointment was palpable. On arrival, they found a hall that was practically empty: only 300 people out of the 15,000 Muslims living in the region. Furthermore, half of them had come from France, mostly from the suburbs of Lille and Lyon. In fact the "silent majority" of the Swiss Muslim community had boycotted the event, despite the colossal publicity provided by the press. The journalists were quick to understand why, when they listened to the preachers on the rostrum. Ushered in by Ramadan, each speaker proved to be more radical than his predecessor. Hassan Iquioussen, a preacher close to Ramadan, introduced as a promising candidate to invigorate Islam, explained that: "Wives must obey their husbands, since for them it is the best way to approach God."[44] He was followed in the same vein by Malika Dif, another of Ramadan's close associates: "Algerian women who demonstrate for recognition of their rights have understood nothing. Islam gives them all these rights. On the contrary, it is from a lack of Islamization that Algeria suffers."

Instead of serving as the promised opportunity to reconcile Swiss citizenship and Muslim identity, the congress turned out to be a get-together of fundamentalists. The journalists who attended were accused of wanting to "annihilate Islamic civilization"[45] or at another moment of "favoring free speech contrary to the rules of the Koran."[46] One speaker even treated them publicly as "insects." Shocked by what they heard, most journalists left the symposium. On the steps leading up to the meeting hall, they found themselves face to face with FIS sympathizers handing out tracts in which it was explained that "true Muslims are those who take up arms to fight for the survival of Islam." The same tract urged Muslims to "follow the edifying example of our Algerian brothers," all of this with the approval of the sponsors.[47] Neither the association nor Tariq Ramadan could continue to fool the people. In particular, *L'Hebdo*, a Swiss weekly news magazine, expressed its disappointment: "What was officially presented as a symposium of dialogue and exchange turned out in fact to be a meeting of confrontation and tension."[48] Criticism of the first association founded by Tariq Ramadan was unstinting: "His minority movement is playing with fire. Even worse: he runs the danger of stirring up tensions vis-à-vis the Muslim community in general, which is diverse and many-sided and obviously not supportive of the MMS." The editor-in-chief of *L'Hebdo*, who had often published opinion pieces submitted by the preacher, explained that he was putting an end to their collaboration: "In the weekly column that we provided him, we were looking for a religious dialogue. Unfortunately, it was used as a political platform."[49] As he always does when in trouble, Tariq Ramadan called it "Islamophobia," but his reputation appeared to be seriously compromised in the Swiss Confederation—for the time being at least. Ramadan has, in effect, lots of journalist friends who are ready to defend him whatever he says and whatever he does. And, above all, he had learned one lesson: when the message fails to get through in one place, go and establish a reputation elsewhere. That is what he has done every time he has got into trouble, thanks to his chameleon-like talent, inherited from his father. The very same year, in 1994, when he appeared washed up in Switzerland once and for all, he went to Belgium, the Dom-Tom (the French overseas territories), and France itself to rest and recharge his batteries. He claims to have taken part in more than 120 meetings in the years 1994 and 1995 alone, often by invitation from networks closely linked to the Brotherhood, but not always. In 1997, he was to found a new association, Présence Musulmane, designed to successfully achieve in France what had not been achieved in Switzerland. In the meantime, Saïd Ramadan's son had become his heir.

Inheritance and the assignment of roles

Saïd Ramadan, the patriarch, the European Brotherhood's Guide, died on August 4, 1995. The Islamic Center, together with the Ramadan family, published an obituary in three languages (Arabic, French, and English): "The Islamic Center of Geneva sadly announces to the Muslim world the death in Geneva on Friday 4th of August of Doctor Saïd Ramadan. He was the founder and general director of the Islamic Center of Geneva, which was the first center established in Europe. He was one of the spiritual sons of the Imam martyr Hassan al-Banna, the founder of the Muslim Brotherhood Movement." Unlike al-Banna, Saïd Ramadan did not die a martyr, but from illness, in a Swiss hospital bed. His friends and relatives were, however, given the opportunity to claim martyrdom when Saudi Arabia refused them the right to bury him in Medina. And why should the Saudi authorities, known to have been at loggerheads with this Egyptian citizen for years, have granted the request? Instead, Saïd Ramadan was buried in Egypt, his native country. Tariq Ramadan was not able to attend the funeral. He was obliged to return home to his family when his wife, who had arrived in Egypt a few days earlier, informed him that the Egyptian authorities were planning to arrest him if he set foot in the country. It was not the first time that his entry into the country had run into problems. Going through the security checkpoints always took longer for him than for any other visitor, but this time it seems that a concerted decision had been taken before he even boarded the plane.

In late June, an Egyptian daily published by leftist supporters of Nasser, *Al-Ahali,* asserted that "one of Saïd Ramadan's sons" had been seen on the terrace of a Geneva café, seated next to Ayman al-Zawahiri, who was sought by the police as the leader of the Al-Jihad group suspected of involvement in the attempted assassination of President Mubarak in Addis Ababa on June 26. Tariq Ramadan denied these accusations, which appear highly extravagant. Is it reasonable to suppose that one of the most wanted men at the time would meet in public with his friends from the Islamic Center for a cup of coffee in broad daylight on the shores of Lake Geneva? The explanation did not convince the European press, which sided with Ramadan, treating it as a false accusation manufactured by the Egyptian government. But the government had reason enough to be worried by the arrival of Saïd Ramadan's heir. It was a period of high tension following the attempted assassination of the president. Some forty-nine members of the Muslim Brotherhood were accused of "having incited hatred of the government among the people" and of "belonging to an illegal organization." Their trial was then taking place behind closed doors in a tense atmosphere, and the arrival of one of the Brotherhood's ambassadors in exile could only fuel the unrest.

After the death of his father, Tariq continued his Islamization project with renewed energy. In the months that followed, he went to Mauritius for conferences lasting several days, and there he was surrounded by Brothers and Sisters who came to present their condolences. Ramadan was greatly moved. On the last day he could not keep from paying tribute to the man from whom he had learned all he knew: "It is my father's image that has been with me from the mosque all the way here," he said, his voice trembling. "You know, he lived forty-one years of exile far, far from his native land [*author's note:* here Ramadan stops to shed tears], and what I feel now is exactly the message that he passed on to me from Islam, namely our message is one of love."[50] He then evoked the fraternal ties existing within the Muslim community, and especially the ties within the Brotherhood, as something that enabled them to withstand adversity. At this moment, more than at any other, it is clear that Tariq Ramadan realized to what extent he owed his status as a sought-after preacher to his inheritance and to his name: "It is thanks to the parents I had, and the family I had, that I am here with you today; the merit is not mine." This was a sentence that he would repeat several months later in a lecture, given in Brussels, to a Muslim audience with ties to the Brotherhood: "I deserve no credit for being here with you. None at all. Because I had a grandfather who gave birth to a father who gave birth to a son. And I myself will be judged according to what I will transmit to my son, not according to what you see now. The day when you will see my son here before you, or see my daughter live as she should or my other son, and if they find the way to speak to you in the true way, then you can say 'Tariq has passed on the message.'"[51]

This admission amounts to a political confession. Even if he sometimes gives the impression of wanting to go it alone, Tariq Ramadan is much less autonomous than one might think. He is limited by his status as heir, by the fraternal ties that bind the Brothers together, and, above all, by his own family. After the death of the patriarch, it is the evanescent, but increasingly decisive presence of Wafa al-Banna that reigns over the family and the administration of the Geneva Islamic Center, which, at the time of his death, had twenty dues-paying members and a public of roughly 500. The family's children all joined the executive board so as to ensure continuity and share the various responsibilities. A memorandum emanating from European intelligence services even asserted: "After the death of the patriarch, the family divided up the apparently considerable sum that Saïd Ramadan had administered on behalf of the Egyptian Muslim Brotherhood. The result was a spectacular increase, both in quantity and quality, of the products and activities of the Al-Tawhid bookshop in Lyon, as well as the As-Salah bookshop in Ferney-Voltaire."[52]

If this memorandum is correct, it would mean that Tariq Ramadan himself finances the Tawhid publishing house, and thus the production of his own books and cassettes, the sales of which provide him with an income. It appears highly probable. Yamin Makri of Tawhid affirms that every month he pays Tariq Ramadan a fixed sum of 2,000 Euros in the form of royalties. But even on the basis of a generous estimate, the number of books and audiocassettes actually sold would not seem to account for such a high income. Does the money invested in Tawhid, and thus in Tariq Ramadan's productions, not come then from the funds divided up among the children when they became administrators of the Geneva Islamic Center after the patriarch's death? That is what the French intelligence services assert. The same source refers to an open conflict, which broke out when the funds were divided up between the Geneva administrators and the Egyptian headquarters of the Muslim Brotherhood. The latter insisted that certain activities linked to the *dawa* be speeded up. If we are to believe the intelligence memorandums, the hyperactivity displayed by Hani and Tariq must not have come as a disappointment. The two brothers were, indeed, more visible and more productive from this moment on. Up to then, between 1992 and 1994, they had competed to demonstrate which of them was capable of taking over from their father. Hani set up a "Muslim cultural space" within the Center, while his younger brother created an autonomous "Muslim Cultural Community Center" equipped with a library, As-Salah, in Ferney-Voltaire.[53] During this period, their relations even became strained. But in the Ramadan family, quarrels are short lived. The mother sees to it. After their father's death, the brothers were already reconciled when it came time to choose which of the two was to replace him at the head of the Islamic Center. At the time, Tariq was already better known, but also more likely to create scandals. The resounding failure of the MMS congress indicated that he was not really taken seriously by the Swiss Muslim community. On the other hand, he was undeniably gifted in attracting the outside world. It became obvious how to assign the tasks. For Tariq the outside world; for Hani the world within.

Hani Ramadan

A lot has been written about the difference in character between the two brothers and their relative degree of charisma. Tariq Ramadan is seductive and full of nuances; Hani Ramadan is forthrightly austere and extremist. As director of the Geneva Islamic Center, he is the official head of the Muslim Brotherhood at war with "Europe's atheistic materialism," and in particular with secularism that "enforces in school programs the separation that eliminates the vertical relationship to God."[54] Which is a bit disturbing to hear, coming as it does from a product of the Swiss state school system . . . Like his grandfather, Hani Ramadan hardly ever recognizes the difference between education and propaganda. He is also as haunted as was his grandfather by the idea of being contaminated by Western decadence: "Is it not in fact true that today, in our modern societies, despite scientific progress and material comfort, we are prey to all sorts of evils that draw us constantly towards worship of the *taghut* (the irreligious) in all its forms? To cite only the unbridled sexuality that results in adultery, prostitution, homosexuality, harassment, rape, paedophilia, and incest."[55] The specter of a loosening of moral standards obsesses him. In interviews, the director of the Geneva Islamic Center never misses an occasion to recall the fact that for Islam "homosexuality is a dead end, both in law and logic; you can't open a door with two keys.[56]

In 1998, Hani Ramadan brought out a book entitled *La femme en Islam* [*Women in Islam*] published by Tawhid, a book that many found shocking.[57] In it, he developed a strictly fundamentalist view of the world that is highly moralistic. In his eyes, "if a society encourages hedonist values and unrestrained individualism; if it becomes more permissive and extols self-serving pleasures; if it calls for the 'loosening of moral standards' and authorizes fornication, it will then lose the sense of mutual confidence necessary for marriage to subsist." For which reason, "Islam advocates a restriction of freedom so as to preserve mutual confidence and fidelity." Hani Ramadan has in mind, of course, that these restrictions on liberty, intended to guard against adultery, be applied first and foremost to women, called on to behave with decency and wear the Islamic headscarf. "The headscarf, in Islam, is the sign that faith obeys the divine commandments. Why then should a young schoolgirl be prevented from expressing her belief? Forcing her to remove the headscarf, is it not repeating what the merciless inquisition and the communist executioners have done?"[58]

The Geneva Islamic Center consistently urges women to wear the headscarf and to go to court if they are asked, as a teacher or a jury member, to remove it. Hani Ramadan is the first to protest against attacks on religious liberty. On the other hand, the Center's director never thinks of himself as an inquisitor or an enemy of freedom when he requires women to wear the headscarf so as to protect men against temptation, while at the same time granting their husbands full rights, including polygamy. His writings are conceived as testimony to the infinite superiority and the loftiness of soul of Islam: "In its struggle against the secular extremists, Islam will, whatever comes, remain a haven of wisdom and tolerance: 'No compulsion in religion' says the Koran. A lesson that the secular torturers never taught us!" Yet secular democracy offered a good number of advantages for those who knew how to abuse its weak points.

Saïd Ramadan's sons knew full well that they could play on the neo-colonial complex and, above all, on the open-mindedness of the democratic system to use and abuse the right of free speech. Here is what Hani Ramadan had to say in 1995 to his followers, massed in front of the European headquarters of the United Nations to call for "an international campaign against the ungodly": "The advantage of our being in Europe is that we can make use of the free zones within the democratic regimes."[59] Why indeed do without? In 2001, the director of the Geneva Islamic Center published a collection of articles on "Islam and Barbarity," dedicated to those Muslims of Bosnia, Kosovo, Chechnya, and Algeria "persecuted on account of their faith."[60] The contents are alarming, but the most terrifying thing is that all the articles were published in the mainstream Swiss press. In his preface, Hani Ramadan warmly thanked the Swiss daily newspaper *Tribune de Genève* and *Le Courrier* for their "open-mindedness." One can well understand why, on reading the legion opinion pieces that Hani Ramadan managed to have published in the press during the 1990s, almost one per month—sometimes published simultaneously by three mass-circulation newspapers—with titles like "The West is out to dominate Islam!"[61] Always in the name of open-mindedness.

In a text entitled "The Sharia Misunderstood," published in *Le Monde* on September 10, 2002, the director of the Geneva Islamic Center justified stoning as "a punishment, but also a purification." He spoke of AIDS as a divine chastisement: "Who created the AIDS virus? You will notice that a person who strictly obeys the divine commandments is safe from this infection, which cannot—except in cases of blood transfusion errors—affect anybody who has no sexual relations outside of marriage, who is not a homosexual and who does not take drugs." The moral lesson: "Muslims are convinced of the necessity to return to the divine law, in all places and at all times." This opinion piece did not seem to have greatly upset the editors of *Le Monde*, who agreed to publish it, whereas, had it been written by a Christian fundamentalist, they would surely have refused. Moreover it was not the first time that this newspaper had opened its columns to Hani Ramadan—let alone his younger brother Tariq. On September 22, 2001, just eleven days after 9/11, the same Hani Ramadan took advantage of the "Horizons" section of *Le Monde* (a page reserved for opinion pieces) to put the corporal punishments advocated by Islamic law "in their proper perspective," and by the same token to justify them.

Yet at times democracy will turn against those who exploit it so aggressively. In Switzerland, where Hani Ramadan teaches, his opinion piece on the "sharia misunderstood" sparked a scandal. *Le Courrier* informed Hani Ramadan that it would no longer publish his pieces "whatever the subject."[62] The editor-in-chief published his correspondence, some of it quite harsh, with the Muslim Brotherhood's European representative. In one of his letters Hani Ramadan spoke of "an absolutely stupefying exclusivist dogmatism" and concluded with a menace: "Man is worthy only in so far as he submits to God. Perhaps it is not only me, a Muslim, that you are betraying by defying divine law. God will pass judgment." In the meantime, it was the Geneva State Council that was to pass judgment. After investigating the question, the members of the council decided unanimously that "Mr. Ramadan has violated the obligation of loyalty and the duty of confidentiality that apply to all public servants." He was suspended from his post as teacher of French for the Golette Orientation Program. In the end, the decision was annulled by the conciliation commission, but the State Council stuck to its guns. They had taken the political decision to get rid of Hani Ramadan and were prepared to pay damages rather than have him return to teaching.

Throughout the affair, Tariq Ramadan had interceded in the press on behalf of his elder brother, in particular in the columns of the newspaper *Le Courrier* (which still publishes contributions by Tariq): "I don't agree with what he said, but I am against preventing him from expressing his views on the pretext that, outside his employment context, he supposedly violated the 'duty of confidentiality,' a duty for which there is no clear definition. They make use of their authority to attack an easy target, a public servant who is said to be a model teacher, in order to prove to the world that they can stand up for their values."[63]

Two sides of the same coin

Tariq Ramadan is constantly being called upon to make it clear that he is different from his brother. He is obliged to do so if he intends to continue his *dawa* in the outside world without being unmasked, applying the Muslim Brotherhood's time-tested principle of keeping those sections most in the public eye separate from the more radical ones. That is why he makes a point of stating that he is out of tune with his brother: "The truth of the matter is that, for the last fifteen years, we have followed separate paths. I respect him for his intellectual integrity, but I don't agree with his way of thinking."[64]

This assertion comes as something of a surprise, if one takes the time to compare the speeches and articles of the two brothers over the past fifteen years. In reality, Tariq Ramadan plays with words and takes advantage of the ignorance of the general public. He does indeed have some differences of opinion with his elder brother, in particular as to whether or not (and how) to re-examine corporal punishment and its application, but their disagreements are minimal and occur within the framework of an ideology that is in itself *integrist* (political-fundamentalist). They have the same guiding principles and the same objectives. It is only the style that can, on occasion, differ—for purely tactical reasons. Tariq has to be acceptable to the general public if he is to continue being invited to appear on television. On the other hand, Hani, as director of the Geneva Islamic Center, has nothing to lose; he says what he thinks clearly and without beating around the bush. That does not mean that he never imitates his brother and never tries to be tactful. If you listen closely, you can even recognize some of the rhetorical subterfuges used by Tariq. Like him, he says he respects the law and the need to be modern: "I belong in this country as a citizen who respects its laws and accepts the ingredients of modernity."[65] He also claims the right to be integrated, while simply campaigning for a form of secularism that is more "open." He also reminds us that Islamic law stipulates that a woman cannot be married without her consent, nor be forced to wear the headscarf. He also defends the return to modesty and the wearing of the headscarf as "Islamic feminism."[66] And he condemns violence and the attacks of 9/11: "The Muslim religion, a religion of peace, cannot give birth to such acts."[67]

Le Progrès is good at describing the unsettling effect that Hani Ramadan's ambiguity is capable of producing. It speaks of "a brilliant intellectual, an inspired prophet, a shrewd politician practiced in the art of dodging questions and captivating people's souls."[68] This same type of description will, in turn, be applied to Tariq Ramadan himself, but only after a certain time. How is this time lag to be explained? No doubt it is because Hani Ramadan has none of his young brother's charisma. And less patience. Since he is in contact almost exclusively with an Islamist public, he tends to forget himself and lose track of the distinction between what one can say on the "outside" and what can be said within the community but not in public. Tariq, on the other hand, is on permanent assignment to the outside world. Which means he has the time to fine-tune his presentation for different audiences. For instance, Hani Ramadan sees no reason not to say frankly what he thinks of homosexuals. But Tariq, who is in close contact with the political Left, knows better than to broach the subject. He reassures the respectable circles he frequents by recounting his efforts to keep young Muslims from wanting to stone homosexuals, while omitting to recount that he encourages them to think of homosexuality as deviant for Islam. Aside from this, it is a mistake to think that the two brothers do not share exactly the same view of Islam and of society. They are not in conflict nor even on bad terms. They continue to appear together frequently. They intended to take part together, on May 1, 2004, in a day of boycott of Israeli products, where the leader of the Syrian Muslim Brotherhood was expected.[69] Moreover, why would the audience for the Union of Young Muslims or for the Tawhid publishing house continue to consider the two brothers as models if they were in contradiction? If Tariq really had a moderating influence on young people, why would they continue to idolize Hani? The answer is that their approaches are not different but complementary. Hani Ramadan admits as much himself: "Tariq and I are complementary. We are like two sides of the same coin. We know perfectly well what we are doing and where we are going."[70]

A martyr and his supporters

For the last fifteen years, Tariq Ramadan has always managed to get by through claiming that he is a victim of "Islamophobia." It was in those terms that he accounted for the wave of unfavorable articles that proliferated in the Swiss press in the early 1990s. "In six months my reputation has been turned upside down: after having been a model for Geneva's efforts to promote solidarity, I have become a bogeyman. In 1990, Geneva journalists elected me as one of the ten Genevans of the year in recognition of my work with young people in a program designed to foster solidarity. A few months later, I had become suspect, deceitful, and dangerous, for I had dared to present myself as a Muslim."[71] Tariq Ramadan has a lot of nerve. Defended body and soul by some on the Left and by some newspapers, he came under criticism not because he was active as a Muslim—that had already been the case—but because the opinions he expressed in public were increasingly *intolerant*. Such was the campaign he launched in 1993 to prevent Voltaire's play on Mohammed from being performed, on the pretext that it could discredit Islam in a fragile international context. The play was to be given as part of the tercentenary of Voltaire's birth, organized by the federal government and the city of Geneva. It is true that the international context was at the time strained, as it has been for the last fifteen years, but the play belongs in the classic repertory of Voltaire's works and it makes fun of fanaticism. At the time, its critical perspective on religion would have been a healthy thing. Hervé Loichemol, the director, called it censorship, but no one listened to him. Ramadan tossed back at him his right of free expression and free creation in an open letter published by the press: "In this case, my dear sir, your right to say whatever you please is an assault on the sensitive sphere of intimacy. You call it 'censorship,' I call it tactfulness."[72] Coming from a Christian preacher, such a stand would no doubt have caused an uproar. But coming from Tariq Ramadan, it was met with understanding—to the extent that the subsidy for the play was finally cancelled. In particular, this was thanks to the intervention of two friends of Ramadan: the socialist Jean Ziegler and his wife Erica Deuber-Pauli, at the time directress of cultural affairs for the city of Geneva.

Three years later, Tariq Ramadan was at the center of another furore, this time sparked off by his own writings, namely his book *Les musulmans dans la laïcité* [*Muslims in a Secular Society*], in which he explained that "School biology courses can include teachings that run counter to Islamic principles."[73] He did not suggest that students skip the course, but rather urged Muslim parents to indoctrinate them with a "creationism" more in accordance with

Islamic teaching, but the text nonetheless was sufficient to attract the attention of his colleagues in the Saussure school. In December 1995, one of them, Serge Flueler, left a polite note in his mailbox asking Tariq Ramadan to reassure him: "Dear Tariq, I read with interest your book *Les musulmans dans la laïcité*.... So as to avoid a sterile, dialectic confrontation, I would appreciate it if you would reveal to us what teachings are in question and let me know what is of concern to you. My thanks in advance for your explanations." It was no more than a note between colleagues, a natural reflex and, above all, most cordial. But Tariq Ramadan did not reply. Since there was no word of explanation, a number of teachers decided to hold a meeting. The minutes of the meeting posed a question: "In terms of deontology, it would perhaps be useful to know if it is morally acceptable to teach in a school while disparaging what is taught in a program given by other colleagues." The teachers wanted, above all, to reaffirm the principle of the separation of Church and state, which meant that "no religious group can interfere in our courses." This time Tariq Ramadan was obliged to reply. He produced a lengthy letter in which he expressed his surprise at the manner in which his colleagues had brought up the question, spoke of quotations that were misrepresented, and affirmed the following: "My position consists of inciting young Muslims to participate and understand these issues, while at the same time remaining aware of the replies that are furnished by their religious teaching." And he stipulated, "it is the same thing for history and philosophy." His colleagues had little reason to be reassured, but it was Tariq Ramadan who claimed to be upset: "Your attitude disturbs me: you criticize me for being close-minded, yet your interpretation is itself tendentious. You decide that dialogue is not possible before even attempting it . . . you're making groundless accusations against me." It is Ramadan's standard reply. Every time he is criticized, he speaks of "quotes out of context," of "groundless accusations based on mere suppositions," sometimes implying that his opponents are prompted by "Islamophobia" or even Zionism. In this case, it was not necessary to go this far. He was content to speak of "petty rumors," "facile amalgams," and "dangerous suspicions" so as to make others feel guilty, a technique that had often worked—and did so this time as well. The press that looked into the affair was of two minds, but the school's headmaster, Jean-Jacques Forney, saw no reason to be upset: "There's not the sort of tension that justifies manning the barricades." Whereas the creationist theories advocated by the Christian fundamentalists did indeed alarm Forney, he considered Ramadan's remarks not worth getting excited about: "The book tries to give a true explanation of our Western concepts; if anything, it encourages integration."[74]

There is no room here to calculate the number of times that this form of naiveté, encouraged by cultural relativism, has protected Tariq Ramadan. This "martyrdom" strategy worked perfectly during the furore sparked off by his opinion piece attacking the "communitarian intellectuals."[75] At a time when anti-Semitism was on the rise in France, the preacher caused an outcry by accusing a list of intellectuals, described as "Jews," of insidiously serving the interests of Israel because of their origin. The article immediately caused an uproar that spread to the pages of the leading newspapers, tending to demonize Tariq Ramadan, but also to make of him a media figure. In retrospect, one can well wonder whether it was a mistake or a deliberate provocation that came at just the right moment for him to reassume leadership of the French Muslims and, in the process, count up his supporters on the Left. Among progressives and anti-globalists, many militants were tired of being "suspected of anti-Semitism" every time they criticized Israel. Ramadan was well aware of this potential and, thanks to the outcry, succeeded in putting together an impressive group of allies on the eve of his participation in the European Social Forum, held in Paris on November 12 to 15, 2003. The martyr strategy also helped him bounce back after his disastrous television performance face to face with Nicolas Sarkozy.

100 Minutes to Make Your Case

On November 20, 2003, watched by nearly six million viewers, the French Minister of the Interior, Nicolas Sarkozy, challenged Tariq Ramadan to an eagerly awaited face-to-face encounter. He condemned Ramadan's piece on the "intellectual Jews" as "a moral failure": "When one writes one thinks with one's head and not with one's race. Your article was not just a blunder; it was a moral failure. Because Jews are not like people from Auvergne or Parisians.

There was the Holocaust." Ramadan replied that he had always condemned anti-Semitic attacks, and in particular the fire that had destroyed a Jewish secondary school in Grigny, a Paris suburb. But he did not see what was wrong in characterizing intellectuals by their religion: "They call me a Muslim intellectual; I wrote about Jewish intellectuals. I don't see any harm in that." His replies became decidedly more muddled when Nicolas Sarkozy attacked his brother. "Your brother Hani published a piece in which he justified the stoning to death of adulterous women. It's monstrous. Only someone out of his mind could say a thing like that!" At that point, in front of millions of stupefied Frenchmen, Ramadan failed to utter the sentence that could have saved him, something along the lines of "I condemn stoning" or "I don't agree with my brother." Instead, he preferred to stop the clock by calling for a moratorium: "I'm in favor of a moratorium so that they stop applying these sorts of punishments in the Muslim world. What's important is for people's way of thinking to evolve. What is needed is a pedagogical approach." The audience was stunned. "A moratorium? What does that mean? We're in 2003!" exclaimed the minister. He unsettled Tariq Ramadan for good by alluding to his preface to Zaynab al-Ghazali's book. The reference was totally incomprehensible to the general public, but everyone saw Tariq Ramadan turn white on a live program and understood that he had indeed something to hide. But no one knew exactly what.

The next day the press was unanimous in its praise of Sarkozy's knockout. The left-leaning *Libération* trumpeted: "Sarkozy clobbers Ramadan's double talk." It seemed as if the preacher was permanently sidelined. But that was to forget the workings of celebrity, the public's curiosity, and, above all, Tariq Ramadan's way of working. He bounced back as always, sending off to *Libération* a riposte, in which he offered a point by point analysis: "For the last month, hardly a day goes by without an article critical of me appearing in the press. Up to now I have had neither the time nor the desire to reply to this avalanche of comments, the answers to which are already to be found in my articles and books."[76] And indeed, he had never taken the time to reply to the accusation of "double talk" that had been clearly directed at him over the preceding fifteen years. The reply that he provided for *Libération* also sidestepped the issues. Ramadan objected: "When it came time to expose me for the benefit of an audience of six million, he [Sarkozy] had nothing in hand as proof of my double talk, except my brother's statement and the remarks made by a woman in a book for which I wrote the preface. You must admit it's next to nothing; it's high time for the French to take note." As to the question of stoning that he had not convincingly condemned: "My position is clear and bears repeating here: I have said and written that, for me, stoning is something that can never be applied." The moratorium was a pedagogical tactic to allow for an evolution of opinion in the Muslim world where, Ramadan claimed, his position was in the minority. The subtleties of this remark will become apparent in Part II.

The French Council of the Muslim Faith and Nicolas Sarkozy

There was a background to the settling of scores between Tariq Ramadan and Nicolas Sarkozy in the television program *100 Minutes to Make Your Case*. The preacher had given the Minister of the Interior a hard time when the French Council of the Muslim Faith (CFCM) was being set up. After 9/11, political leaders and a number of French intellectuals thought it a matter of urgency to create a council that could provide a structure and, more importantly, provide institutions for French Islamism so as to isolate it, in particular, from the Algerian, Moroccan,and Saudi Arabian influences that plagued it. The project had been brewing for some time, but Nicolas Sarkozy's predecessors had not carried it through, lest, in so doing, they should grant the Union of Islamic Organizations of France a certain legitimacy to the detriment of the secular Muslims of the Paris Mosque.

The first elections to the council, held in April 2003, marked the rising power of the UOIF, which was now on an even standing with the Paris Mosque. As if it was not enough to have set a place at high table for the association with the closest ties to the Muslim Brotherhood, Sarkozy decided to celebrate the event by attending the annual UOIF congress held in Le Bourget on April 19, 2003. On arrival, he received an ovation from an audience in which the women (wearing headscarves) were seated on one side and the men on the other. The atmosphere got a bit chillier when Sarkozy reminded his listeners that French law required identity card photos to be taken bareheaded. He was booed by the militants, even though they were under tight surveillance. The scene was immediately broadcast on all French TV stations, and this rekindled the debate on the banning of the headscarf in schools.

The UOIF, which had wanted to reopen the debate, had reason to be pleased. But Tariq Ramadan remained skeptical. Not that he was against launching the headscarf debate; on the contrary he was most amenable to it, but the timing was not to his liking. Ever since 1997, he had been working within the Islam and Secularism commission to win acceptance for the idea of negotiating a redefinition of secularism. The commission had first been attached to the Education League before being sponsored by the Human Rights League. A few more years of effort and the proposal would come from the political Left and not from the UOIF itself, giving it a far greater chance of success. The Le Bourget provocation, however, ran the risk of alerting the secular, anti-fundamentalist Left. Tariq Ramadan was, in addition, hostile to the French government's having any say regarding French Islamism. It should not be forgetten that his grandfather had been assassinated after negotiating with the Egyptian government, and that the Muslim Brotherhood was decapitated after the failure of the negotiations with Nasser. Even if he knew that times had changed, he saw the establishment of a French Islamism under the aegis of the French state in the same light. No doubt state interference would have been less painful to accept if he had been chosen to be part of the CFCM. Instead of which, the increasing influence of the UOIF within this organization diminished his personal power. He was extremely reticent and expressed his objections in articles published in *Le Monde*, in which he criticized, in particular, the "breakneck speed" enforced by the Minister of the Interior and the rush to wind things up with the risk of failing to respect "the autonomy of religion guaranteed in a secular state."[77] The dispute between the two men was to explode publicly in *100 Minutes to Make Your Case*. Nicolas Sarkozy, after granting the UOIF a legitimate place within the CFCM, then unmasked Tariq Ramadan's double talk on prime time. As for the preacher himself, he seized the occasion to challenge the Minister of the Interior to make the

French Council of the Muslim Faith "independent." He had lost a battle, but refused to lose the war.

More discreetly, Tariq Ramadan sent "a message to the Muslims of France" in the form of an audiocassette, distributed by the Islamist bookshops, in which he revealed the reasons for his anger.[78] He adopted the tone of a warlord making use of a clandestine radio frequency to transmit his final instructions. The recording, obviously made shortly after the Le Bourget affair, was put out by the Ligue Nationale des Musulmans de France (National League of French Muslims). Tariq Ramadan was furious: "I'm angry at my own community, I'm not angry at Nicolas Sarkozy." He berated those who had replied to Sarkozy's provocation, which was foreseeable, by provoking him in return. "Dear Brothers and Sisters, you are no longer children, we lack maturity," he said, before exhorting French Muslims to exhibit more "discernment." Ramadan reminded his followers that the essential thing was a *dawa,* far more silent but far more efficacious. He cautioned them: "Don't be zealots in your Islamic activities . . . our work has several different dimensions." His directives were clear: "Do not abandon the suburbs on the pretext that you belong to the university . . . because if you don't take things in hand, no one will!" but "I find that the field work is being abandoned." He congratulated "the Brothers and Sisters who are dependable," who had been coming to listen to him for years and who represented "the true strength of this community": "Here in Rosny [a Paris suburb] and throughout the region, I know that the people here will not necessarily be reliable and hang on, but I can tell you one thing: if in the neighborhood there are five or fifteen people who stand out, who are patient, and who set high standards for themselves, who work together at an overall project, that's how we'll change things."

The tone, which was already melodramatic, became sinister when Tariq Ramadan brought up the CFCM. He feared a clash with the liberal Muslims, but, above all, he was concerned by the aftereffects of his quarrel with the UOIF, and he issued a warning: "The major problems will involve our brothers." The warning continued: "Today, in the national community, they will try to sow dissension, to set us one against the other, to find hypocrites in our ranks" and "among us there is the gypsy [the devil]." Tariq Ramadan's harshest criticisms were reserved for Muslims who did not share his plans for the future. He spoke of "people who are capable of lying, traitors who are all smiles when they are with you and insult you when speaking to others." It is to be an ordeal, but Tariq Ramadan loves playing the role of the martyr. At any rate, he explained, "the Prophet has experienced failure, he knows that men can betray and tell lies, he knows that the serpent lies hidden behind some people." The most frightening was yet to come. Tariq Ramadan informed his supporters of hard times ahead: "The coming years will be as difficult for Muslim society as our progress has been rapid, because this time they will be there waiting for us."

The most disturbing thing about this speech is not the warlord-like tone, which reveals a Tariq Ramadan very different from the one we know from watching television; no, the most alarming thing can only be understood if one keeps in mind the Muslim Brotherhood's history. The tone, but also the words and even certain sentences, come amazingly close to the speech given by Hassan al-Banna shortly before his death, in which he announced that the progress made by the Muslim Brotherhood was to cause them problems; the speech in which he announced the transition to another stage. All very disturbing when one knows of the Geneva Islamic Center's contacts and the company it keeps.

Denied entry into France

On frequent occasions, the Ramadan brothers' shady reputation has caught up with them; they have even been suspected of inciting hatred or acts of terrorism. Despite his angelic looks, which have often beguiled the general public, Tariq was the first of the two brothers to have caused concern to the French authorities. On November 26, 1995, as he was about to cross the frontier between Switzerland and France at Verrières-de-Joux on his way to Besançon to attend a conference, he was informed that he was being denied entry into France as "a menace to public order." Ever since the bomb explosion in the Saint-Michel metro station, the French authorities had feared that the terrorists of the Armed Islamic Groups (GIA) would renew their attempt to export violence to France. The arrival of a preacher acting as the spokesman for the

Muslim Brotherhood's version of *dawa* was not really welcome. In effect, there was good reason to believe that the Geneva Islamic Center—of which Tariq Ramadan is still an administrator—served as a European stopping-off place for militants of the FIS and even the GIA.

In 1994, Islamists calling for support for the jihad in Algeria took part in the first congress of Tariq Ramadan's association, the Muslim Men and Women of Switzerland. The following year, on March 11, 1995, members of the FIS and the GIA co-organized a meeting with the Geneva Islamic Center in front of the United Nations headquarters. It was, in effect, a sort of outdoor prayer meeting: each participant had his prayer rug, while the speakers took turns at the rostrum. Two orators, microphone in hand, conducted the public preaching session: Saïd Lalli, a former FIS deputy, and Hani Ramadan. Tariq Ramadan also took part in the gathering. Richard Labévière and a French-speaking Swiss TV crew tried to record the event, but the event stewards violently attacked them and prevented them from filming. The "ambassador to the outside world" was not supposed to keep the same company as the "interior ambassador," even if, in fact, he did.

The event's logistics, in particular the supply of the sound system, was handled by Ijra, an organization run by former members of FIDA, a group with close ties to the GIA that has been responsible for the murder of Algerian intellectuals.[79] On March 7, 1993, for example, FIDA claimed responsibility for the assassination of the director of the Algiers School of Fine Arts. Since the "civil concord," a government measure that provided guarantees for ex-Islamist terrorists in order to bring peace back to Algeria, Mourad Dhina (alias Sheikh Amar) and Moustapha Brahimi, two of its leaders, had been in exile in Switzerland, where they took advantage of the freedom of speech provided by the European democracies to publish a propaganda bulletin, *Al-Qadât* (*The Cause*), distributed in French, Belgian, and Swiss Islamist circles. The bulletin paid a vibrant tribute to Saïd Ramadan on the occasion of his death. It claimed to continue in the same tradition, which implied being close ideologically to Saïd Ramadan's official heirs.[80] For Richard Labévière, author of an investigative piece on the "European Networks of Algerian Islamists" for *Les Cahiers de l'Orient*, there is no doubt that Saïd's two sons were in touch with the editors of *The Cause*: "Mourad Dhina, as well as Moustapha Brahimi, had close ties to the Ramadan family, whose two sons, Tariq and Hani were also in Switzerland. The latter were instrumental in teaching them the virtues of pragmatism in a complex political and social setting."[81] Dhina and Brahimi continue to frequent the Geneva Islamic Center. On September 18, 2004, Brahimi gave a talk on "the personality of Imam Shafii." On October 2, it was Mourad Dhina's turn. The Ramadan headquarters thus still retains official links with the GIA veterans who publish *The Cause*.

The journal *The Cause* claimed to be the "Voice of the elected representatives of the Islamic Salvation Front." Though the body is (unfortunately) legal, this is far from reassuring. In fact, the editors—Mourad Dhina under the pen name Abou Omar and Moustapha Brahimi under the name Mustapha B.—were both active members of the FIDA-GIA, and *The Cause* served to relay their message. But in order not to lay themselves open to arrest, the authors were careful never to refer explicitly to calls for an armed jihad, except for traditional invocations, for instance those of Ibn Taymiyya. There were exceptions when it came to obituaries, as, for example, when Mustapha B. published an article entitled "Sheikh Chérati, my brother, my friend" in tribute to the FIS theologian known for his *fatwa* calling for a holy war in 1992. He had just been killed by the Algerian security forces.[82] But for the rest of the time, only a well-informed reader could catch the jihad references that come in the midst of internationalist, anti-globalization articles, some simulating concern with human rights. *The Cause* on occasion alluded favorably to the Zapatista movement in Mexico or quoted from an Amnesty International report, but of course only when it was a question of denouncing torture in Algeria. But the obsessions of this official mouthpiece of the FIS, which was in effect run by FIDA members, would rapidly resurface. The journal made a practice of targeting French intellectuals, often Jewish (Bernard-Henri Lévy, André Glucksman, and Jean Daniel), accusing them of attacking Islamist ideals. French secularism and the French Revolution, which gave birth to "liberty, equality, fraternity," were pilloried on every page, particularly when it came to rendering the murders committed by the GIA more palatable by explaining that the French Revolution had done worse. You would think that the Algerian Islamists had not got used to the idea that France no longer governed Algeria; *The Cause* regularly dispatched menacing letters to French deputies. In 1995, shortly after the presidential election, the group again threatened Jacques Chirac: "Since you want to symbolize change, allow me most humbly to advise you to stop French meddling with what is happening in Algeria. Begin by admitting that what is happening now in Algeria is part of the plan scrupulously carried out by the stooges that the French administration planted in our country before 1962 . . . . But our people are determined to get rid of these puppets and break the hand that takes pleasure in manipulating them."[83] The menace was taken seriously. All the more so as the group reaffirmed its commitment to armed jihad in a letter addressed to a French deputy: "War is declared against the junta in power and its allies until the day when an Islamic state is established in Algeria."[84]

This background is necessary in order to understand the context in which the denial of Tariq Ramadan's entry permit took place. The French police sent a report to Jean-Louis Debré, then Minister of the Interior, to remind him of the ties between Tariq Ramadan and the Brotherhood, as well as his participation in Secours Islamique. The report also specified that Tariq Ramadan had translated "newspapers published by the Hamas movement in the occupied territories." It concluded that "the intellectual influence of such a person could be particularly dangerous" in a climate of such tension.

The refusal of an entry permit for Ramadan immediately set off a scandal. A defense committee was set up, including radical Islamists close to the Center and to the Geneva Mosque, but also leading figures from the Left, the Catholic Church, and the Human Rights League, to request that the ban be lifted. Ramadan had, in effect, brought all his talents to bear to appear as the victim of an unjust conspiracy. Ten days after learning that he had been denied entry, in the course of a lecture given in Brussels, he adopted a particularly melodramatic tone to reassert that the ordeal would not deter him from his mission: "Because the path before us is not determined by circumstance, but laid out by destiny."[85] Once again, his speech curiously brings to mind Hassan al-Banna's last address, shortly before his death, in which he announced to his companions that, once their true nature was revealed, they should be prepared to face adversity. Tariq Ramadan made a point of claiming that he was heir to this mission, even if it meant confronting the same "injustice" that his father and grandfather had known: "I will continue to speak this message, for it is our inheritance and our destiny." He explained to his companions the strategy that he planned to implement: "You will not hear of revolt; you will hear an insistent call for justice." Which is far more efficacious. Putting this strategy into effect, Tariq Ramadan adopted a quite different tone for the outside world and cried out for justice. He contacted any and every association or journalist willing to listen to him. Was he accused of being an Islamist linked to the Secours Islamique? He spoke of documents riddled with errors and claimed, for example, that Hany al-Banna was no relation. In the meantime, he omitted to mention that he did indeed serve as one of the high-ups of the organization in question, which was, in fact, what he was accused of. He insisted that he was 100 percent a pacifist, a victim of a misunderstanding—and he was to have his way. All the more readily in that the French Left was, at the time, fully mobilized against the security policy of the government, convinced that it was acting in the great anti-colonial tradition by accusing the governments of the newly independent nations of exaggerating the risk of terrorism in order to step up their persecution of Islamists. Tariq Ramadan recounted to anyone who would listen that he had been banned at the request of the Egyptian government, as a way of getting back at him for having, on a French TV program, submitted the Egyptian ambassador to aggressive questioning over the lack of respect for human rights in his country (where the Muslim Brothers continued to be arrested and harassed). Many people were to believe his version of events, especially in view of the campaign waged against him in Egypt at the time of his father's death. As a result, Ramadan once more came through as a victim: "The damage has been done. Mistrust is in the air," he declared to the press, adding that the ban would keep him from going on with his "salutary" work in drawing young French Muslims into dialogue. The Human Rights League even wrote to the Minister of the Interior, requesting that the ban be lifted on Tariq Ramadan—"whose beliefs and opinions are perfectly respectable." While some Swiss journalists wanted nothing to do with him after the Muslim Men and

Women of Switzerland congress, others called it a scandal and stepped up to defend him. The French journalist Elisabeth Lévy, who at the time was favorable to Ramadan, even took up the Egyptian conspiracy thesis in the *Nouveau Quotidien*: "We knew that, when it comes to hunting down Islamists, France does anything the Algerian regime asks. Now it seems France is also ready to pursue those whom the Egyptian regime considers enemies."[86] As for *La Tribune de Genève,* it recalled that Tariq Ramadan had just published a book, *Islam: le face-à-face des civilisations* [*Islam: The Confrontation of Civilizations*], that proved the preacher's "open-mindedness." Above all, the press was impressed by the defense committee. Close to 17,500 people (10,000 in France, 6,000 in Belgium and 1,500 in Switzerland) signed the following text: "The dialogue between communities is essential for our future. Tariq Ramadan, who in his writings and teachings embodies the commitment to dialogue and tolerance, has the right to be heard, the right to free speech and movement."[87]

The offense to Tariq Ramadan's honor was a subject that could bring together historical revisionists, as well as pro-Third Worlders; the liberal minded, as well as anti-secular Christians; professors, as well as political figures—all of them siding with the Islamists.[88] Nobody appeared upset by the fact that Roger Garaudy—known to be a negationist—signed; nor by the fact that the defense committee's address was "care of H. Ouardiri," that is to say the rector of the Geneva Mosque, known to be close to the Wahhabite Saudis. To be more precise, this "Committee for the defense of the right of free speech for Muslims" was orchestrated by Yahia Basalamah, Hafid Ouardiri, and Yousouf Ibram. This last is today the most active member of the European Fatwa Council, the governing religious body of the UOIF, through which he issued a *fatwa* banning abortion. But none of this far from respectable backing disturbed Michel Rossetti, the administrative councilor for the city of Geneva for whom "Tariq Ramadan represents a link between our communities."[89] Jean Ziegler went so far as to call on the lower house to request that the Federal Council intercede with the French government so as to lift the "arbitrary" ban. In his text, the Swiss deputy really laid it on, explaining that Ramadan came from a tradition that favored a tolerant form of Islam! The Swiss Socialist Party, in the person of Bernadette Gaspoz-Brede, a municipal councilor, also gave vent to its indignation at the ban imposed on the preacher. Mobilization became more intense once the ban began to have secondary effects within Switzerland. Informed of the decision taken by the French authorities, the Department of Public Instruction and Religious Affairs chose to postpone Tariq Ramadan's talks in the secondary schools. He was refused the right to give a lecture in a Lausanne lycée gymnasium, but the Department of Public Instruction ended up rescinding this decision, clearing him of "any suspicion of fundamentalism," according to *Le Journal de Genève*.[90] In the meantime, the Besançon administrative court, on May 9, 1996, annulled the Ministry of the Interior's decision, which appeared to vindicate all those who had defended him. The lifting of the ban afforded him the opportunity for a triumphal return. He was more listened to than ever on the Left, which considered him a victim of racism, a defiant political opponent.

His brother Hani was not treated with the same solicitude when something similar befell him the following year. On February 1, 1997, when he was about to cross the frontier to give a lecture in Lille, he was informed that his presence was unwelcome. The French authorities spoke of "a leading figure in the European Islamist movement" connected to the UOIF—which the ministry had no difficulty in establishing was on friendly terms with "the Palestinian Hamas movement." The authorities considered that the comings and goings of Hani Ramadan constituted a public danger, specifying, however, that "even if this intellectual cannot be suspected personally of sympathizing with the Islamic circles that advocate recourse to violence, the recent murderous attacks that have taken place on French soil oblige the authorities to increase their vigilance to include all those whose behavior can contribute, directly or indirectly, to the progress of extremist ideologies within France." On May 22, 2001, the decision was to be annulled by the administrative court of Lyon as irregular; there had also been a failure to observe the provisions of the ordinance governing the entry and residence of foreigners. But in contrast to what had happened in Tariq Ramadan's case, the accusations failed to elicit a reaction from the French Left. Hani had to be content with a statement of support issued by the UOIF denouncing the decision as "an affront to the Muslims of France." Once the ban was lifted, he was welcomed as a hero by the Union of Young Muslims of Lyon—which had had to make do with Tariq during the period that Hani was held up at the frontier. The association organized a conference to celebrate the return of their second-favorite lecturer. On October 4, 2001, only a few months after having been authorized to re-enter France, Hani Ramadan, speaking to a packed municipal conference hall, began by pleading for observance of the law: "We are not in a Muslim country; we must act in keeping with the existing associative and cultural structures, and keep up the contacts and dialogue with the authorities and political representatives; but we must also develop inter-religious relations." This did not prevent him from reasserting that "a secular state worthy of the name, a state that prides itself on being truly secular, should admit the wearing of the headscarf." And then, as always in the end, the mask came off. His text got out of hand when he launched into international affairs: "Wherever a Muslim is attacked, wherever a country's territory is invaded, it is our duty to mobilize, here and elsewhere. Obviously this commitment holds true for Pakistan and for the Taliban."[91]

The speech was given less than one month after 9/11, and Hani Ramadan was clearly calling on Muslims to refuse to serve in the NATO army ranged against the Taliban. He also announced a massive demonstration in support of Palestine. One year earlier, on October 6, 2000, in response to an appeal from the Geneva Islamic Center, a thousand demonstrators had assembled on the steps of the UN for this selfsame cause. Hani Ramadan had, on that occasion, uttered the following words: "When an army kills children and adults armed with nothing but stones, the reply is not speeches and negotiations, but the jihad!"[92] To be sure, he, like his brother Tariq, was to defend himself in the press by explaining that the jihad was "a defensive war," and therefore legitimate. In the meantime, on the terrace of the United Nations, the preacher, Yahia Basalamah, imam of the Geneva Mosque, Tariq Ramadan's childhood friend and one of the organizers of his support committee, gave his version of defensive war: "The Koran reminds us that the territory of Jerusalem and the Al-Aqsa Mosque are sacred places. We will never accept that they be administered and desecrated by Zionist aggressors."[9]

Repeatedly suspected of terrorist links

The Ramadan brothers, and in particular Tariq, have quite frequently been suspected of maintaining cordial relations with Islamists involved in terrorist activities. In a report delivered to Judge Garzon, who was assigned to investigate the 9/11 attacks, the headquarters of the Spanish national police stated that Ahmed Brahim, an Al-Qaeda leader arrested and imprisoned in Spain, was "in frequent contact" with Tariq Ramadan.[94] An association of victims of the World Trade Center, represented in particular by Jean-Charles Brisard, an expert on Islamic financing, went public with the affair, arguing on the basis of the record that the Geneva Islamic Center and Tariq Ramadan had maintained relations with a bin Laden "cell," or at least with one of its heads. Contacted by several newspapers, such as *Le Temps*, Tariq Ramadan said he "had never been in touch" with Brahim, and then added: "I don't even know of his existence." The assertion comes as a surprise. Ramadan certainly knew the Algerian millionaire, at least by name.

The files of the Spanish, Belgian, and French intelligence services, readily made available to journalists, began to pile up. According to these sources, a telephone tap dated April 22, 1999 recorded a conversation between Brahim and a certain al-Amin (which the police suspected was a code name for a militant with ties to the Tawhid bookshop that distributed Ramadan's works):

> Al-Amin: Tell me, is Tarek to come with me? . . .
>
> Ahmed Brahim: No, he can't right away, it's not urgent. I have an idea how to get things started and I will be seeing him in the al-Dawa Center in Madrid, Paris, or Geneva. The instructions come from Riyad . . .

From the rest of the conversation we learn that it involves "an important project" that "must not be rushed" and that concerned the production of audiocassettes in Spanish. The conversation is—to say the least—vague and not very enlightening. It is quite possible that it refers to the Tariq (also pronounced Tareq) associated with the Tawhid publishers, but this is not certain. On the other hand, the existence of ties between an Al-Qaeda outpost and the Lyon bookshop that serves as the preacher's headquarters is disturbing. Another memorandum from the Spanish national police head office, dated May 10, 1999, confirmed that Brahim did, in fact, telephone the bookshop that serves as Ramadan's headquarters: "Another telephone call of interest was recorded on April 21, 1999, when Brahim dialed the number corresponding to the Tawhid bookshop in Lyon and spoke of a certain Mohamad Amine; it appears that the latter was involved in the Ahmed Brahim project." As the years pass, so the number of investigations featuring the name of Tariq Ramadan increases. In his role as administrator, he is obliged to report on those who frequent the Geneva Islamic Center; listed among them are representatives of organizations suspected of terrorism by the association of victims of the attacks on the World Trade Center.

Since 1991, the press and the Egyptian authorities have suspected the Ramadan sons of having organized a meeting in Geneva with Ayman al-Zawahiri, the Egyptian second-in-command of Al-Qaeda and the man who, in 2004, declared that the French law banning the Islamic headscarf was proof of "the rancor of Occidental crusaders against Muslims." The news broke on the occasion of Saïd Ramadan's burial, and then subsided. At the time, the accusation appeared far-fetched and was denied by the Swiss police. However, in 2003, this time via the Swiss police, the charge reappeared on the front pages and became more explicit. The Swiss police had in their possession a sworn statement dated December 1, 2003, in which a former associate of the Geneva Islamic Center guaranteed that he had heard one of the Ramadan sons inform his followers that the "Islamic warrior" Ayman al-Zawahiri was coming to France: "I attest also attending the Friday prayer session conducted by Mr. Ramadan, who announced the arrival of the Islamic warrior Ayman al-Zawahiri. Mr. Ramadan then invited us to come to the lecture to be organized to welcome Mr. Zawahiri the following week in Geneva." The conference is supposed to have taken place at the Penta Hotel in Geneva in 1991, and was supposedly set up by the two Ramadan brothers, and attended by Zawahiri, as well as by Omar Abdel-Rahman, the brains behind the World Trade Center attacks two years later. This categorical testimony is troubling. Nevertheless, this "secret source" must be handled with care. The same witness asserted that Abdel-Rahman was the Ramadans' "uncle," which is highly improbable. Unless he expressed himself poorly. In Arabic the term "uncle" is often used for a person whom one addresses in affectionate terms, without necessarily being a relative. The episode provided an occasion for Tariq Ramadan to indulge in sarcasm: "These self-proclaimed terrorist experts think nothing of redoing your family."[95] Nonetheless, despite this error of interpretation, the rest of the testimony is plausible. At the time, Zawahiri and Abdel-Rahman were not high on the list of wanted men, as they are today, and Switzerland, since it takes a more or less neutral stance on these matters, is a perfect place to organize a conference. Finally, and most importantly, it is quite likely that the Geneva Islamic Center, the headquarters of the Muslim Brotherhood in exile, would organize a meeting with two Egyptian jihadists belonging to the Muslim Brotherhood.

For years, Egypt has raised this connection and insisted on an investigation. For years, the Swiss intelligence services have simply replied that they possessed "no information by way of confirmation," which encouraged the press to conclude that it was an Egyptian maneuver. In reality, the Swiss investigation at the time was strictly minimal. According to the information published in *Le Temps* by the journalist Sylvain Besson, "the inquiry consisted essentially of checking the hotel registers for the name of al-Zawahiri, despite the fact that the latter used pseudonyms and forged identity papers."[96] It appears, then, that the Swiss were not particularly zealous. Too much was at stake. On the other hand, after 9/11 the net began to close in on the Ramadan family.

The Al-Taqwa lead

The Islamic Center again found itself in the midst of a media storm when the Islamic bank Al-Taqwa was closed down on December 31, 2001, after having been singled out by the American intelligence services as one of the financial sponsors of terrorism. Paul O'Neill, the Secretary of the Treasury, accused it of having "transferred funds in cash to Al-Qaeda," via its subsidiaries located in Lugano, Liechtenstein, and the Bahamas. Backed by the United Nations, the American Treasury Department affirmed that

> the Al-Taqwa Bank was founded in 1988 thanks to a sizeable financial contribution coming from the Muslim Brotherhood. They invested in the financing of radical groups such as the Palestinian Hamas movement, the Islamic Salvation Front and the Islamic Armed Group in Algeria, as well as An-Nahda, the principal Islamist group in Tunisia, and Osama bin Laden and his Al-Qaeda organization. Each year Hamas received 60 million dollars via Al-Taqwa, even after a storm of protest in 1997, when half of the Hamas budget was siphoned off by an intermediary.[97]

Up to this point, the investigations had not caused much of a stir. But after 9/11, at the request of the victims' families, things became clearer. Jean-Charles Brisard, an expert on Islamist financial networks, was called in to investigate. A Washington federal court became involved, as did the Swiss Ministry of Public Affairs. Some of the material in the files began at last to appear in the press. Thus it was that the Ramadans and the Geneva Islamic Center appeared on the list of beneficiaries of Al-Taqwa, almost all of which were linked to the Muslim Brotherhood. Tariq Ramadan outdid himself explaining that it proved nothing: "We have never had any sort of contact with the bank. The fact that our name appears in its address file doesn't mean a thing. My name also appears in the address files of Bordeaux wine . . . which, of course, I never drink."[98] Once again, Tariq Ramadan's denials are too vehement to be credible. It is a falsehood to say that the Ramadans never had "any sort of contact" with the bank, since they were well acquainted with its chief administrators, beginning with its president-founder, Youssef Nada, one of Saïd Ramadan's best friends.

Like Saïd, Nada was one of the Muslim Brothers who had fled Nasser's Egypt to take charge of the international branch from abroad. Like him, he established a privileged relationship with the Saudi Arabian princes. This *éminence grise*, now in his seventies, is today a highly influential Islamist billionaire. Dividing his time between Lugano and Campione, he is well established in financial and political circles. He served, in particular, as an intermediary for Saddam Hussein in the negotiations on the withdrawal from Kuwait. In

1977, after twenty years of exile, he founded an Islamic bank in Cairo, in association with Mohammed al-Faisal al-Saud, the son of King Faisal (the leading sponsor of the Brotherhood). In 1988, the bank became Al-Taqwa. In other words, he is someone who is almost untouchable. On Al-Jazeera TV, he was self-confident. "They can prove nothing. I challenge them to prove the slightest thing." And he had reason to be confident. In view of the Saudi backing that the investor enjoys, many observers are already counting on the investigation being dropped. The financial records of the bank are kept in Saudi Arabia and the Saudi authorities appear to be in no hurry to produce them.[99] And who is in any position to put pressure on them? In addition, Swiss legislation prevents fact-finding investigations concerning "political" questions from going too far. Meanwhile, Nada has only to deny the whole thing: Al-Taqwa is not the Muslim Brotherhood's bank, even if he has to admit the bank's links with the Brotherhood and its role in the international organization.[100] According to Abdelkader Soheib, the assistant managing editor of the weekly *Al-Mussawa*, there is no doubt about it—the Al-Taqwa bank was set up to finance the international expansion of the Muslim Brotherhood with capital from the Gulf: "Initially, Al-Taqwa was conceived as the principal financial instrument of the Muslim Brotherhood, particularly of the international branch."[101] The bank's religious guarantee is none other than the Muslim Brotherhood's theologian, Yusuf al-Qaradawi, another of Tariq Ramadan's friends. How can one imagine that Saïd Ramadan and his Center were not in touch with Al-Taqwa and Nada? Not only were they closely linked, but Saïd was one of the founders of Al-Taqwa. Even the Supreme Guide Machour does not deny the fact. Richard Labévière, who interviewed him, recalls: "The guide confirmed that Youssef Nada and Saïd Ramadan were involved from the start in the creation of the Al-Taqwa Bank."[102] So Tariq Ramadan lied.

The investigation into Al-Taqwa had several beneficial side-effects. First of all, it revealed a bit more about the behind-the-scenes financing of the Muslim Brotherhood. But it also brought to light the longstanding association between the Brothers and Nazism, as well as today's pro-Nazi sympathizers. The Egyptian secret service has in its files a dossier on Youssef Nada that deals with his activities during the 1940s.[103] He was then suspected of having planned the assassination of King Farouk with members of Admiral Canaris's *Abwehr*. Richard Labévière, author of the exhaustive investigation into Islamist financing, *Les dollars de la terreur* [*The Terror Dollars*], suspects that the Al-Taqwa Bank has links with the Swiss pro-Nazi banker François Genoud: "I interviewed him several times and he told me he assisted the Muslim Brothers in exile in Europe."[104] Genoud's chauffeur, Ahmed Hubert, is, curiously enough, a former administrator of the Al-Taqwa Bank, as well as an old acquaintance of the Geneva Islamic Center. He readily confirmed knowing Saïd's two sons: "Hani is a friend, as is his brother Tariq."[105] Despite his good-natured appearance, Ahmed Hubert is no angel. This Swiss citizen, converted to Islam, is a great admirer of Hitler and Khomeini, whose photos are prominently displayed on the wall of his office, alongside that of Jean-Marie Le Pen. He first developed a passion for National Socialism thanks to Nasser, whom he got to know during his years in Egypt. He speaks of the great man with emotion, which often results in his being told to keep quiet by his friends at the Geneva Islamic Center! It was at the Center in 1962 that he converted to Islam. The following year, in 1963, he was in Cairo when he met Johann von Leers, Goebbels' former right-hand man, who "opened his eyes to the true meaning of the great adventure of the Third Reich."[106] Ever since, he has had but one obsession: to convince his skinhead friends that Hitler admired Mohammed and convince his Islamist friends that Mohammed would have adored Hitler; in short, to convince them that they should start working together—and start by defeating the Jews. For a while, he thought he could wage this campaign from within the ranks of the Swiss Socialist Party, where he served as the press representative for forty years before being expelled for "revisionism, Khomeinism and anti-Semitism"—but not until 1994! Before then, in 1989, he had been fired from the largest Swiss press consortium, Ringier, for having approved of the *fatwa* condemning Salman Rushdie to death. He got over it by saying that he had picked the right horse, since the European extreme Right and the Islamist movements were beginning to come together. "You know, Jean-Marie Le Pen has understood a lot of things," he is apt to say. According to him, both Jörg Haider and the German far-Right NPD were to come to the same conclusion. Hubert does his part, giving lectures on the potential synergies between the Crescent and the Swastika for New Right and neo-Nazi groups, for Iranian television (for which he is an advisor)—and also for the Geneva Islamic Center, where he held several conferences up to the time that Al-Taqwa was closed down. "I said to Hani, it's just as well that I no longer come here, so as not to get you into trouble." One thing should be clear: it is as embarrassing for the Geneva Islamic Center to be seen to be close to Al-Taqwa as it is for Al-Taqwa to be thought of as close to the Geneva Islamic Center. Even after the liquidation of Al-Taqwa, Hubert is obliged to continue protesting high and low that the Islamic bank was never linked to terrorist organizations and that the Americans lied. He does so, but without really convincing people: "You know the Americans also accused me of being Islamist, Khomeinist, and neo-Nazi simply because, as a Muslim, I had a somewhat different opinion of the Third Reich and of the past! They also accused me of being anti-Semitic, whereas I am against Judaism, as is the Koran, that's clear." What is also clear is that Ahmed Hubert is as talented at doublespeak and euphemism as are his friends Hani and Tariq—but in his case it is accompanied by a sense of humor. Even if Tariq Ramadan does not share his enthusiasm for Nazism and Nasserism, this type of acquaintance tells us a bit more about the radical atmosphere of the Geneva Islamic Center in which the preacher is plunged. Do we really need to show that the Center is a meeting place for militant terrorists? Is it not enough to demonstrate that it is unquestionably the hub of Islamism in Europe? Hani Ramadan (who perhaps does, after all, possess a sense of humor) once declared with a straight face: "Our activities are transparent. We do nothing that is incompatible with an authentic Islamic commitment."[107] Need one say more?

As for Tariq Ramadan, he was now aware that any sort of connection with the Geneva Islamic Center could blur the image that he was trying to project to the outside world, for it would prove he is lying when he says he had no functional link with the Muslim Brotherhood. When he cannot deny the connection, he attempts to minimize his role in the Center, as during an interview given to Manuel Grandjean for *Le Courrier*:

Grandjean: The Geneva Islamic Center has been suspected of having links with

> certain disreputable figures. Are you still one of the administrators of the Center?
>
> Ramadan: When my father, Saïd, the founder of the Center, died in 1995 he left an organization in debt. It was then that my brother Aymen, a doctor, took charge of the bookkeeping, and it was decided that the official board of directors would be made up of family members. The Center is a property belonging to the family. The running of the Center is in the hands of an association of which my brother Hani is the director. I have no official role. However, I insist that what is said about us is nothing but rumors; no proof has ever been provided concerning the Center.[108]

Ramadan contradicts himself and plays on words. He does indeed hold a position in the Center, since he is one of its administrators. Moreover, he defends the Center against the slightest accusation, which proves that he identifies with it and feels part of it. And he defends it in bad faith, since the charges for which the Geneva Islamic Center is held to account are no mere rumors. It is undeniable that the Geneva Islamic Center and its administrators contribute to the spreading Islamism that incites hatred throughout the heart of Europe. It remains to be seen whether Tariq Ramadan, as an individual, produces the same effect. To add an additional touch to his image as a moderate, he makes a point of saying that he is under permanent surveillance by the intelligence services, but that no one has ever provided proof of his doublespeak. As if the fact that he travelled throughout the world preaching Islamism does not prove that he has been involved in spreading a radical and dangerous Islam. Who does he think he's fooling? The police are not empowered to lock up preachers just because they preach fundamentalism. When it comes to speech rather than activity, their mission is limited to one of surveillance. And in terms of his speeches one can say that Tariq Ramadan has been the center of a good deal of attention and is highly suspect to most Arab, European, and American intelligence services. That he was denied entry into France and that his visa for the United States was refused by the Department for Homeland Security provides sound evidence of this. Alain Chouet, former head of the security intelligence service of the French Foreign Intelligence Agency (DGSE), has stated categorically that fundamentalism and terrorism cannot be contained without taking action against a Brotherhood ambassador such as Tariq Ramadan:

> Al-Qaeda is only a brief episode and an expedient instrument in the century-old existence of the Muslim Brotherhood. The true danger is in the expansion of the Brotherhood, an increase in its audience. The wolf knows how to disguise itself as a sheep. Tariq Ramadan, for instance, is not part of Al-Qaeda but of the Brotherhood. If one were to clearly denounce the power and the strategy of the Brotherhood, those who spread its influence and recruit in its name would be forced to give an account of themselves rather than showing off on TV or in international forums.[109]

Concerning Ramadan's double talk, the 2001 report of the Belgian Permanent Committee for the Control of Intelligence Services is no less severe: "State security also reported that the moderate speeches that Tariq Ramadan gives in public do not always correspond to the remarks made in confidential Islamic settings, where he is far more critical of Western society." A number of individual cases can serve as confirmation.

Djamel Beghal, a Lyon Islamist arrested for terrorist activities, declared to Judge Jean-Louis Brugière: "In 1994 I took courses given by Tariq Ramadan, who is an Egyptian with Swiss nationality belonging to the Muslim Brotherhood." Tariq Ramadan dismissed this sworn statement with a wave of his hand: "It's impossible. I only began those courses in 1997!"[110] The explanation is a bit too succinct. In reality he had given lectures—considered by the associations that invited him to be training seminars—since 1994. They took on a more official character in 1997, but they existed well before. It is, therefore, possible and even probable that Djamel Beghal did attend, as he affirms, Ramadan's lecture-conferences. Moreover why would he lie? It does not mean that Tariq Ramadan himself urged Djamel Beghal to become a terrorist. One can simply register the fact that his influence does not have the moderating effect that he makes so much of when with journalists.

A danger for the United States; a "wise man" for Great Britain

In the autumn of 2004 Tariq Ramadan was scheduled to be "in charge of the study program devoted to religions, conflicts and the establishment of peace" for the Joan B. Kroc Institute that is part of Notre Dame University. A magnificent university, founded in 1842 by a priest of the Congregation of the Holy Cross, equipped with a basilica, numerous chapels, two liturgical choirs, departments of theological studies, and a program of Catholic education by satellite. The man who recruited him, Scott Appleby, has written for several books on religious fundamentalism, such as *The Fundamentalist Project*,[111] and was perfectly well informed of the polemics set off in France by the preacher. "It's precisely because he was at the heart of these polemics in Europe that we wanted him here," he declared to the magazine *Lyon Mag*.[112] Officially, his decision to bring Tariq Ramadan to the United States was in keeping with the Kroc Center's policy. In the beginning, the idea was to foster dialogue between Americans and communists, but since the fall of the Berlin Wall the Center has focused rather on Muslims, with the objective of finding "non-violent solutions to conflict." How did a specialist in fundamentalism come to think of Tariq Ramadan for such an assignment? Appleby claims to have listened to Tariq Ramadan's tape recordings. He admits that Ramadan is a skilled speaker, but refuses to consider him an Islamist: "He knows perfectly well that if it was proven that he was an Islamist he would no longer be welcome."[113] This is false; the proof is there. And yet the director of the institute defended him: "Tariq Ramadan is neither an extremist nor anti-Semitic." As regards the struggle against secularism in the West, Tariq Ramadan is on the right side in the American's eyes. Although he is anti-fundamentalist, Appleby supports the Islamo-Christian alliance against secularism. In an article published in *Foreign Policy*, he suggests that the next pope forge a sort of alliance with Islam. Compared to what he describes as a "new and aggressive secularization," he presents Islam as "the great world religion that is both the Church's main rival for adherents and its potential ally against a purely materialistic concept of human development."[114] From this perspective, Tariq Ramadan most certainly has a lot to teach American Catholics. But from a security perspective, on the other hand, the United States had no need whatever of someone like Tariq Ramadan. On July 28, 2004, the Department for Homeland Security decided to revoke his visa—a blow for the preacher, whose image in Europe suffered, except in England, where

Tariq Ramadan surprisingly bounced back, thanks to relations between the Muslim Brotherhood and some members of the Labor Party. The Mayor of London, Ken Livingstone, is very close to the Muslim Brotherhood's most listened-to theologian, Yusuf al-Qaradawi. On July 12, 2004, the two men fell into each other's arms at a meeting of the pro-*hijab* association (an organization "to put pressure on European parliaments" to accept the Islamic headscarf). The meeting was set up by the English branch of the Muslim Brotherhood, thanks to the patronage of the mayor—and was attended by Tariq Ramadan. The Swiss preacher has been much in demand in England ever since the government decided to counter the influence of the Salafist jihadists by promoting leaders representing a fundamentalist Islam, officially non-terrorist, such as the Muslim Brotherhood. Only a few days after the attacks of July 7 and July 21, 2005, Tariq Ramadan was invited by the London police to give a lecture on Islam. In autumn of 2005—stupefaction: he was being considered for membership on the government's working group for "Preventing Extremism Together" — set up to advise Tony Blair on how to "combat Islamic extremism." It was taken as a joke. But the Prime Minister stood fast and defended his choice. And the left-wing press backed him up, all the more so since the foremost attacks on Tariq Ramadan came from the *Sun* and were thus considered "Islamophobic." Yet Ramadan's presence on this working group is alarming. The group's first proposal was to abolish commemoration of the Holocaust Memorial Day, on the basis that it was "wounding" to Muslims. Iqbal Sacranie, a Muslim Brotherhood member of the Muslim Council of Britain, who was knighted by the Queen in 2005 for "services to the Muslim community," explained that he had always boycotted Holocaust Memorial Day because it was "offensive to Muslims." For Tony Blair's working group, this day of commemoration did not do sufficient justice to the atrocities suffered by Muslims, and thus gave the impression that "Western lives were of greater value than non-Western lives." The committee proposed replacing it with a national Genocide Day that would mark the genocide of the Palestinians, the Bosnians, and the Chechens. Another member of the group, Ahmad Thomson of the Association of Muslim Lawyers, took advantage of his appointment to furnish the press with his version of the war in Iraq: "Tony Blair decided to wage war on Iraq after coming under the influence of a 'sinister' group of Jews and Freemasons."[115] In 1994, he wrote a book claiming that the European and American governments were controlled by Jews and Freemasons, that the Holocaust was "a big lie," and that the Jews were not a pure race.

How can one explain Tony Blair's decision to set up an advisory committee on "Islamic extremism," in which the Muslim Brotherhood and their propaganda are given a starring role? The decision would appear to confirm that, within the British government, there are some who are toying with the idea of making a deal with the Muslim Brotherhood: a stop to terrorism in exchange for concessions that reinforce their position in the community. This hypothesis is by no means far-fetched. After having served for years as a haven for the most virulent jihadists, Britain has been obliged, since 9/11—and even more so since 7/7—to re-examine its legendary tolerance of Islamists, without, however, subjecting its communitarian (and vote-catching) approach to similar scrutiny. Over the last few months, mosques that were under Salafist influence have been taken over by the Muslim Brotherhood, a radical movement but one that is prepared to give voting instructions and that is considered more "controllable" by the British authorities—but wrongly so. As in the case of Nicolas Sarkozy in France, who also chose to institutionalize the Muslim Brotherhood, backing a fundamentalist movement in order to combat terrorism could well prove not only counterproductive, but dangerous. The Salafist jihadists are far too radical to be restrained by the political Muslim Brotherhood, whom they despise for their "softness" and consider to be "innovative." The Salafists can only be rendered harmless through thorough intelligence work, and by politicians who do not feed the fires of religious identity, which is exactly what the government is doing by choosing to entrust the future of the Muslim community to the Muslim Brotherhood—an organization that has always known how to take advantage of a state's failures in order to pursue its goal of conquest. As we shall see, Tariq Ramadan is counting on the Islamization of the European Muslim communities to fulfil the dreams of his father and grandfather. Yet he still needs to ponder the advice of Hassan al-Banna, who recommended advancing stealthily, step by step.

The loss of his post at Notre Dame University and the ban on his working in the United States were obstacles in Ramadan's path. By accepting the position of "visiting research fellow" (that is to say, without pay) at the prestigious St. Antony's College, Oxford, and thanks to his being officially appointed by the British government to a working group on "Preventing Extremism Together." Tariq Ramadan can hope to re-establish his legitimacy. And, after all, he might well hope that the United States will lift its ban on his working there . . . That is, unless decisionmakers, the press, and all those who believe in Tariq Ramadan's good faith finally take the time not just to read him and listen to him, but also to decode his message.

PART TWO

DISCOURSE AND RHETORIC

In principle, it is not that difficult to see that Tariq Ramadan speaks with two voices: you have to read him and listen to him, and then you have to decipher what he is saying. The trouble is that few newspaper reporters have the time or the space required both to recount his career and to analyze his message. Journalists are, by their nature, drawn to the telling of events, and they prefer to adduce biographical facts rather than dissect rhetoric, which means that Tariq Ramadan can often claim that he is attacked on account of his family background or the people he is in contact with, rather than for what he says. A few magazines have made the effort—*Islam de France* and *Nunc* spring to mind. But their circulation is such that they are no match for the media attention that Tariq Ramadan commands.[1] Until now, therefore, he has managed by challenging his interlocutors to cite a single sentence of his that is in any way compromising. It is no simple matter; as a preacher he has worked hard, almost obsessively, at redefining his terminology, so that a very ordinary sentence can have different meanings according to the context in which it is spoken. Complex and far-fetched though this may seem, and contrary to what I thought when I wrote *Tirs Croissé* [*Crossfire*], this double-speak does indeed exist. To dig it out, dissect it and demonstrate how it operates is not something that can be done in a sentence or two. It is like the works of a Swiss watch (no play on words intended!) that you have to dismantle wheel by wheel. All of this takes time. This part of the book is, therefore, entirely devoted to analyzing the content of Tariq Ramadan's public speeches, newspaper articles, books, and recorded tapes, so as to put them in perspective and measure their impact.

Chapter 3

A "Reformist" but a Fundamentalist

Tariq Ramadan claims to be a "reformer." The term touches on two commonly held notions—that of political reform pursued in a spirit of moderate renewal, and the Protestant reformation. But these images are confusing to those who have heard him spoken of as an Islamist. Tariq Ramadan is aware of the fact and never misses an opportunity to insist on the term "reformer" being used. Here is the definition that he gives of the word "reformer" in the glossary published as an annex to the French edition of *Etre musulman européen* [*To be a European Muslim*]: "According to traditional prophecy, a reformer will appear in each century to renew the Muslims' understanding of their religion. It is this renewal—not a renewal of the texts themselves but a renewal of their interpretation—that will give further impetus to Islamic teachings and allow for their adaptation to the context of the time."[1] Recalling this prophetic tradition is by no means irrelevant. Obviously, one is expected to think of him in this connection. This messianism with a reformist touch works wonders with American journalists. In 2000, *Time* magazine chose to name him as one who would bring about a renewal of his religion, as an "innovator." Others have gone so far as to speak of Tariq Ramadan as "Islam's Martin Luther King." Such prophecies may not go down so well in France, where skepticism in regard to religion is widely accepted. But in France, Tariq Ramadan often compares his reformism to liberation theology, which clears him of any suspicion of bigotry, even in the eyes of radical left militants who are, for the most part, anti-clerical. He is seen as a thinker who will reform Islam, make it more rational, modern and even more secular. This is an objective to which Tariq Ramadan has never laid claim, but which he takes care not to repudiate—just as he is careful not to inform the journalists who have not read his books of the real history of the term "reform" in Islam. Let us fill in the background for him.

The ambiguities of the term "reform"

In Islam there exist two quite different reformist trends. The first is a liberal reformism that is intent on making Islam more progressive and open-minded, more rational and modern—an Islam that is cultural rather than political. The second is Salafist reformism that is turned towards the past, towards an Islam based on founding principles, more archaic and more political. To understand what is at stake, one has to grasp the basic features of liberal reformism—contested by the Salafists:

1. *Islam is not a political system.* Along the lines of the analysis developed by Abd al-Raziq in *Islam et les fondements du pouvoir* [*Islam and the Origins of Power*], liberal reformism points to the fact that Mohammed never set up a government during his lifetime and made no provisions for designating a successor or instituting a political system that would survive him. We are also reminded that the great majority of the verses of the Koran (more than 70 percent) deal with questions that are strictly religious and not social. Regulations such as those concerning the wearing of the veil are altogether trivial matters by comparison with the overriding importance that the Koran accords to the five pillars of religion: the profession of faith, prayer, pilgrimage, the observance of Ramadan, and the obligation to give alms (*zakat*).

2. *Islam is compatible with secularism and democracy.* The Koran, in a sura entitled "Consultation" (*choura*), explicitly proposes that "men consult between themselves on their affairs." Which indicates—even more conclusively than the Biblical phrase "Render unto Caesar the things that are Caesar's"—the extent to which Islam is open to the idea of a democratic dialogue separate from the realm of the sacred.

3. *Islam calls for recourse to reason and thus for adapting to changing times.* Islamic jurisprudence (*fiqh*) provides for account to be taken of commonly held opinions (*ijma*) to allow for evolution and adaptation to the times. Liberal Muslims encourage efforts at interpretation and personal reasoning (*ijtihad*).

4 *Islam is not intent on proselytizing.* Liberal reformism considers that religious faith is not something to be forced on others, in accordance with the verse of the Koran that explicitly bans proselytizing: "If your Lord had so willed, the whole of the universe would have espoused the faith. Is it then for you to force men to believe?"

On all these points, the Salafist reformism of the Muslim Brotherhood is totally opposed to the liberals. They sometimes cite the same references and the same verses, but ascribe to them a totally different meaning. For them, religion and politics are inseparable, practically indistinguishable, to the extent that they often attach more importance to campaigning on social issues, such as the Islamic headscarf, than to questions of ritual or theology. According to the Muslim Brotherhood—which is the principal school of Salafist reformism—the call for "consultation" is not to be taken as acceptance of the principles of secularism or democracy, but as a call for pluralism in terms of religious obedience. They use it as a pretext in pleading for political representation when confronted by one-party systems that block their access to power in certain Arab/Muslim countries, but they dream at the same time of reducing this pluralism, once in command, to a dialogue between Islamist scholars. When that day comes, the law will be based on the sharia and there will no longer be any question of taking "commonly held opinions" into account, but only of being as faithful as possible to the Koran and the Sunna (made up of the *hadiths* or words spoken by the Prophet and taken down by his companions). The Salafist reformers often express a certain disdain for Islamic jurisprudence, which has enabled Islam to evolve over the last fourteen centuries, since they want to return to a pure, original Islam. To have their way, they are prepared to use any means—though they often repeat the passage from the Koran that condemns proselytizing, in order to prove that Islam is tolerant, they never actually take it into account. On the contrary, they are obsessed with the idea of the *dawa*, that is to say the transmission of the faith, and conversion.

Far from being complementary, the progressive and Salafist reformers have been at war for almost a century—perhaps even from the very beginnings of Islam. The vicissitudes of history, the Crusades, and the colonial context have, until today, benefited the latter to the detriment of the former, preventing Islam from pursuing its *aggiornamento*. So, even today, Salafist reformers have an easy time discrediting reason and modernity as Western and thus *enemy* qualities; only a return to the foundations of Islam will restore the vigour and cohesion of the early days—that is to say, revive the Golden Age of the caliphate and Muslim expansion. Liberal reform symbolizes for them subjection to the Western colonizer, whereas the Salafist reform will re-establish a Muslim world that is strong and triumphant—in short, a colonizing power.

Tariq clearly belongs to the second tradition, rather than the first. In one of his most recent books, *Les musulmans d'Occident et l'avenir de l'Islam* [*Western Muslims and the Future of Islam*], published in 2003, he openly attacks "liberal reformism" that is based on reason and that is progressive in spirit.[2] It is not the first time that he has dropped his mask. The outspoken hatred of liberal Islam is already to be found in *Etre musulman européen* [*To Be a European Muslim*], written while attending the Leicester Islamic Foundation, and published by Tawhid in 1999.[3] In these two works, Ramadan makes no secret of his disdain for "liberal reformism," which, he tells us, "resulted from the influence of Western thought beginning with colonialism."[4] In order to equate the liberals with secular atheists, he includes in the liberal camp the advocates of the secularization project of Mustafa Kemal Atatürk in Turkey, whom he obviously detests as much as did his grandfather. Above all, he accuses the European theoreticians of liberal reformism of being "assimilated": "In the Occident, the supporters of liberal reformism advocate the integration of Muslims, which they expect will result in the adoption of Occidental styles of life."[5] He clearly has in mind the official representatives of the Muslim faith, such as the mufti of Marseille (Soheib Bencheikh) or the rector of the Paris Mosque (Dalil Boubaker).

According to Ramadan, three facts illustrate the assimilation of the liberals. First of all, they do not "insist on the daily practice of religion" but rather on "a form of spirituality that is experienced individually and in private or else as an attachment to one's native culture."[6] This statement reveals the extent to which Tariq Ramadan refuses to envisage any way that religion can develop into an individually held faith that is not to be forced on others, or into a culturally based faith that is to be shared as a source of enrichment instead of being instituted as an ideology. Ramadan is even more explicit on the subject of the two other characteristics that supposedly condemn liberal reformism. He reproaches the liberals for not considering the Islamic headscarf an obligation and for combating fundamentalism: "Most of them," Ramadan says of the liberals, "are opposed to any difference in people's way of dressing, which they consider synonymous with sequestration or even fundamentalism." Which makes of them traitors, corrupted by the influence of Western rationalism. "Taking the evolution of society into account, they consider that the Koran and the Sunna can no longer serve as a guide for proper behavior; it is the exercise of reason that henceforth sets the criteria for social conduct." The moral of the story? "The term liberal refers here to the meaning that the term has taken on in the Occident; it privileges rationality and is founded on the primacy of the individual." Thus Tariq Ramadan, speaking as a professor of philosophy, openly accuses the Muslim liberals of promoting rationalism and individualism. In other words, if Muslims attempt to reform their religion—bringing it up to date in an intelligent manner, so as to encourage the development of an individual faith more cultural than political—instead of sticking to a dogmatic Islamist view, then they have automatically become renegades who have sold out to the West. As a way of finishing them off once and for all, Ramadan explains that, although the liberals are "a minority within the Muslim world," they have intermediaries in Europe because "their rhetoric is immediately picked up by Western ears."

These extreme and fraudulent accusations appear not to have the slightest effect on those who insist on seeing Tariq Ramadan as the representative of an open-minded Islam. But they have been picked up by truly liberal Muslims, such as Leïla Babès: "By treating this school of thought as radical secularists, and by ignoring the intellectual work being accomplished within the Muslim faith—as in the case of Ali Abd al-Raziq, Mahmoud Muhammad Taha and Muhammad Sa'id al-Ashmâwi, whom he never mentions—he is suggesting that the liberal Muslims are Muslims . . . without Islam."[7] This analysis is most accurate. In a cassette, "Islam and the West," Tariq Ramadan refers openly to "Muslims that are "secular" as "Muslims without Islam."[8] He effects a skilful shift of meaning, by which the Islamists—the fundamentalist Muslims—become simply Muslims, and the others, the secular or liberal Muslims, become sub-Muslims, or even non-Muslims. Whilst he is openly critical of the liberal Muslims, he never utters a word against the fundamentalists. A "fundamentalist" or "Islamist" is one who makes use of religion for freedom-destroying political ends. However, Ramadan never uses the term in speaking of Islamists. As long as they are close to the Muslim Brotherhood, the most radical of theologians and militants—from Yusuf al-Qaradawi to Sayyid Qutb and al-Banna—are always referred to in flattering terms, such as "political Muslims" or "scholars." This is a way of denying their fundamentalism that fools those who don't know how to differentiate between a Muslim and an Islamist.

Laying claim to the middle ground—an absolute priority

It never ceases to amaze me how a preacher who is so adamantly opposed to liberal Islam can pass himself off as a modern, enlightened Muslim in the eyes of observers. By way of excusing them, it must be said that Tariq Ramadan relies on a multiplicity of rhetorical tricks to maintain this ambiguity. He constantly takes advantage of people's lack of knowledge of the Muslim world to present a vision of Islam in which he ends up by representing a sort of middle ground—even if this middle ground is a million miles from a progressive, enlightened Islam. In *To Be a European Muslim* (1999) and in *Western Muslims and the Future of Islam* (2003), Tariq Ramadan readily assumes his role as supporter of the Salafist reformism of al-Banna, Mawdudi, and Qutb, but he does so in such a way that this school of thought is not immediately recognized for what it is, namely a movement firmly opposed to liberal reform.[9] He takes advantage of the fact that he is one of the few Islamist intellectuals listened to and read in Europe to propose an interpretation of Islam divided into six major currents:

- Scholarly traditionalism (linked to one of the four great schools of thought of Islam)

- Salafist traditionalism (a "literalist" fundamentalism inspired by Arab traditions not necessarily Islamic
- Salafist reformism (fundamentalist, but not literalist, the reformism of the Muslim Brotherhood
- Literal political Salafism (a literalist political current, openly jihadist)
- Liberal reformism
- Sufism (a mystic Islamic school).

This way of breaking Salafism up into three currents out of six is pure politics. To be truly pedagogical, one should distinguish four principal schools: the scholarly tradition, the liberal reformist current, Sufism and Salafism, within which coexist three tendencies: reformist Salafism, literal Salafism and traditional Salafism. Literal Salafism is most simplistic: it consists of simply applying to the letter the Koran and the Sunna. Traditional Salafism is hardly more developed, since it combines the defects of literalism and those of archaic non-Islamic traditions—such as forced marriage and female circumcision. In comparison to these two Salafisms, the third—that is to say reformist Salafism—obviously stands out as more moderate. Indeed, by advocating a reform that consists of returning to founding principles, it rids Islam of certain traditional customs without necessarily being literalist. This categorization explains how a militant Salafist reformer such as Tariq Ramadan can reject both Saudi Wahhabism and the traditionalism of the Taliban, and vehemently criticize literalism without himself being a modern, liberal Muslim. Presenting Islam as formed of six different schools reduces liberal Islam to the smallest possible share (one sixth) on the fringe, and situates Salafist reformism in the middle ground, equidistant from both the "excesses" of rational reformism, considered as too Western, and of literalism or traditionalism, seen as too archaic.

While accepting his role as heir to Salafist reformism, Ramadan bristles with anger when he is suspected of being influenced by the Muslim Brotherhood's philosophy: "My way of thinking draws on interaction and dialogue with all tendencies, and I do my best to propose a theoretical development that takes account of this diversity by combining reformists (including the Muslim Brotherhood among other groups), the Sufis, the rationalists and embracing even Salafist traditionalism and the Tabligh."[10] One understands why Ramadan chooses to bury the reference to the Muslim Brotherhood in the avalanche. But the statement is troubling. Note that it does not specify the proportions of the mix. In reality, Tariq Ramadan draws principally on the philosophy of the Muslim Brotherhood, but sprinkles his theory with a minimum number of references to the other sources—all of them, with the exception of Muslim rationalism, apparently far too radical for him. When he quotes "rationalism," Ramadan is speaking not of Muslim rationalism—which he loathes—but of non-Muslim rationalism, which he cites here and there to avoid being suspected of Islamism, and only then when the reasoning in question is in line with his own thinking. He does not repudiate Sufism, which also influenced his grandfather, so long as it is orthodox Sufism and not a Sufism that would allow for innovation regarding the basic principles of Islam. As for the other two references, the Tabligh and Salafist traditionalism, there's nothing to be proud of. The Tabligh—often called the Jehovah's Witnesses of Islam—is an Islamist pietist movement, obsessed by the *dawa* (in other words by proselytizing), that is responsible for the many conversions to Islam that have taken place in France over the last few years. It is understandable that Ramadan, whose mission is *dawa* for Europe, should take the Tabligh as a model, but why cite them? As for Salafist traditionalism, this is the most reactionary and fundamentalist ideology of Islam, and Ramadan claims to be combating it in order to appear more moderate. To this extent Ramadan is right: his way of thinking is, in effect, based on this patchwork. But once we take account of the relative weight attached to each of the schools, and once we correctly identify them, we realize that these multiple influences have nothing very reassuring about them. But never mind. The preacher has developed thousands of ways of throwing any accusers off the trail.

To convince his audience, he likes to say that he is detested by the extremists: "In the eyes of the fundamentalists, I am a traitor!" Without ever specifying who these "fundamentalists" might be. Yet, for him, the term can only refer to the literalist jihadist Salafists, in other words to Al-Qaeda, Al-Muhajiroun or Hizb ut-Tahrir; that is to say, to those in favor of immediately waging holy war to establish a worldwide Islamic dictatorship. From this perspective, he is indeed more moderate. But does this mean he stands for the modernization of Islam? Many people think so, forgetting that his "middle ground" has often helped turn events in favor of the Islam of the Muslim Brotherhood, to the detriment of progressive Muslims.

Reformist Salafism as a bulwark against . . . Salafism!

Tariq Ramadan has scoured his imagination to find ways of protecting his Salafist reformism from accusations of extremism, in particular by tailoring his rhetoric to fit the audience in question. When speaking to a "friendly" audience, he is forthright in declaring the school of thought to which he belongs, but he takes pains to avoid being too explicit about it when speaking to a public that might disapprove. Interviewed by the community radio station Beur FM in November 2003, he admitted adhering to Salafist reformism: "There is the rationalist reformism and the Salafist school, in the sense that the Salafist tries to remain faithful to basic principles. I belong to the latter; that is to say, there's a certain number of principles that are, for me, fundamental and that, as a Muslim, I refuse to betray."[11] It is impossible to be more explicit. Ramadan is indeed a reformist, but a Salafist reformist, in the fundamentalist tradition (the word *salaf* in Arabic means "our pious ancestors"). The term "reform" indicates his willingness to renew our understanding of Islam, but the adjective "Salafist" reveals in which direction this reinterpretation is to take us—namely backwards. Tariq Ramadan is prepared to adopt this stance—except when speaking to the general public, when he plays on words. On February 25, 2004, less than four months after his interview on Beur FM, he spoke quite a different language in a symposium organized by UNESCO. Painted into a corner by Ghaleb Bencheikh, known as a representative of the liberal reformist school, Ramadan turned the audience in his favor by claiming his opponent had falsely accused him: "I am not a Salafist! 'Salafi' means literalist. I am not a literalist."[12] The denial worked so well that members of the audience took the floor to say how reassuring they found it . . .

In truth, this was a brilliant stroke of trickery. Here we have Tariq Ramadan caught red-handed indulging in doublespeak. *Salaf* refers to the basic principles of Islam, not to literalism. And Ramadan is indeed a Salafist, even if he is not a literalist. He does advise Muslims to be faithful to the spirit of the text rather than to the precise wording—"what is absolute is not the letter, but the spirit"[13]—but nonetheless considers the precepts formulated in the seventh century, in a specific historical context, to be "in essence eternal truths." Which means that his non-literalist Salafism is a way of refusing to modernize or rethink principles that date from the seventh century.

"No" to patriarchal traditions . . . unless they are Islamic

The Muslim Brotherhood understood early on that they could pass their fundamentalism off as a form of progress if they were to emphasize the fact that their puritanism has rid Islam of some patriarchal traditions—traditions that were not Islamic. Journalists who are not familiar with Islam are often surprised to hear Tariq Ramadan condemn archaic, sexist practices, such as female circumcision and forced marriage. If they have heard experts in the field refer to him as a dangerous fundamentalist, they then assume they have been lied to and that Ramadan is, in fact, a progressive Muslim. But there is nothing progressive about his enterprise, even if he contests certain injustices inflicted on women. Tariq Ramadan is devoted to Salafist reformism. It is just that the basic principles of Islam are less misogynous than one tends to think. Even if the Koran dates from the seventh century and is taken literally, it is less sexist than the majority of twenty-first century Islamist groups.

Coming seven centuries after Jesus and twenty centuries after Moses, the Koran is the first monotheist text that does not view male domination as justified by original sin. An entire sura is devoted to women, basically in order to grant them rights they did not up to then enjoy. The Koran grants women the right to inherit half of what a man inherits—which marks considerable progress at a time when women had no financial autonomy. The Koran also forbids men from disinheriting the wives they repudiate: "But if you intend to take one wife in place of another, even if you had given the latter a whole treasure for a dowry, take not the least bit of it back; would you take it by slander and a manifest wrong?"[14] What is not generally known is that most of the sexist practices ascribed to Islam are actually patriarchal traditions that many Muslims refuse to reconsider, despite the more advanced views contained in the Koran and the Sunna. Forced marriages, for instance, are in total contradiction to the teachings of the Prophet—who authorized a woman to refuse to marry a man her father had chosen for her. The four schools of jurisprudence of Sunni Islam agree on this, basing their opinion on the following *hadith*: "The widow has more rights over her marriage than her tutor, and virgins cannot be married without their consent." The same intransigence exists regarding female circumcision—in reality practiced out of respect for patriarchal traditions, but said to be of religious origin. During his lifetime, the Prophet attempted to calm the zeal of his fellow citizens. In particular, he advised a woman whose vocation it was to practice circumcision not to cut too deep into the clitoris since "it is better for the woman and affords the husband greater pleasure." There was hardly anyone to listen to him . . . Despite the injunctions of the Koran—and even if it is against the law in many Muslim countries—female circumcision continues to be practiced on some one million young girls in Egypt every year, as well as on millions of others in Ethiopia, Kenya, Nigeria, Somalia, and Sudan.[15]

As a fundamentalist Muslim who claims to be modern, Ramadan is opposed to these non-Islamic practices, but has never written a book devoted to them. He is content to remind his public, in the course of a conference or an interview, of the extent to which these practices sully Islam's image and of the fact that they are not to be attributed to religion. Very often, he does so to defend Islam against any form of criticism. In 1998, when giving a lengthy conference on "The Muslim woman" in Senegal, a country in which female circumcision is widely practiced, he disposed of the problem in one sentence: "Female circumcision is not Islamic."[16] Full stop. Nor, as far as I am aware, has he ever given a lecture on the subject in Sudan, where he has contacts at the highest levels. Ramadan could take advantage of his status, of the prestige he enjoys in the eyes of Islamists worldwide, to devote all his energy to a real modernization of Islam. He can sometimes be critical of the Muslim community and of Muslim traditions, but at heart he remains deeply conservative. The liberal reformers wear themselves out waging this battle; they dare to call for a real reform of the sexist practices stemming from tradition or the Koran. But the Salafist reformers devote far less time to the subject. This difference in the way the two schools invest their energy is no accident. The modern-minded reformists consider it a priority to put an end to the injustices committed in the name of their religion, whether sanctioned by the Koran or not. The Salafist reformers, on the other hand, make strategic use of the fight against non-Islamic customs to demonstrate that a return to basic principles can mean progress, and to protect Islam from the criticism of Westerners. Appearing as champions of anti-traditional reform is one of their tactics for avoiding criticism, without, in fact, contributing to the evolution of Islam. Even if the status of women could thereby be slightly improved (circumcisions that cut less deep, fewer forced marriages), one must remember that these concessions are granted in the context of a broad-based return to an archaic way of life, modeled on standards of morality established in the seventh century, without any modernization of their basic principles.

Matahed Shabestari, an Iranian intellectual, was right in saying that Mohammed was a more or less feminist leader. "He did away with some of the flagrant injustices that penalized women within the limits of the idea of justice that existed at the time."[17] Unfortunately, the seventh century in which the Prophet lived was a long way from meeting the standards that today we consider to be a minimum in terms of human dignity, with the result that the meagre accomplishments due to the Koran remain locked into the patriarchal context in which the Prophet made his appearance. Sura IV, entitled "Women," thus reads: "Men are the protectors and maintainers of women because Allah has given them more strength than the other . . . "[18] As sacred texts, the Koran and the Sunna rigidified the traditions that they did not condemn; thus dozens of practices now considered barbaric, such as corporal punishment, the killing of apostates, or the ban on Muslim women marrying non-Muslim men, were given the stamp of legitimacy for centuries to come. This marks the limits of Tariq Ramadan's fundamentalist reformism. He no doubt defends an Islam that is less archaic than the Islam of the Taliban, but his reform does not go beyond the progress accomplished during the time of the Prophet. He is in favor of ridding Islam of certain discriminatory practices, but not to the extent of challenging the patriarchal principles of the seventh century: "We are not told: 'Be Muslim in this twentieth century as were the Muslims in the seventh century.' Rather: 'In this twentieth century be respectful of and faithful to the principles of the seventh century.'"[19]

When "contextualizing" does not mean "actualizing"

So as to render his faith dynamic and alive, a liberal reformist is ready to adopt his religious practice in accordance with his times. Applying the principle of *choura* (consultation) and *ijma* (consensus), Ghaleb Bencheikh, for instance, is clearly in favor of bringing up to date, and even rescinding, certain verses of the Koran if they run counter to human dignity as understood today. Tariq Ramadan by no means shares this approach, which he considers to be a betrayal, even a denial, of Islam. He says he wants to situate the teachings of the Prophet in their context; but for him "contextualizing" never means "actualizing." He speaks of "principles that are eternal" but also of "the relativity of intelligence and their understanding."[20] The ambiguity of such a position provides the preacher with ample room for maneuvering. In practice, he leaves it to the liberals to implement the real reforms, while treating them as "Occidentalized" behind their backs. For himself, he will forgo insisting on the strict application of certain principles only if he can thereby avoid accusations of archaism. Unlike the literalist Salafists, the Salafist reformers claim the right either to contextualize or to maintain the literal interpretation of Islamic principle in accordance with their political objectives. But this relative freedom never allows for reinterpreting a principle set down in the Koran.

Apostasy as a test

Islam decrees death for a Muslim who renounces his faith. It is in the name of this principle that all the dictatorial regimes based on the sharia have persecuted their political opponents or secular Muslims. In Egypt, for example, Nassr Abu Zeid and Ibtihal Younès were forced to divorce because Abu Zeid had been accused of "apostasy." In 2001, Nawal el-Saadawi, an Egyptian feminist, was likewise arrested and prosecuted for the same offense. The Ramadan brothers never miss an occasion to castigate the Egyptian government for not respecting human rights. However, in cases of this sort, one never hears a squeak from them. How can Tariq Ramadan claim to be fairly tolerant and open-minded if he does not fight for the right of a man or woman born into a Muslim family to choose to be Muslim or not? The liberal Muslims do, referring to two verses of the Koran: the verse that bans proselytizing and the verse that proclaims "No compulsion in religion." On this basis, they refuse to accept such practices. Tariq Ramadan is never as explicit, despite the constant pressure coming from his friends on the Left. He did finally concede the right to change one's religion, but in a half-hearted way, in the course of an interview, and on one condition: "My point of view, a minority point of view in historical terms but justified in religious terms . . . is to recognize the right, but to ask of those who change their religion what one asks of all human beings: Change your soul and your conscience, but do not insult or cause prejudice to those whom you leave behind. Wherever you go, whoever it is you forsake, leave them in a noble and dignified manner.'"[21]

Once again, this declaration is designed to reassure "the outside world." It comes in reply to a question in the context of an interview; it is couched in such a manner that the speaker does not appear to be a fundamentalist and is thus left free to continue with his charm offensive. In other circumstances, Ramadan is in no hurry to wage war on this disgraceful custom—current in all Muslim countries—in which the ulemas, often associated with the Muslim Brotherhood, separate couples or kill individuals for apostasy. It is simply not a subject of much interest to him within the Muslim community, where his energy goes into discrediting the liberal reformers. This was made painfully clear to Leïla Babès, who felt quite isolated when she tried, over the years, to talk to scholars close to the Muslim Brotherhood (such as Tareq Oubrou from UOIF), hoping to convince them to encourage this reform: "Tariq Ramadan does state that Muslims have the right to practice their religion or not. But for him, those who reject the laws founded on texts that are unequivocal 'have abandoned religion,' since they are no longer Muslim." Leïla Babès, however, adds: "The right to change one's belief, like the right to have a different opinion, is considered as the equivalent of apostasy."[22] To say nothing of the fact that the apostate is requested to leave Islam "with nobility and dignity," without causing prejudice to Muslims—whom Tariq Ramadan insists on equating with the Islamists. This is an important point. Most Islamists condemn "apostates" not because they have ceased to be practicing Muslims, but because they turn against Islamism or because they contribute to the "desacralization" of Islam by advocating a critical view, both historical and secular. Tariq Ramadan is well aware of the fact, since he was apprenticed to the network that led the campaign in England against Salman Rushdie. He did not agree with the *fatwa* declared by Khomeini in Iran—the jihadists most virulently opposed to Rushdie, like Omar Bakri, were incensed to see a Shiite leader steal the show. But Ramadan did, like them, condemn *The Satanic Verses* and did approve the campaign against Rushdie. He spoke of the book as "a stupid and disgraceful provocation." But, as we have seen, Tariq asks Muslims to renounce Islam "with nobility and dignity," otherwise they are to be considered apostates. And that, according to the theologians that counsel him, can mean death. His stand is not all that courageous.

Polygamy: yes—mixed marriages: no

Tariq Ramadan has not been of much help in fighting against the patriarchal customs contained in the Koran. He has nothing to say against polygamy, even if he does point out that the Prophet authorized it only in periods when marriages were scarce, and provided the existing wives agreed (a first wife can refuse this in the marriage contract) and that the husband was prepared to treat his wives equitably: "Polygamy is permitted in Islam, up to four wives," wrote Ramadan in *Peut-on vivre avec l'Islam* [*Can One Live with Islam?*], in an edition revised and corrected in 2004, "but it comes with explicit conditions attached."[23] On this question, as on others, his opinion does not differ from that of his brother Hani, whose book *La femme en Islam* [*Women in Islam*] created a scandal. But the most blatantly scandalous stand taken by Tariq Ramadan is, without doubt, his position on mixed marriages. Given that Islam is a religion bent on expansion, a male Muslim can marry a non-Muslim woman, but never the other way round. It is in the name of this principle that the majority of "crimes of honor" are committed, including in the heart of Europe. In 1993, in Colmar, a young girl succumbed after several torture sessions conducted by her mother, her brothers and her uncles—all because of her liaison with a non-Muslim. On November 5, 2001, Latifa, a Franco-Moroccan student, suffered a similar fate in Nice. Her father stabbed her with a knife because she was about to marry a non-Muslim. What did the leader of the European Muslims do about these injustices? Did he take up arms against the ban on mixed marriages? Absolutely not. In theory, the European Fatwa Council, for which Tariq Ramadan wrote a preface for the first compendium of religious edicts, issued an opinion authorizing mixed marriages. This *fatwa* is always prominently displayed by the Union of Islamic Organizations of France (UOIF) to show how adaptable their fundamentalism can sometimes be. It remains to be seen whether the authorization is respected in practice. In the course of a conference given in Chambon-Feugerolles, Tariq Ramadan appeared very embarrassed when asked whether the Koran banned mixed marriages. He would not answer until he was forced to reply when the question was asked for the third time. "It's true, the Koran forbids a Muslim woman marrying a non-Muslim man. Which means that every time you let one of your sisters, one of your friends, or a woman of your family marry a non-Muslim, it means she has left the community." And he concluded: "A loss for the community is a loss to the umma."[24]

Ramadan never risks distancing himself from the seventh century. Above all, if it is a question of discouraging habits that run counter to the *dawa*, the expansion of the Muslim faith, which is his primary mission. He himself, who married a former Catholic, is the first to approve of a man capable of winning the heart of a non-Muslim and thus converting her. But he remains inflexible in the opposite case. In his books, he urges that everything be done "upstream" so as to avoid mixed marriages: "It is better to curb passions at the start, rather than be faced by catastrophe after several years."[25] His prognosis was very pessimistic: "Sometimes mixed couples survive like others, but very often it goes tragically wrong." A husband can always convert to Islam, but there again Ramadan is most skeptical: "What can appear as a solution 'for today' is almost sure to produce problems 'for tomorrow.' A conversion that does not commit both heart and mind is null and void. One can try to fool oneself, but one cannot fool the Creator, and tomorrow the couple's agonizing separation will teach the lovers they once were that an authentic act of faith must, of necessity, be sincere. The only act of faith worthy of a human being."[26] Decidedly, freedom to love is not really a priority for this man of the faith, obsessed with proselytizing.

As for corporal punishment . . .

Tariq Ramadan's lack of determination when confronted by barbarity is particularly evident when it comes to corporal punishment. The Koran specifically recommends that women who are not obedient be beaten: "As to those women on whose part you fear disloyalty or ill-conduct, admonish them first, next refuse to share their beds, and lastly beat them lightly; but if they return to obedience seek not against them means of annoyance."[27] Once again, what is most shocking is not that this practice should have existed in the seventh century, but that the twenty-first-century fundamentalist preachers should refuse to challenge it. A liberal reformer has no difficulty whatsoever in considering it outdated. At the time, the Prophet recommended that the wife's punishment be administered with a stick cut from an arak, the equivalent of a cinnamon stick. In other words, he was suggesting that the husbands of his time control their temper and show restraint in dealing with their wives. A Salafist literalist does not see it that way. In April 2004, in the course of a wide-ranging investigation into the rise of Islamism in the Lyon suburbs, the magazine *Lyon Mag* published an interview with a Salafist imam, Abdelkader Bouziane, in which he declared that the Koran authorized a husband to beat his wife if she was unfaithful. The affair provoked an uproar; the imam was expelled (though he was allowed to return to France). In condemning this expulsion, the UOIF and its training institute for imams claimed it stood as a bulwark against these Salafist imams . . . while forgetting to specify that the Union was itself reformist, but also Salafist! The theologian who advises the Union imams, Yusuf al-Qaradawi, is the first to say that, according to the Koran, beating one's wife is legitimate. Here is what he recommends for young

Muslims living in Europe in *Le licite et l'illicite* [*The Lawful and the Unlawful*], a book available in all shops associated with the Muslim Brotherhood:

> When a husband detects in his wife signs of pride or insubordination, it is up to him to rectify the situation by all possible means, beginning with well chosen words, convincing arguments, and wise advice. If this method bring no results, he is to shun her in bed so as to awaken her feminine instincts and thus persuade her to obey him, so that their relations once again become tranquil. If this proves to be useless, he must punish her, using his hand, but not hitting her too hard and avoiding blows to the face.[28]

This indicates just how minimal the differences between a literalist reading of the Koran and a reading that is simply fundamentalist can be. Tariq Ramadan also stands as a guardian against Salafism that is not reformist. He warns Muslim husbands not to succumb to the temptation of using the authorization to beat their wives as a pretext for making slaves of them: "Some men treat their wives' bodies in ways that are so offensive that I dare not speak of them here. They have heard it said that wives must obey their husbands as if they were their servants, and they treat their wife's body as if it belonged to them, that's not Islam."[29] One can only be thankful to hear him profiting from his aura of prestige to provide this clarification for the benefit of his audience. Unfortunately, this does not mean that he is willing to condemn the verse authorizing the beating of wives. Moreover, it is not his job. Tariq Ramadan is not a theologian. The authority he refers to when speaking to Muslims is none other than Yusuf al-Qaradawi. In his books, Tariq Ramadan describes him as the scholar "who is accustomed to attending numerous meetings devoted to the problems of our modern life in order to elaborate appropriate Islamic solutions."[30] He is the one to whom Tariq Ramadan's followers are directed, in order to learn what is lawful or not. In so doing, they will rapidly find it confirmed that beating one's wife is within the law.

A moratorium to decide on the size of the stones?

Furnishing a somewhat loose interpretation of the basic principles of Islam, so as to continue attracting the outside world, while at the same time shifting responsibility to Islamist "scholars," who will anyway block whatever progressive ideas he expresses in a private capacity, is a classic Tariq Ramadan strategy. This hypocrisy finally came to light in the course of the television debate with French Minister of the Interior Nicolas Sarkozy (November 20, 2003), when he proposed a "moratorium" on stoning women to death as punishment for adultery.[31] Even if it may appear well intentioned, this proposal represents a step backwards compared to the progress that the Koran itself had marked. Like Jesus before him ("He that is without sin among you, let him first cast a stone at her"), Mohammed had intended to put an end to this disgraceful punishment. Aisha, his second wife, was falsely accused of adultery, and he did not want this kind of injustice to be repeated. The Koran proposes explicitly that stoning to death be replaced by a hundred lashes. Before any penalty can be carried out, four witnesses must swear that they were present on the occasion of the adultery.[32] Which is obviously almost impossible. This provision was designed to render the punishment inapplicable. Mohammed himself was not content to decree a "moratorium": he stripped the archaic practice of its legitimacy! Thirteen centuries later, Tariq Ramadan was not so courageous.

Shortly after his televised confrontation with Nicolas Sarkozy, Ramadan set forth in an opinion piece exactly what he meant by the establishment of a moratorium:

> My position is clear and bears repeating here: I have said and written that, for me, stoning is something that can never be applied . . . . I have vigorously condemned all practices (in particular in Saudi Arabia and Nigeria) concerning capital punishment and corporal punishment. Among the ulemas of the Muslim world, this is a minority opinion and most of them systematically refer, but without always being very clear about it, to "the conditions in which the punishments are to be applied." Confronted by this situation, I ask, therefore, for an absolute moratorium on all punishments, so as to allow the ulemas to hold a thoroughgoing debate on this issue (and discuss their interpretations); in the meantime, let a stop be put to the use of Islam to oppress the poor and women. The objective here is clearly to open the way to abandoning these practices; but we will not succeed without an in-depth debate within the community.[33]

And he added: "I address audiences throughout the Muslim world, and my aim is not limited to expressing my own personal condemnation (which is evident), but to bringing about a change in mentalities, which is why I spoke of a 'pedagogical attitude.' I speak the same language in France, in Asia and in the Arab world."

This statement of intent, which once again came in response to outside pressure, raises several problems. First of all, by limiting himself to the call for a moratorium, Tariq Ramadan, who is speaking from the point of view of European Muslims, gives the appalling impression that European Muslims are still debating whether or not to stone someone to death for adultery! Declaring that he cannot display more tolerance for fear of no longer being listened to proves that he prefers to remain credible in the eyes of Islamists, rather than to take the risk of offending them by adopting a firm stand for progress. This is why he will never be a moderating element, but rather a radicalizing one. One has difficulty imagining that Iranian political leaders are going to change their minds after discussing things with Tariq Ramadan . . . On the other hand, considering it acceptable to debate the pros and cons of stoning certainly has an effect on European Muslims under his influence. Lila and Alma Lévy (who are sisters) said they listened to cassettes by both Hani and Tariq Ramadan. Recently, they published a book in which they defended the right to stoning as a free choice.[34]

Finally, one must understand what Tariq Ramadan means by "moratorium." He speaks of a consultation (*choura*) that is supposed to take place not between citizens, but between scholars. But Tariq Ramadan only recognizes as scholars those theologians close to the Muslim Brotherhood—that is to say, political fundamentalists. That is really why his view is in the minority. But is he in the minority among European Muslims? No. He is in the minority among Islamist scholars. So what does it mean to propose a moratorium to be discussed among Islamist scholars, who are generally in favor of stoning, other than to propose a moratorium that can open the way to maintaining the practice? This is exactly what happened in Iran . . . But that will not distress Ramadan. In the revised and corrected edition of a book published in 2004, he explained that, even if it was not applicable, corporal punishment was there to recall "by way of teaching" that "fornication and adultery are most serious matters in the eyes of God."[35]

An all-encompassing Islam

If he were simply a fundamentalist, Tariq Ramadan would hardly be more than an archaic religious figure, a bit sectarian and reactionary. Unfortunately, he is the product of a movement, the Muslim Brotherhood, that has always put politics ahead of religion. Obsessed as he is by the idea of influencing politics and society in the name of Islam, there is nothing that exasperates him more than believers who practice their religion only in the private sphere. His *dawa*, the mission that he considers his priority, propagates a political Islam intent on becoming a model for society. In France and certain other European countries, this proselytizing is immediately perceived as integrist (politically fundamentalist). Ramadan is well aware of the fact, and encourages his followers not to state point-blank that Islam makes no distinction between religion and politics. Not that he considers such an approach to be wrong; it is just that he finds it inept, which is not the same thing. In order not to shock people, he advises practicing "communication strategy": "You must know how to speak to those who don't come from the same background as we do."[36] He explains that the subject is "sensitive," that Christians might take it badly as submission to a dogma, whereas the fusion of politics and religion should appear as something positive. He himself has recourse to an ingenious approach.

He never speaks of political Islam, but always of an "all-encompassing" Islam, the only way to be faithful to one's religion: "The Muslims of the West cannot avoid this task; if they want to follow the "Way of the Faithful," if they want to trace out their "path to the source," they must commit themselves, inspired by the all-encompassing character of Islam's message."[37] Once again, the liberal Muslims who want to keep their faith within the sphere of the spiritual and the private are singled out as unfaithful. But as always, in order to avoid being identified as a fundamentalist, Tariq Ramadan makes a point of presenting his proposal as if it were the middle ground. In a cassette on "Islam and politics, between confusion and separation,"[38] he begins by setting up a framework that will allow him to situate his position as a median between confounding religion with politics and separating one from the other. Which is a way of saying, implicitly, that separating religion and politics is an extremist view. "When you say such a thing, your public is at a loss," he explained, referring to his favorite technique that has protected him over the years from accusations of fundamentalism: invoking the distinctive nature of Islam in order to justify the claim that his way of merging religion and politics is in no way similar to the negative manner in which Christians do so.[39]

The virtues of cultural differentiation

What would people think of a fundamentalist leader who defended an "all-encompassing" Christianity that forbids mixed marriages, considers men superior to women, and argues that corporal punishment is a good way of teaching that "fornication and adultery are most serious matters in the eyes of God?" Certainly not that he belonged to the Christian Left . . . The political views that Ramadan espouses are close to those of another fundamentalist, Jerry Falwell, one of the moving spirits behind the American Christian Right. The comparison is obviously not welcome. Which is why Tariq Ramadan tries at all costs to insulate his school of thought from such criticism by invoking a "specific history" that renders the comparison inapplicable.[40]

Ramadan refuses to accept the terms "integrist" or "fundamentalist" being applied to Islam: "The term 'integrist' cannot be used because it refers to Catholicism, just as 'fundamentalism' refers to the Protestant religion," he explains in his interviews.[41] A flagrant case of doublespeak. He himself uses the term "fundamentalist" as the equivalent of "Salafist" when there is no danger of being taken for a literalist. And he also brands as "integrist" the Islamist movements that are not in full agreement with the Muslim Brotherhood. Yet he rejects these same terms when not used inside the movement, but voiced by people outside. Adopting a pseudo-scholarly stance, he contends that fundamentalism and integrism are concepts applicable only to Christianity: "Fundamentalism, which has often been criticized in the Christian tradition, has nothing to do with our way of going back to founding texts."[42] Invoking this cultural difference has an enormous advantage: it avoids criticism that treats the two traditions (Christian and Muslim) in the same terms, convincing those who are not familiar with Salafist reformism and Christian fundamentalism not to compare the two for fear of committing a cultural blunder, or even being taken for a racist—even at the risk of forgiving Muslim integrism what we don't forgive the Christian sort.

There are, to be sure, cultural differences stemming from the history of each religion. In Judaism, the radicals call themselves "orthodox" or "ultra-orthodox," since they believe in strict application of their religion. In the Catholic tradition, the radicals are called "traditionalists," since they believe in returning to pre-Vatican II interpretations. In the case of the Protestants, the term "fundamentalist" is used. But this term applies as well to movements such as the Muslim Brotherhood, because they, too, want to return to the fundamentals of their religion. Ramadan is well aware of this, since he uses the terminology himself. He has nothing against the word "fundamentalist" when he uses it to define his approach and that of the Muslim Brothers. It is just that he takes offense when the term is used by way of criticism, lumping him in with fundamentalist Christians. It is true that the two fundamentalisms, Christian and Muslim, arose in very different historical conditions. The former was born in the West in reaction to the theory of evolution; the latter, in the East, was born in reaction to the decline of Muslim expansion due to colonialism. But the former is engaged in a battle with liberal Christians, just as the latter is engaged in a battle with liberal Muslims. Despite his much-advertised enthusiasm for dialogue and clarification of terminology, Tariq Ramadan does little to clear up the misunderstanding when he addresses his allies on the Left.

In the same way as he refuses to be criticized for his fundamentalism, he never uses the word "integrism" when speaking of Islam. "What is meant today by integrism is when people do not distinguish between the religious sphere and the public sphere. And they enter the public sphere armed with dogmas that they want to impose *without resort to reason*," he explained.[43] In reality, integrism is a political term that refers to the aim of prescribing an "integralist," all-encompassing vision in the name of a religion, whatever it might be. It is thus a political approach that is applicable to all religions. But Ramadan obviously wants at all costs to preserve his "all-encompassing Islam" from such slander. So he redefines the term "integrism" as a feature that can only concern dogmatic religions and non-rational religious practices, before explaining to us that this temptation could never exist in his own religion, since it has recourse to individual reasoning (*ijtihad*).

To hear him speak, one would think that, in Islam, there was no conflict between faith and reason because, I quote, "the Koran forces us to think."[44] Which is one way of implying that this is not the case for the Bible. Christians, and Jews will welcome the news! Similarly, he will tell you that "it is normal for a Muslim to read the Koran in a state of adoration," since the Koran is "a fountainhead that vivifies the intelligence" and not one that "shackles the mind."[45] For him, "all the difference is there." A splendid way of getting across the idea that fanaticism is no threat in Islam. Undoubtedly, if the Koran "vivifies the intelligence," then placing this text above the law and above all human concerns should not be interpreted as fanaticism, but as the sign of intense faith.

In the same vein, he argues that Muslim fundamentalism can never result in integrism, simply because it is not literalist. But, as we have seen, the literalism of fundamentalist Protestantism and the non-literalist Muslim fundamentalism amount to roughly the same thing: both of them consider the principles proclaimed in their founding texts to be revealed truths that are eternal, and not open to question just because we live in modern times. The faithful are obliged to apply these principles, even though they were determined by a different context. Thus, the Protestant fundamentalists are persuaded that all the stories recounted in the Bible are untouchable truths, beginning with the story of Adam and Eve. But that doesn't mean they practice their religion naked in a Garden of Eden, refusing any and every modern development not anticipated by the Bible! They, of necessity, make use of their reason in order to implement, in the twenty-first century, the Biblical principles dating from the first century. They are even at the forefront of evangelical technology, thanks to the Internet and television. Tariq Ramadan would have us believe that Christianity is so dogmatic that fundamentalist Christians are incapable of adapting to the times or of reasoning. His efforts to protect Islam from criticism by invoking differentiation lead him to be contemptuous of the two other monotheistic religions.

When reason equals faith

Tariq Ramadan often reassures the journalists who interview him that he is a preacher who has "no problem whatsoever with reason." As a result, they are convinced that Ramadan stands for a sort of Islam of the Enlightenment. "The particularity of Islam," he is fond of saying, "is that faith is the light and reason the guide."[46] These terms, obviously borrowed from the vocabulary of Enlightenment philosophy, were not chosen by accident. As a teacher of philosophy, the preacher is aware of the historical significance of the word "reason," and he deliberately uses it in order to reassure those who would be foolish enough to consider him a fanatic. But we should not be too hasty to interpret what he says as an invitation to take a rational, and thus critical, look at his religion. It is not at all in these terms that this mystic philosopher defines the word "reason." Encouraging "reason," in the sense of the Salafist reformers, is ferociously opposed to all Muslim reasoning. It is a rhetorical ploy to present individual reasoning, or *ijtihad* (searching with one's own intellect for answers to questions that are not already answered in the Koran or the Sunna), as a safeguard to protect Islam from fanatical heresies—and it results in his public being duped. They come away convinced that Tariq Ramadan stands for a rational Islam, in harmony with Enlightenment philosophy; whereas, in his cassettes, he condemns Kant and Pascal categorically as counter-models. Reason, as represented by a critical spirit, is abhorrent to him—a conception that he describes as an extremism typical of the Occident. He is distressed to see that, in the West, everything is subject to critical scrutiny, to the extent that people come to consider that "everything is relative." He wants at all costs to protect Islam from this critical spirit, thanks again to the virtue of cultural differentiation, by explaining, with a straight face, that "doubt is linked to historical circumstances." In a cassette entitled "Islam, modernity and modernism" he went so far as to declare: "We do not doubt everything in the same way."[47]

This is a terrifying confession for a professor of philosophy. Descartes' "I think therefore I am" is jettisoned, and then it's the turn of Dostoevsky, whose aphorism "Everything is permitted" he caricatures in order the better to refute it: "You are familiar with Dostoevsky's expression 'if God does not exist, then everything is permitted'; we say, and it's just the point, 'God exists, therefore everything is not permitted.'"[48] He contrasts the reason that ends in the permissiveness characteristic of the moral decadence of the West, with the "reason guided by the divine," designed to have us discover that all has been foreseen by God. A conception of reason that he presents as the true grandeur of Islam: "In Islam," he explains, "the whole conception of man is different . . . . In fact, what is asked of reason is to show us the way of faith in our hearts, not to explore its limits so as to extend our faith."[49] In particular, he takes up the Koranic metaphor that makes of faith a veiled treasure until the day "reason" comes to break the seal and save our sick hearts. A pleasing prospect, which explains why Ramadan says that, as a Muslim, "he has no problem with reason"—because, for him, reason equals faith.

Chapter 4

An "Islamic feminist" — but puritanical and patriarchal

In July 2003, the French-language magazine *Yasmina* published an interview with Tariq Ramadan, introducing him in these terms: "He owes his success to the radically innovative way he speaks of Islam: not as a religion of coercion, interdiction and repression, but as a religion of free choice, freedom of will, and liberation, particularly for women. Meet a thinker who is promoting an "Islamic feminism" and who challenges those for whom the return to religion means regression."[1] Tariq Ramadan does, indeed, defend an "Islamic feminism," which he defines as a "women's liberation movement in and by Islam." In theory, this feminism is supposed to counter the "overrated" idea that the more restrictive something is, especially in regard to women, the more "Islamic" it is. In practice, it means combating feminism in the name of Islam.

"No compulsion in religion" but the veil is obligatory

The veil is one of those typical patriarchal traditions that a "feminist" such as Tariq, who intends to reform Islam without giving in to anti-Westernism, should be eager to combat. This custom, which dates back to the Mesopotamian era, has successively been adopted by Judaism, Christianity, and Islam, but only the fundamentalists of the three religions are in favor of maintaining it, the better to mark the distinction between men and women. The Torah speaks of Rebecca, who covers herself with a veil when a stranger approaches, but only a limited number of orthodox Jewish women wear a veil or a wig to set themselves off from men. In the case of Christianity, St. Paul strongly advises women to wear the veil rather than cutting off their hair or shaving her head, for "every wife who prays or prophesies with her head uncovered dishonors her head."[2] In practice, only certain nuns, some traditional activists, and a few orthodox women continue to wear a veil or a cornet as a sign of "submission."[3] In the same epistle, St. Paul also reminds us that it is unfitting for a woman to "address an assembly."[4]

The Koran is less explicit and markedly less sexist. For the first fifteen years after the Prophet's coming, Muslim women did not wear the veil. The custom first appeared in Medina in very particular circumstances.[5] In retaliation for having been robbed of their influence in the city, certain leading figures of Medina—whom the Koran qualifies as "hypocrites"—decided that one way of dishonoring the Muslims was to take sexual possession of the Prophet's wives. In the face of this danger, and urged on, in particular, by the future caliph Omar, Mohammed finally agreed to heed the Koran's injunction: "Prophet, tell thy wives and daughters, and the believing women that they should cast their outer garments over their persons when abroad: that is most convenient that they should be known as such and not molested."[6] A second verse specifies the parts of the body concerned: "O Prophet! Say to the believing women that they should lower their gaze and guard their modesty; that they should not display their beauty and ornaments except what must ordinarily appear thereof; that they should draw their veils over their bosoms and not display their beauty except to their husbands, their fathers, their husbands' fathers, their brothers, their brothers' sons, their women, their slaves, and their eunuchs, or the prepubescent."[7] That is what it says in the Koran. Nothing more, nothing less. The Koran simply advises the wearing of a veil, intended to cover a woman's bust; a veil that, in many circumstances, can be dispensed with. As in the case of all religious texts, many different translations exist for each verse. Every translator uses a different word to indicate the part of the body to be veiled—sometimes it is called the "bosom," at other times the "cleavage"; but all interpretations agree: the area concerned is none other than . . . the bust. How is it that a unique recommendation, adopted in very particular circumstances, concerning the covering up of a woman's bust and her arms, became the imposition of an ever more intrusive veil?

It is a question to ask of the fundamentalists. Even though they say their only intention is to conform scrupulously to the Prophet's precepts, they do everything they can to make things more confining for women. The head-to-toe veil that its advocates call the *niqab*—a veil that covers the whole body, with the exception of two little slits for the eyes—is never mentioned in the Koran. Insisting that it be worn is a way for radical Muslims to prove that, unlike Western husbands, they are masters over their wives. Similarly, it is not because of Islam, but because of Islamism, that some Muslim women, in defiance of Western values, began once again wearing the *hijab* towards the end of the twentieth century, even though this tradition had almost disappeared. Even if a woman wanted to respect the Prophet's advice, why could she not wear a hat or a wig? Why is she obliged to wear a *burqa* or a *chador*, dark clothes that cover the body from head to toe even when it is 40 degrees centigrade in the shade? Qaradawi, the scholar most frequently cited by Tariq Ramadan, has an explanation: "This garment must not resemble what is worn by infidels, Jewesses, Christian women, and idolaters. The attempt to imitate these women is forbidden in Islam, which requires that Muslims be different and independent in both their appearance and being. That is why the Prophet decreed doing the opposite of what infidels do."[8]

This example shows that, despite their proclaimed objectives, the Muslim fundamentalists' insistence on strict religious obedience is less an attempt to follow in Mohammed's footsteps than a means to oppose and resist Western values. Their rhetoric varies according to the context and the immediate needs. Khomeini—when it was not a question of building an Islamic state, but, on the contrary, of enlisting the support of women who could help him take power from the Shah—declared: "There is absolutely no difference between men and women." And he added: "According to Islam, women must wear the headscarf, but are not obliged to wear the *chador*. A woman can choose any kind of clothing to serve as a veil."[9] During this period, the future ayatollah even promised women education, freedom to travel, and the right to take part in economic activities—promises that he lost no time in breaking once his theocratic dictatorship was established. Less than one month after coming to power, on March 7, 1979, Khomeini adopted the slogan "a veil or a crack on the skull." As for his successor, Khatami, even though he promised change, he never revised the policy. On the contrary, his two counselors, Massoumeh Ebtekar and Zahra Chodja'i, reaffirmed that the *chador* was "the superior form of national dress for Iranian women."

What did Ramadan, the great "reformer," do when faced with this crude and sexist exploitation of the veil? He did nothing to influence the use made of the veil in Iran; quite the reverse, for Iran was a model when it came to "promoting women."[10] We return later to this subject. On the other hand, in all that he has written, and in all his conferences, he savagely attacks the Muslim moderates who try to oppose what Leïla Babès calls "the doxa of the veil," that is to say, a dogmatic conception in the service of political ambitions, rather than respect for the original intention of the Koran.[11] He berates the liberal reformers who are faithful to the spirit, and not the letter, of this Koranic precept. The liberal Muslims interpret the two verses that deal with the veil as expressing the desire to protect women from "offense." In keeping with this intention, they encourage everything that can protect a woman and promote her integration into society. From this perspective, whereas, in the context of seventh-century Arabia, the veil served as a shield and a sign of discretion, in the context of twenty-first century Europe it has the opposite effect: not only is it openly provocative, but it can be a social handicap that, far from protecting women, renders them more vulnerable. Soheib Bencheikh, the Marseille mufti, puts it this way: "Paradoxically, today what protects young women's personality and promises them a future is schooling. It is by learning that women can defend themselves from offense to their femininity and their dignity. Today, the veil for Muslim women in France is the school—secular, compulsory, and free."[12]

This is not at all how Tariq Ramadan sees things. Even if he claims to be interpreting the spirit of the Koran and not the letter, he reads these verses literally and considers that a worthy Muslim woman must wear a headscarf that covers her hair: "According to scholars . . . it's an obligation in Islam."[13] To be sure, he immediately adds: "The headscarf is an obligation, but it cannot be forced on someone."[14] Here we touch on the very heart of Ramadan's rhetoric, a subtle blend of "voluntary coercion." He knows perfectly well how, in order not to antagonize young European Muslim women, to speak of the headscarf as an object of pride and not of submission. There is no question of forcing it on them, but rather of making them understand on their own how much freer they will feel by willingly adopting this symbol of submission to Islam. "The veil is an act of faith," but "it took fifteen years [after the coming of the Prophet] to have women understand it as such," he explained.[15] Taking this as an example, Tariq Ramadan claims to respect women who make the effort to similarly "discover their way." Even if, of course, there is no question of their getting lost in transit. In terms of "discovering their way," it would be more accurate to speak of finding the way mapped out for them. For if Ramadan speaks of respecting the "stages of faith," then the wearing of the headscarf stands as the final stage for all women who aspire to be good Muslims. "There are women who have gone the whole way and who wear the headscarf. It's a good thing. Next to this there are, to be sure, women who are still seeking their way.... They can't be forced to wear it, but there is one thing on which we must all agree if we want to create a real Muslim community—one thing that is a necessity for all of us—and that is decency."[16] In a word, a Muslim is not forced to wear the headscarf right away, but a good Muslim must be chaste. And the height of chastity is the wearing of the headscarf. How many of his sisters would turn down the chance of appearing as the ideal Muslim in the eyes of Tariq Ramadan? Certainly not those who have a hand in running the Muslim associations influenced by the preacher, all of whom end up wearing the Islamic headscarf.

Rallying around the Islamic headscarf

In the last fifteen years, the preacher has persuaded many young girls to wear the Islamic headscarf—a concrete illustration of the profoundly conservative influence he wields. Whereas the 1989 cases in France concerned young girls forced to wear the headscarf because of family pressure, recent cases have had to do with young girls firmly determined to wear the headscarf in the face of their family's disapproval.

The immigrant women of the first generation wore the headscarf in the traditional manner. Their daughters, because they had been to school and were in contact with secular society, wanted to be free of these traditions. The third generation—totally integrated and, for the most part, culturally assimilated—suddenly took to wearing the headscarf as a reproof to their mothers, even if they did not always understand its religious significance, but saw it rather as a symbol of pride in a newly discovered identity. The October 14, 2003 edition of *Le Monde* published a long report on young girls who wore the headscarf "from choice." Included was a particularly lively exchange between Leïla, sixteen years old, and her mother of Moroccan origin. The latter simply could not understand why her daughter insisted on wearing such a cumbersome headpiece at her young age: "You're not the sort of girl to be pushed around. You're not submissive." Leïla's reply: "I am submissive to God." The exchange tells us a lot about the family quarrels set off by those who take advantage of the generation gap to encourage young girls to wear the headscarf despite their parents' advice. It so happens that Leïla had been attending the UOIF mosque in La Courneuve. She had thus been fed sermons encouraging the abandonment of tradition for the Ramadan brothers' version of Salafist reformism. Her father, Algerian by birth, was so upset at this radical turn of events that he threatened to throw out any headscarves he could lay his hands on! As for Leïla, she just kept repeating over and over again that it was "her choice," In reality, even if they are determined, these young girls have not always taken the time to study the matter or to think it over before making a choice that will be decisive in the formation of their identity as a woman. In the same article, we are introduced to Nadia, whose parents are active supporters of the UOIF. At the age of seventeen, she had just been expelled from the Saint-Ouen lycée, where she was a student in the "economics and society" program, for having refused to remove her headscarf as was required by school rules. For her, wearing the headscarf was a religious duty, and therefore non-negotiable. However, when the reporter asked her on what verses of the Koran she based her decision, the young girl was embarrassed. She searched in her room, returned with Hani Ramadan's books and Tariq Ramadan's cassettes, then tried to find the right verses in the Koran, but without success. Never mind, it's written there, "she's sure of that." Later on, she wants to be a schoolteacher but only if she can keep on wearing her headscarf. Meanwhile, she would rather take correspondence courses or go to a private school than take the headscarf off and return to the lycée. Tariq Ramadan would not be the one to dissuade her.

One of the fifty demands in the program of the Muslim Brotherhood is that it is necessary "to combat all forms of provocative or ostentatious behavior and to summon women, in particular teachers, schoolgirls, students, doctors, etc., to behave respectfully."[17] Tariq Ramadan is in full agreement. Whereas the fight against forced marriage is not one of his priorities, this issue certainly is. In one of his cassettes on the "duty of women to participate," he warmly encourages women not to be intimidated, to wear the headscarf, and to go to court if this right is denied them: "It's also necessary to call on the law and on our rights, so that we're taken seriously in those terms."[18] He added that it is out of the question to give way in the face of difficulty, or through fear of having "problems with colleagues" or "at school." Paying tribute to the young girls who had demonstrated "the courage it takes," he asked the Muslim community to support them: "They need to have the community behind them." In this regard, the Geneva Islamic Center worked hard to encourage Swiss schoolmistresses to come to class wearing the headscarf and to target regulations forbidding teachers to display their religious preferences in class. Whenever a case concerning the Islamic headscarf makes headlines, Tariq Ramadan and his brother are not far off. In his role as spokesman for the outside world, the preacher makes a point of explaining to Muslims how to justify their decision, so as to bring about change, have the headscarf worn more and more frequently, and then have it finally accepted: "The more we make ourselves known, the more women with their *hijab* make their appearance in society and in debates, explaining their approach, explaining who they are . . . the more the mentality will evolve and the more things will change."[19]

On this point, there is one thing Tariq Ramadan understands: a woman who stands up in favor of the Islamic headscarf is far more credible than a man. He knows full well that his vision of society, patriarchal and religious in nature, could not take hold unless it is backed by women: "We are not regarded as credible when we speak for women . . . ," he explained to his followers.[20] Hence the idea of "developing a discourse" to be produced for and by women: "I promise that when a woman speaks, when she is understood, when she says: 'Listen to me, the headscarf I wear, it's not forced on me by my father, it's not forced on me by my husband, it's a requirement of my faith, and an act of my heart. I ask all of you who look at me to consider me as a human being and not simply as a body; to see that I am made for God and not for your eyes . . .' Well, when women speak this way, I promise you they will have an effect on a great many women, for there are a great many women in the West and elsewhere that suffer from having become objects . . . ."[21] That should be sufficient to convince husbands that it's worth letting their wives speak to journalists. Acting as the benevolent elder brother, Tariq Ramadan induces women to speak in moving terms: "You are witness to a totally new way of speaking: be human beings who will become beings in the eyes of him who accompanies them." He suggests that they put things this way: "I don't want to be looked at any old way. I order you, I require you, I command you to respect what is in my heart. That is the message of women for the future."[22]

One can catch a glimpse of the future that Tariq Ramadan envisages for women by taking a look at the way his acolytes are treated. Malika is more or less his "second in command." He taught her everything she knows, and she follows him everywhere, carrying his personal belongings and his briefcase. Jacqueline Costa-Lascoux remembers having known her during the period she was with Tariq Ramadan at the Education League. She was struck by Malika's evolution, by the way she become more and more discreet, even self-effacing: "In the beginning she would often intervene. Then she came wearing a headscarf, then two headscarves, and then three. In the end, she made a habit of sitting at the back of the room and no longer taking the floor. One day I asked her what had become of her plan to be a teacher. She replied: 'I let it drop. With the headscarf they would never hire me.'"[23] No matter . . . Like other disciples of Tariq Ramadan, she can always serve as one of the preacher's spokeswomen. Or be like Asma Lamrabet, who published a book, *Musulmane tout simplement* [*A Muslim Woman, No More, No Less*], that urged women to discover "Islamic feminism."[24] The contents were "cut and pasted" from Tariq Ramadan's lectures.

Sisters in the service of the Brothers' Islam

Even the most reactionary and anti-feminist movements have always needed women to campaign against . . . women. In the United States, a fundamentalist Christian movement, named the Promise Keepers, openly calls for a return to masculine domination; and yet it is not made up solely of men. The activists' wives have been granted the right to organize a "women's commission" to help their husbands re-establish masculine domination in the name of Christianity. Anti-feminist movements have always worked this way. The Islamist movements are no exception. Even an Islamist as radical as Mawdudi, the father of Pakistani fundamentalism, when he saw a war of independence looming, preached that women should be taught to fight alongside men.[25] He did, however, stipulate that they were to be sent back to their proper place (i.e., taking care of the household) once the war was won. By so doing, he demonstrated the respect for women that supposedly distinguishes Islamic civilization from the West: "The difference between us and the Occident is that Occidental civilization gives women rights only if they become likenesses of men and take on men's duties. Islamic civilization honors and respects women by permitting them to remain women."[26]

It is almost laughable when you consider that the fundamentalist Christian groups in the West say almost the same thing. For example, the militant anti-abortion groups also claim they are defending the right of women to rediscover their "true nature"—that is to say maternity—in the name of a pro-life feminism that is resolutely anti-feminist.[27] This way of disguising anti-feminism as a means by which women can adopt a feminism that respects "women's nature" is a classic tactic, invoked whenever a totalitarian or fundamentalist movement wants to put a stop to women's liberation. And this is exactly the direction that Tariq Ramadan's "Islamic feminism" takes. His argument comes down to promoting an "Islamic femininity" which, he asserts, is founded on "the dignity and the autonomy of the feminine being, equal [to men] in law and complementary in nature."[28] "Which certainly doesn't mean that, to be a liberated woman, one must of necessity resemble the Western model of liberation."[29] Women's liberation in the West is clearly seen as a model to reject. And then he adds: "We must introduce a new model of feminine presence; a presence that is in her very being and not her appearance; in her intelligence and not her charm."

This way of presenting European or American feminism as simply a feminism of charm does have one thing in its favor: it is a change from that other anti-feminist discourse that berates feminists for being prudes because they campaign against the treatment of women as sexual objects! Taking the opposite tack, Tariq Ramadan attacks feminism as a movement working for looser moral standards, in the domain of sexuality in particular. That is what he objects to, but he cannot be open about it. Instead, he prefers to caricature the Women's Liberation Movement the better to discredit it: "We are not about to get involved in the sort of thing that has happened in European countries, where women have become feminists in opposition to men, and where some of them refuse even to greet a man because he is the enemy. We don't want to have anything to do with that approach."[30] One can find the same caricature, almost to the letter, ten years earlier in a speech by Soraya Djebbour, a teacher active in the women's commission of the National Front, who also wanted women to rediscover the virtues of masculine domination.[31] Yet one must admit that Tariq Ramadan is far more gifted than the French extreme Right when it comes to passing off his anti-feminism as feminism. Nobody in France takes seriously the "feminist pro-life" movement or the "feminism" of the National Front that purports to help women accede to dignity and maternity. On the other hand, the European press regards as credible the groups close to Tariq Ramadan that claim they want to defend the right of women to wear the headscarf and behave with propriety in the name of "Islamic feminism," little realizing that this feminism is to be used as a weapon against feminists, including those coming from a Muslim culture who have been treated as "Westernized" if they campaign for true equality between men and women. Tariq Ramadan makes no secret of the fact. He berates Taslima Nasreen[32] for her "simplistic, totally Occidentalized rhetoric."[33] On the other hand, just consider the women that Tariq Ramadan cites as models: Zaynab al-Ghazali or his mother, Wafa al-Banna. In terms of feminism, Ramadan's objective is to have women take part in the Islamic renaissance alongside men: "We must build together an Islamic society, a society of morality, of true beings and spirituality."[34]

This feminist element is all the more precious in that it promotes an anti-feminist agenda in the heart of Europe, at a time when observers reproach Islamists for their sexism. As Ramadan explained to the faithful: "There are lots of people who will listen when it is a Muslim woman because it is a Muslim woman speaking, many more so than if it were a man. And this is part of our influence here in Europe."[35] It is from this perspective, and this perspective only, that one should interpret his obsession with educating women: because Islamic education is the only way to turn them into effective Islamic militants. On his courses, education is always linked to being effective as an activist. "We need women who are cultivated, who read widely, who understand things. We want women who can say 'I know what's happening to the men and women of such and such a country.'"[36] The point of learning is not to become free and autonomous, but to join the rank and file in the service of the Islamist cause: "You should be human beings who remind us of our spirituality, who guide the community and take part in its reform."[37] It was with this idea in mind that the European Fatwa Council—in a book with a preface written by Tariq Ramadan—advised husbands to encourage their wives to attend "Islamic seminars":

> It's all the more urgent in that, on the one hand, forces hostile to Islam are constantly at work, mobilizing women in this area; and on the other hand, the women called "secular," the atheists and the Marxists, are active night and day within Muslim countries trying to cut the community off from the true reality of their religion, propagating concepts that are foreign to Islam and combating the true preachers of Islam that are calling for reform, revival and renaissance.[38]

Like Mawdudi, Ramadan believes that the revolution cannot succeed with men alone, and he has welcomed women into the ranks of Islamism: "In all the countries I have visited, the number of women in almost all the Muslim movements quadrupled."[39] And he cited the example of Pakistan, where "the mobilization of women is even greater than that of men." But rest assured, these women are closely supervised: "The people in charge tell you that women have taken things in hand; they are intelligently trained and instructed in religion."[40] Phew! One might be tempted to think that their taking part in the revolution would liberate them. But not at all. Women are asked to do their bit without ever forgetting that they are women; they will be relegated to the status that men have assigned them once the objectives have been met. Their participation will in no way serve to liberate them, but only to help reconstruct a society in which masculine domination is reinforced.

In a series of cassettes devoted to "The Muslim woman and her duty to participate," Tariq Ramadan made a point of defining the limits of women's participation. He determined the sort of militant activities that are compatible with women's natural capacities and their duty to remain chaste.[41] According to him, women are, by nature, equipped to act in three areas: solidarity, education and culture. By solidarity, he means in particular the fight against prostitution: "Don't be the judges of these lost women, but act as their sisters and help them."[42] To save these women from a life of debauchery, he advises reaching out to them through activities "that will have them understand the meaning of faith." The important thing is "to communicate with these young girls who have lost their way, which is not possible for the Brothers." But the mission that Tariq Ramadan considers a priority concerns "the social education and schooling of these young girls, but also their Islamic education."

The idea that women are to be educated so as to take part in Islamic reform is by no means new. The leading theorist of the question is none other than Hassan al-Banna. Tariq Ramadan never misses an opportunity to pay homage to him when urging women to go to school so as to be more effective militants: "I come from a family in which my grandfather, every time he set up a school for men, provided one for women as well . . . . It was an obsession with him. You can't create an Islamic society with only half of the population."[43] As early as 1944, the founder of the Muslim Brotherhood had, in effect, constituted a feminine branch: the Muslim Sisters. Their mission? "Fight against unwelcome initiatives, absurdities, lies, false ideas and bad habits that circulate among women," influenced, of course, by the West.[44] In theory, Tariq Ramadan advocates an Islamic feminism that is neither traditionalist nor seen as a way of countering the Occident. In practice, his feminism is exactly the same as Hassan al-Banna's. Ramadan, moreover, explains that "colonization permitted and proposed models of women's behavior that in no way corresponded to Islamic principles."[45] Today it is no longer a question of combating political colonization, but cultural colonization, Tariq Ramadan's mania: "In our society, there has developed a feminine discourse that borrows ideas from outside our sphere of reference; you can see young women who have become lax in their behavior and their faith, and in their relation to God." And he warns: "Woe betide those who speak the language of liberation, but who shut themselves away, forgetting God."[46]

Equal rights, but not an equal nature—so no equal jobs

Tariq Ramadan is willing to admit that men and women are equal "in the eyes of God," but not at the social level. Yet when listening to him quote this magnificent *hadith* issued by the Prophet, one could well believe they were: "He who treats his daughter no differently from his son will go to paradise." Unfortunately, the equality holds true only until puberty, at which point women's education must be adapted to their "capacities" and to the complementary role that Ramadan intends them to play in social and political life. Ramadan is quite prepared actively to support women who demand "equal pay for equal work," since the slogan is, after all, in line with the Koran; but he does not agree that women should have access to all types of employment, nor that they should succeed professionally in certain areas; in brief, he is not in favor of their having "equal jobs." "Allowing women to work does not mean opening up all types of work to them," the preacher has warned in his lectures.[47] The most important thing is not to choose a type of work that runs counter to their natural inclination, that is to say the chastity that is required of them: "As to working, women have a right: that they should not have to provide for their livelihood. But this does not mean that work is forbidden. Women have this right, but in accordance with their capabilities and their aptitude to play a role in society; if the rules are, as for men, rules that respect individual decency, then it is perfectly possible for a woman to take part in social life and acquire a civic education."[48] Later, Tariq Ramadan insists on defining a woman's "work" more as "social commitments" or "participation." In reality he thinks of women's work outside the home as a fill-in job, preferably a mere social occupation; something in the way of a service that a woman can render the community in accordance with her "capabilities."

This type of discourse comes strikingly close to that of the Catholic fundamentalists. They, too, have nothing against women working, but consider that a woman's natural disposition suits her almost "hormonally" for charity or social work; in any case, suits her for social activities that are but an extension of her role in the family. To be sure, they do not openly say that they want to keep women in subaltern jobs as assistants; they prefer to present it as a way of orienting women in accordance with their natural inclinations. This subterfuge, which is pure sexism, is also one of the classic tactics of National Front anti-feminist rhetoric. Claudie Lesselier in *L'extrème droite et les femmes* [*Women and the Radical Right*] puts it this way: "The statements of doctrine and the 'worldview' to be found in the theoretical and cultural magazines of the extreme Right invariably begin by recalling a few fundamental principles: nature (and on occasion divine law) has assigned different functions to men and women that are hierarchical and/or complementary."[49] Tariq Ramadan does the same when he distinguishes between employments that are fit for women and those that are not: "There are many areas in which women can be active, including medicine, social work, community work, or community service. We are not going to go to the lengths you sometimes see in Western society and say that, in order to prove they are liberated, women must become masons or truck drivers [*the audience laughs*]. For us, that makes no sense. We're not going to be so stupid as to say: prove you're liberated, be a truck driver, drive a truck, whore [*sic*] you'll show that . . . . Take a job in the areas for which you are fitted, which belong to you, once you have found the right balance in your family life."[50]

I shall not dwell on Ramadan's use of the word "whore," which came up suddenly when he was talking of women in men's jobs, when he is never vulgar in his lectures; nor on his choice of the metaphor "truck driver," traditionally used to caricature lesbians. Tariq Ramadan's audience knew very well what he thought of women who took jobs without regard to their "nature" and their obligation to act with "modesty." It is in the name of those two requisites that Saudi Arabia encourages men and women to receive different educations. Article 15 of Royal Policy stipulates: "The state is responsible for the education of girls and for providing them, as far as possible, with the means to satisfy the needs of all those of school age, so that they will have access to those disciplines that correspond to their natural aptitudes." Despite the obvious handicap of their "natural aptitudes," and despite the many barriers created by the government, women nonetheless represent 55 percent of the nation's university graduates.[51] Unfortunately this rate of success is not reflected in the job market because of provisions that prevent them from occupying positions that would not be in keeping with their duty to act "modestly"—that is to say, any employment that might bring them into one-to-one contact with men.[52] Thus, those women who do manage to engage in a profession do so in a closed-off environment, or one reserved for women only: banks and universities that cater to women, health care and teaching exclusively for women and young girls, etc. In theory, Tariq Ramadan, like all the Muslim Brothers who have held a grudge against Saudi Arabia since the Gulf War, denounces this treatment of women, their segregation and the ban on women driving a car as "malfunctions" characteristic of Saudi society. He even goes so far as to speak of "men's behavior that is nothing short of perverse."[53] Yet it is important to understand that these criticisms are not aimed at sexual segregation *per se*, since Saudi Arabia is close to the model advocated by the preacher ever since he was in Switzerland. Hassan al-Banna himself considered it indispensable "to revise the educational methods for young girls" so as "to distinguish between such methods and those appropriate for boys at all levels of schooling."[54]

Tariq Ramadan is, indeed, highly critical of the situation of women in Saudi Arabia, but only as a prelude to his approbation of women's status in another country that he considers to be a model of its kind: Iran! "Iranian society today is, compared to other Muslim societies, the most advanced as concerns the promotion of women," he explained, in all seriousness, in one of his recorded lectures.[55] He returned to the issue in his book of interviews with Neirynck, republished in 2004: "It must be said that Iran is, without doubt, one of the Muslim countries that has done the most, over the last twenty years, in terms of advancing women's rights."[56] Sure of himself, and without ever encountering opposition, Ramadan insists on presenting Iran as the country "in the vanguard" when it comes to women's rights in the Muslim world, way ahead of Saudi Arabia (agreed) and Egypt (possibly), but also far ahead of Tunisia! Which is nothing but out-and-out propaganda, for Tunisia is widely considered to have the most progressive Family Code in the Muslim world, so far as women's rights are concerned, thanks to its secular institutions. But that is the nub of the problem. Tariq Ramadan does not think in terms of equality, and he is not in the least bothered by the segregation that prevails in Iran. He forgets to explain that, if Iran has made tremendous progress, it is because it had such a long way to go. And even if Iranian women have begun appearing in the public domain, this has taken place under a sexist, segregated dictatorship that denies them access to certain professions (as, for example, sitting as a judge) in the name of decency and respect for their "nature."

"No liberation detrimental to the family"

Tariq Ramadan encourages women to take part in the Islamic renaissance, but their participation is always subject to their remaining good mothers and faithful wives. It is what he calls "balancing one's commitments"; that is to say, the family is the number one priority for women: "No liberation for women if it's detrimental to the family."[57] This is a demand that he also makes of men, but there is no secret as to who is to be sacrificed first. As he puts it: "The family is the core of social organization and the core of the Muslim community. We consider it to be the fundamental ingredient."[58] The fact of considering the family as the basic element of social organization is not in itself reactionary. It only becomes reactionary when the concept of the family is reduced to a traditional, hetero-patriarchal definition, in which the family stands as a citadel besieged by modernism and threatened both by the redistribution of male and female roles due to feminism and by the development of new parental models. And it is to counter this evolution, which is part of progress and modernity, that Ramadan calls for the defense of the "traditional" family. "We will take up the struggle; we will be resistance fighters; we intend to spread the idea of what is called the traditional family."[59] And he provides the definition: "What we want is a daddy, a mummy, and children that establish just that sort of harmony. There's nothing worse than single-parent families. There's nothing gloomier than people who try to bring up their children alone." Unlike strict Catholicism, Islam allows for divorce, but Ramadan makes a point of citing this *hadith*: "Of all the things permitted by God, it is the most detestable!"[60] And he adds: "When you see that, in some Western societies, two marriages in three end in divorce, it's terrifying!"

The defense of the family is a war waged as if civilization were at stake. Tariq Ramadan asserts that "in all Western countries, the origins of catastrophe and breakdown are not in the economy, drugs or delinquency, but at the level of the family."[61] Which does not keep him from subsequently linking the decline of the family with juvenile delinquency and drugs, as would any Christian activist of the extreme Right.[62] In 1988, the magazine *Itinéraires*, a Christian political fundamentalist publication, sent out this call to women: "Make of your families mini-fortresses or, even better, houses of prayer and of charity, that will stand up to the assaults of the world and its malevolence."[63] Tariq Ramadan employs the same mystical, melodramatic tone when urging women to protect their families against the evils that hover over them: "The enemy is invisible, just as the devil is invisible; but the enemy is tangible, just as the devil is tangible and real."[64] The preacher is all the more tempted to treat the family as a citadel under siege because he himself grew up in a family in exile, in a family that considered itself beset by adversity. It is almost as if he were bequeathing his own family fears to his Muslim followers when he declared, in emotional tones: "The family, yes the family! I care about it and all of us care about it, and we will fight for it; it's a battle; it's the personal jihad of every one of us."[65]

"A man who has faith and a woman who has faith"

In a cassette on "Married life in Islam," Tariq Ramadan gives us his definition of the ideal couple: "A Muslim couple must be made up of a man who has faith and a woman who has faith."[66] The statement can be taken in two ways: either as a means of encouraging religious practice, or as a refusal to countenance mixed marriages, since it is a common faith that unites the couple. Tariq Ramadan promises women a peaceful home if they submit to God and conform to the family model proposed by Islam: "I promise that you will transform your household if you first transform your own self—if you display to your husband, to your children, to your entourage, to your relatives, that faith has made of you a being who ascends and not one content with mere appearances."[67] Advice that should be taken as encouragement to behave with decency, which means wearing a headscarf, and, above all, not seeking professional recognition that could be prejudicial to home and husband. Under the pretext of offering women a "balanced" family model, it is men's interests that Ramadan has in mind: "We want wives that are pious. The best thing that can be granted a man is a pious wife. And the best thing that can be granted a woman is to be pious."[68] A statement punctuated by cries of "Allah Akbar!" that rose from the Ivory Coast audience listening to his speech.

Within the family, consisting of a man of faith and a woman of faith, Ramadan insists on the maternal role: "The heart of the family, it's the mother."[69] He often repeats the two *hadiths* that reveal with what emotion Mohammed, who was an orphan, evoked the image of the mother. The first reads "paradise is at the feet of one's mother." The second gives Mohammed's reply to someone who asks of him: "To whom do I owe respect?" And the reply: "Your mother, your mother, your mother, and then your father." This way of honoring the mother, while it is tenderhearted, obviously has nothing very feminist about it. It belongs to the classic patriarchal repertoire, by which women are given an almost domineering role within the household, so that they forget all that is denied them in the outside world. Shortly after having recalled these two admirable *hadiths*, Tariq Ramadan sets things straight: "One has heard it said that women must be obedient to men, and it's an excuse to do just about anything! But a woman is to obey a man only if he is a model Muslim."[70] Let us be clear what he means. The statement can appear positive, in that Tariq Ramadan is coming to the defense of women confronted by potentially violent husbands, but it also reminds us that this compassion for women is worlds apart from accepting the principle of equality between the sexes; it argues for a relation of complementarity, in which the woman obeys the man if the man obeys God. It can bring to mind what St. Paul said: "Now I want you to realize that the head of every man is Christ, and the head of the woman is man."[71] Tariq Ramadan is of the same opinion when he says he wants to see "paternal authority" within the family reaffirmed.[72] "Islam proposes a setting that fosters a global conception of human beings, of men, women, and the family. Two principles are vital: the first affirms the equality of men and women in the eyes of God; the second affirms their complementarity within society. In terms of this conception, it is the husband that is responsible for managing the household, but the mother's role is central."[73] On the face of it, the aim is to reassure the father and have him participate more actively,but obviously the statement's primary effect is to reactivate the good old patriarchal reflexes.

"One thing that we hold fast to, even today in our contemporary societies, where people have lost their bearings, is that there exists in Islam the conviction that a man is responsible for his household in financial terms and is responsible for guiding it."[74] It is on the basis of this conception of the couple that *fatwa* number 32, published by the European Fatwa Council with a preface by Tariq Ramadan, authorized husbands to act like domestic tyrants: "The husband has the right to forbid his wife to visit certain women, Muslim or not, if he fears that it will be prejudicial or harmful to his wife, his children or his marital life."[75] Tariq Ramadan can repeat as often as he likes that "being responsible isn't being a dictator," but it is clear that, even if he is in favor of dialogue and exchange between the couple, he is defending a particularly patriarchal and reactionary model.

Long live sex, but only within marriage!

Unlike Christian fundamentalists, Muslim fundamentalists have, in theory, no qualms about speaking of sex. Even Yusuf al-Qaradawi, the Muslim Brotherhood's theologian, who preaches on Al-Jazeera TV, is known for his juicy sexual metaphors. As Gilles Kepel put it: "Islam has never been encumbered by our Victorian prudishness, for while zina (fornication) is condemned on all sides—which results in an apparent desexualization of public society—sex, once it is within the law, is considered an excellent thing, since it provides pleasure (for men at any rate) and perpetuates the species."[76] Heir to the tradition inaugurated by a Prophet who was keen on women, Tariq Ramadan encourages Muslim men to think of sex as something natural, and even to take women's feelings into account. "Don't be brusque." But removing the guilt attached to sexuality has its limits. While they are far from devoting a cult to chastity (as do fundamentalist Christians, following St. Paul's example), Muslim fundamentalists live in constant fear of engaging in unlawful sexual acts. Websites such as Fatwa Bank or Fatwa-Online are inundated with questions that reveal a fear of transgression—a fear that the Islamist leaders are keen to foster. Even in marriage, relations are so codified that certain Islamic publishing houses have specialized in producing instruction manuals. For instance, *Le mariage en Islam: Modalités et finalités* [*Marriage in Islam: Means and Ends*]—a manual you can find in any Islamist bookshop associated with the Muslim Brotherhood—recommends reciting an invocation before sexual relations: "When one of you approaches his wife, if he says to himself: 'In the name of God, O God, keep Satan away from all that you will give us,' and if a child is then granted you, Satan will be helpless to harm him and will have no power over him."[77]

Confronted by this avalanche of taboos, all the more agonizing because they are vaguely worded, Tariq Ramadan seems to provide an alternative for these youngsters, terrified lest they confound what is *haram* (illicit) with what is *halal* (licit). He disapproves of the binary, systematic way of approaching a religion that he sees, above all, as "a religion of the heart": "How have we come to make of Islam a technical system of rules and regulations?" he asked, in vexed tones, of his Muslim audience, which was relieved to hear this sort of language.[78] Unfortunately, the let-up was not to last for long. For the open-mindedness that Tariq Ramadan displays is only superficial. In content he says exactly the same things as is written in the books he refers to, published by houses with which he is on good terms. The rules—Yusuf al-Qaradawi's speciality—governing what is "licit or illicit," end up being applied.

Ramadan asks of young people "an Islamic conception of sexuality," that is to say "exclusively within the context of marriage."[79] He is ready to admit that sexuality is "a natural need," but he asks his followers to exercise self-control "in order to remain worthy in the eyes of God." "Sexuality is natural; it is to be lived naturally," he asserts, before insisting on the necessity of remaining chaste until marriage.

The fact of "exercising self-control until marriage" is presented as a gift comparable to the alms given to "him or her that one loves in the eyes of God,"[80] which is exactly the approach taken by traditionalist Christians. A few years ago, I interviewed a young activist in the movement Love and Truth, an association responsible for promulgating the Catholic Church's position on chastity. He explained his point of view in the same terms.[81] To be sure, abstinence is a perfectly respectable choice, so long as one does not try to make those who have another conception of sexuality feel guilty, especially at a time when talking openly is essential because of the threat of AIDS. What does Tariq Ramadan have to say on the subject? Does he take advantage of his unbelievable prestige to advise young Muslims to "protect" themselves? I have never heard him pronounce the words "AIDS" or "condom" in his talks on sexuality. No doubt because, as with the Catholic Church, he considers that the model he proposes provides the remedy in itself: abstinence, then faithfulness, and too bad for those who lose their way.

On the other hand, unlike many fundamentalist Christians, he has nothing against contraception by natural means, so long as it is between married couples. Mohammed himself permitted one of his contemporaries to practice *coitus interruptus* so as to avoid his wife becoming pregnant once again. Tariq Ramadan specifies that it must be "a natural form of contraception" that is no danger to health, and that it must be performed with the wife's consent. He remained, however, sufficiently vague for a member of the audience to feel it necessary to ask him if contraception involving anything other than natural means was authorized. His reply: "A man and a woman have sexual relations in the framework of a marriage with the idea of founding a family . . . but scholars are in favor of all forms of contraception that respect Islamic values."[82] Which hardly made things crystal clear. In the event, it turns out that "Islamic values" authorize contraception if a couple already have too many children, but not if it is a question merely of protecting what Ramadan calls "a couple"s selfishness." One suspects also that artificial contraception is authorized if there is no health risk or danger of permanent sterilization. On the other hand, at no point in his conference on the "Islamic conception of sexuality" does he say a word about abortion. To know more, the faithful are obliged to solicit the opinion of the European Fatwa Council, the theological apparatus of the Union of Islamic Organizations of France. In one case, Yousouf Ibram, a Union militant, issued a *fatwa* refusing to grant the right of abortion to a woman who had asked his advice, a mother of four children who could not stand being constantly pregnant year after year.[83] The Council's *fatwa* number 22—published in the selfsame book that has a preface by Tariq Ramadan—reiterated that recourse to abortion was forbidden: "Abortion is illicit in terms of the Islamic sharia"[84]—an opinion confirmed by Ramadan himself in his book of interviews with Jacques Neirynck: "Abortion is forbidden, except in cases where scholars have unanimously decided that the life of the mother is in danger."[85] Christian "scholars" have ignited controversy for less than that.

"A man for a woman and a woman for a man"

Tariq Ramadan bans homosexuality for his followers: "Islam, in regard to sexuality, has established limits. God decreed that there be an order. And that order is a man for a woman and a woman for a man."[86] Obviously, it is no invention of his. The Koran, like all the monotheist religions that invoke Sodom and Gomorrah, condemns homosexuality. But some believers have revised their opinion on this prejudice that belongs to another age. Tariq Ramadan is not one of them. For him, fundamentalism always takes precedence over reform: "The ban is unequivocal; homosexuality is not something that Islam permits."[87]

This irrevocable condemnation concerns more than the private sphere. When Jacques Neirynck brought up the question of the Pacte civile de Société or Civil Solidarity Contract (which allows unmarried heterosexual or homosexual couples to legally formalize their relationship), the preacher's reply was unambiguous: "Homosexuality is not allowed in Islam, and the public legalization of homosexuality, which is what is demanded in Europe, is inconceivable in Islam, whether it be a question of social acceptance, of marriage, or anything else. There are limits to what can be considered as normal in society and in the public domain."[88] At least he makes no bones about it. The simple fact that Ramadan does not advocate the death sentence for homosexuals is enough for him to be considered a liberal Muslim. We can be grateful to him for encouraging his peers not to insult those whose lives are, in his terms, "outside of nature." He admits being moved by the numerous letters received from young Muslims suffering from the hostility that they encounter in their communities. He invites his brothers and sisters of the faith "not to pass judgment on human beings, even if they pass judgment on the acts they commit."[89] Which brings to mind the hypocritically compassionate distinction proposed by the Pope when he differentiates "the sinner" from "the sin." As in the case of Christians, the rejection of homosexuality goes together with "an offer to accompany them" on the road to repentance and recovery. What Tariq Ramadan calls "guiding them towards a more righteous way," "that is in harmony with man's creation."[90] As far as compassion is concerned, it is, above all, a means of diluting the intolerance of his message with a semblance of charity—the sort of "charity" that has led Jewish and Christian fundamentalists (and soon their Muslim counterparts?) to set up associations of "reformed homosexuals," in which the faithful who are in the grips of temptation are propelled towards heterosexuality by means of sermons, "guilt" sessions, and sometimes even exorcism. In Tariq Ramadan's case as well, the call for tolerance is rapidly exhausted: "For Islam, homosexuality is not natural; it lies outside the true way and outside the rules by which we become human beings in the eyes of God. Such behavior is a sign of disorder, dysfunction and disequilibrium."[91]

As a result, the problem of homophobia in the Muslim community is by no means resolved. Young people coming from Muslim families who are unlucky enough to fall in love with someone of the same sex are immediately classed as apostates; which, in the eyes of the scholars close to Tariq Ramadan, warrants the death sentence. Sheikh Qaradawi puts it this way: "When a man becomes effeminate and a woman virile, it's a sign of chaos and moral decadence."[92] Tariq Ramadan shares the same obsession: "Just how far can one accept that a young boy acts like a girl, and a young girl like a boy? Where is the border line?"[93] Once more, he is on the same wavelength as his brother Hani.

This intransigence is not limited to homosexuals. Even heterosexual sodomy is a tragedy! According to a *hadith* cited by Yusuf al-Qaradawi, the Prophet is supposed to have said: "Do not visit your wives by the anus" for "it is almost homosexuality."[94] In obedience to this teaching, Tariq Ramadan forbids sodomy: "That sort of act encourages something that is close to bestiality."[95] He says the same thing about pornography, characterized as "bestiality in the form of images."[96] Finally, even if Islam is supposedly less prudish than Christianity, and despite his promise of achieving serenity, the figure of Tariq Ramadan that emerges from his advice on sexuality is very much the puritan.

Keeping watch on the young

In a conference devoted to the "major sins," recorded in Réunion in August 1999, Tariq Ramadan called for mobilization of the Muslim community as a whole to combat fornication among the young:

> It's a monstrous transgression, a monstrosity, to live such an experience outside the bonds of marriage. And young people today, in our Muslim community, here in Réunion, are doing things that are shocking to us and that are not Islamic. We are all of us concerned. Rather than staying behind in the mosque repeating "Please, O God, protect us from that," we must launch a vast campaign of education to bring back our children, our daughters and our sons.

At least Ramadan has the merit of insisting that parents stop making more stringent demands of their daughters than of their sons. Which is certainly worthwhile, given the fact that daughters in some Muslim families are constantly spied on and denied any sort of outing on their own, so strong is the fear that their virginity may be at stake, while their brothers can do anything they like, including mistreating, attacking, or raping girls: "I have not spoken only of young girls, as I don't know where you got the idea that to protect your daughters you should let your sons have their way . . . . In terms of protecting the body, there is no difference between a boy and a girl."[97] Unfortunately, we see that this call to keep as close a watch over boys as over girls is an encouragement not to grant more liberty for all, but rather to impose more restrictions on all.

Woman: Keep us from temptation

As is the case in all the monotheistic religions, Tariq Ramadan is obsessed by the perils of *zina*, that is to say, fornication or adultery. Like all men, he would reform society so as to protect men and their sexual instincts, rather than challenge the ideology of male domination. Tariq Ramadan calls on women to protect men from temptation! If they want their husbands to remain faithful, they are expected to "give themselves over entirely." "What is asked of a Muslim wife in regard to her husband is to be the cloak that protects him from the unlawful . . . to know how to surround him with tenderness and offer him in terms of sexuality what he need not seek elsewhere."[98] It is a recommendation that brings to mind several *hadiths* in which women are clearly presented as sex objects for men: "A woman must never refuse a man, even on the edge of a burning stove";[99] or again, "A woman must never refuse him even on the back of a camel." This recommendation may appear unimportant, but it is one of the prerogatives of Muslim men, and is by no means the least. In the West, men who regard equality between men and women as an offense to their virility are sometimes attracted by a religion that seems to cater to their desires. This patriarchal conception would be a matter of personal morality if it applied only in the sphere of the family. But to Ramadan's way of thinking, these taboos and recommendations are to be extended to the social domain, with the result that women are asked to do everything in their power to avoid tempting men; in other words, they are obliged to hide themselves beneath a veil, so that their feminine silhouette should not excite men's male instincts. Ramadan's explanation resembles the most odious expressions of male chauvinism: "If it is women who are asked to wear the veil, it's because the weaker of the two is not the woman; in reality, the weaker of the two is the man, and the man who looks at a woman is far more vulnerable than the reverse. The veil is a protection for the weaker of the two."[100] So it is the men who are the weak beings, and women, acting as good Muslims, must help them overcome their instincts . . . by hiding! And all of this, of course, in the name of that marvelous strength that women possess, which is always invoked as a prelude to requiring more obedience of them. To be sure, the requirement to act with decency is supposed to apply to men as well as to women; but in practice this recommendation, as always, concerns primarily women. They are the only ones required to wear a veil because "beauty must not suggest seduction." So, Ramadan tells women, "if you try to attract attention, by your body, your perfume, your appearance, or by gestures, you are not on the path of decency, you are not on the way that leads to spirituality."[101]

From the obsession with decency to separation of the sexes

Tariq Ramadan has devoted considerable time to thinking about relations between men and women. According to him, three things can disrupt relations: ignorance of the principles of Islam, the overly restrictive constraints insisted on by certain scholars, and systematically choosing the opposite of what is done in the West, instead of relying on Islam: "In the name of the campaign against certain types of relations between men and women based on seduction," he explains, "we tend to forget the true sense of our relations founded on spirituality, on the sense of our being, and on complementarity."[102] Which leads him to urge Muslims to do away with the atmosphere of suspicion that prevails between them: "The Muslim community—it is brothers and sisters together, respectful of Islamic principles; not brothers against sisters."[103] As an example, he takes campuses where the young Muslim male students speak with other women, but not with their Muslim sisters. "You can speak with your sisters, but only under certain conditions." His grandfather was more adamant on the subject, since his program "banned male and female students being educated together," and considered that "students meeting alone together were committing a punishable crime." Ramadan, however, knows that he has to deal with audiences that are very much in favor of coeducation. Yet his acceptance of open relations between men and women has its limits.

In theory, Tariq Ramadan is very critical of overly staged respect for decency. He makes fun of those who tremble at the very idea of taking a good look around them. In practice, however, a young man or woman, having listened to one of his lectures, will come away convinced that duty requires him or her to make every effort to avoid succumbing to temptation or seduction, according to a conception of life that remains Manichean in religious terms: "Don't forget the angels . . . the one on the right notes down what you have done that is good; the one on the left what you have done that is bad."[104] Behind his apparently reassuring words, Tariq Ramadan turns out to be an outdated bigot, obsessed with chastity and the risk of transgression. After having intimated that caricaturing the West was no substitute for thoroughgoing self-criticism of the Muslim community, he lapses into an apocalyptic portrait of a decadent Western society that is a menace to Muslims intent on remaining true to their principles: "When we witness what is happening in the world, and you can see it via television or the press, then all sense of decency is lost. And when decency is lost, it's just do whatever you please; and when you do whatever you please, there are no longer any values, any limits, any sense; there is only total permissiveness."[105] Posters displaying pictures of naked women are particularly repugnant to Tariq Ramadan. On this subject, his rhetoric comes close to that of certain feminists; except that the feminists—at least the majority of them—protest about sexism, rather than the absence of decency. They reject domination, not seduction. Tariq Ramadan says exactly the reverse: "We live in a society that assaults our senses—that accentuates all that stimulates the instincts, particularly by exploiting what, for men, is the feminine dimension."[106] He explains that publicity material featuring scantily clad women constitutes "aggressive stimulation" for him who "has moral principles and wants to please God."[107] In his course on "Today's Muslim man" that he gave to a Muslim audience in Roubaix in 2001, he even went so far as to recount his own embarrassment when, on stepping onto a moving walkway in an airport corridor, he could not turn his head without coming face to face with an enormous poster of a woman in a bikini. "Which means that when you walk in the street you should keep your eyes glued to the pavement!"[108]

He began his lecture by saying that he wanted to put an end to the atmosphere of suspicion in public places and the child-like fear of looking at a woman; however, he was adamant in warning against "lustful looks": "In this community, there are some who are not sufficiently reserved in their way of looking around them."[109] As an example, he mentioned young boys whose behavior was not beyond reproach during a party organized on a Saturday evening in a community hall. As always, this obsession with decency quickly became a call for separation of the sexes. Of course, he has nothing against a woman and a man talking together in public, but he considers it immoral for an unmarried woman and an unmarried man to be alone in the same room. He would even prefer them not to shake hands, unless it is really necessary so as not to appear too much of an extremist. "Try to avoid it when you can; but if someone stretches out their hand, then shake hands." He also spearheaded a vigorous campaign for separate swimming pools for men and women, as indicated by the anger he voiced in the course of his lecture on the "Major sins" delivered in Réunion. "Today, the swimming pools in Réunion are not Islamic! Certain men go there anyway, saying But I know how to protect what needs to be protected'; but what do you look at while at the swimming pool? You can't go there because you will be looking at things you shouldn't be seeing! Because you go there, and inevitably it attracts you! So we have to provide for places where it's healthy, where there will be swimming pools that are in accord with our ethical principles."[110]

Therein lies the danger to society that a fundamentalist as prudish as Tariq Ramadan represents. If he were content to apply his restrictions to himself alone, he alone would bear the burden of these constraints, born of an extremely archaic vision of spirituality. Unfortunately, his project is not for one individual, but for a community, and even for society as a whole, with the resulting disruption of every aspect of social life. His preaching is directly responsible for the increasing number of Islamic headscarves that are appearing all over France, in particular among third-generation North African immigrants. Following his advice, an increasing number of young girls, instead of choosing to attend private schools, try to have the state schools accept the wearing of the headscarf, putting pressure on the girls of North

African descent who still refuse to do so. More than 1,500 cases were registered in 2003, 150 of them serious, that is to say, accompanied by attempts to proselytize and the refusal to attend certain courses. Since many teachers were at a loss as to how to handle the problem, the French government appointed a commission to look into the situation. During a public debate that lasted for months, France discovered just how bad things were: hospital emergency wards, where women refused to be treated by male doctors in the name of "decency"; female students refusing to take oral exams with male teachers; young girls no longer attending gym classes. Let's not forget the demands for separate hours for men and women in the municipal swimming pools that dot the (secular) landscape. In Lille, the mayor (Martine Aubry) finally gave in. Until the mayor changed her mind in the wake of secularist protestations, the South Lille swimming pool was reserved for women; the personnel were all women; and curtains protected them from the outside world. Other city halls have refused to give in to this blackmail, invoking the principle of secularity, but it is obvious that the pressure is growing stronger. The countervailing secular powers have never been so close to giving way. While they have been most effective in dealing with Catholic fundamentalism acting in the name of moral standards, they tend to lose their willingness to fight when religious minorities ask for special treatment in the name of respecting cultural difference, even if it is the same secular principle that is at stake.

Chapter 5

Muslim and Citizen, but Muslim First!

Tariq Ramadan has impressed many political and media observers by playing the role of the person who will show European Muslims how to find a satisfactory balance between their Muslim identity and their identity as citizens. That is what one might be led to think on going through some of his writings, such as *Les musulmans dans la laïcité* [*Muslims in a Secular Society*] (1994), *Etre musulman européen* [*To Be a European Muslim*] (1999), or *Les musulmans d'Occident et l'avenir de l'Islam* [*Western Muslims and the Future of Islam*] (2003). These three books say more or less the same thing, but the fact that they appeared at intervals several years apart was an advantage, for it provided their author with the opportunity to reappear in public debate on a regular basis in order to spread his message—a message, however, that was ambiguous and difficult to interpret. Here and there, one can find in his writings certain passages that suggest that Ramadan has succeeded in defining a proud and militant Islam that allows European Muslims to find a balance between their religious and civic identities. But he does not make it clear whether this is a sign of progress for Islam, or for society as a whole: "We, in the Muslim community, are experiencing a genuine silent revolution in the Occident. More and more young people are becoming involved, searching for the means to live in harmony with their faith, while at the same time taking part in the societies that are now theirs. French, English and American Muslims—women, as well as men—are constructing a 'Muslim personality' that will come as a surprise to a great many of their fellow citizens."[1]

But just what sort of surprise does he have in mind? Even a close reading does not really tell us. For the most part, journalists and intellectuals prefer to give him the benefit of the doubt. Each of Tariq Ramadan's books is greeted as *the* work that will finally mark the emergence of a generation of Muslims that will enjoy full citizenship, thanks to an Islam that is determinedly dynamic and modern. That is also what certain Swiss journalists thought—until the day they attended the Congress of the Muslim Men and Women of Switzerland . . . How can one explain this discrepancy between the praiseworthy aims announced by the preacher and the concrete impact of his words on the Muslims who listen to him? Once again, the key is to be found in his numerous cassettes, which together outline a conception of citizenship that can enlighten us as to what the "surprise" foreseen by Tariq Ramadan will turn out to be.

Obey the Constitution . . . except when it goes against an Islamic principle!

In theory, even on his cassettes, Ramadan sees no contradiction between the fact of being Muslim and French, or Muslim and Swiss, etc. He encourages his fellow Muslims to say they are "Muslim Frenchmen," just as readily as "French Muslims," without fearing that they are thus being traitors to their identity. This equanimity in regard to terminology could lead one to conclude that there is a form of equality, or equilibrium, between the two identities, the religious and the civic. In reality, if Tariq Ramadan does not want to make an issue out of word order, it is because he considers that religion and citizenship belong to two totally different spheres. In a footnote to his book *Muslims in a Secular Society,* he specifies: "The distinction that is made much of between being first a Muslim or first a Frenchman is, to our way of thinking, a false issue, for the two affiliations are of a different nature and a different order. Being a Muslim means embodying a certain conception of life, a sense of the meaning of life and of death; being a Frenchman means playing one's role as a citizen of a nation."[2] Already, in this book, one sees foreshadowed the idea that the two affiliations are not comparable, and that one is superior to the other: the tension is between, on the one hand "the meaning of life and of death," and, on the other, a role that one plays as "a citizen of a nation." However, the use of the term "citizen" gives the impression that

Tariq Ramadan takes this latter affiliation seriously. This is by no means the case on his cassettes, where the fact of being French no longer entails acting as a citizen, but simply refers to "geographical circumstances."[3] He takes it even further: "Geography cannot take precedence over my life or the meaning I give to my life." If someone asks a French Muslim to say if he is more of a Muslim or more of a Frenchman, here is the reply he suggests: "Muslim, it's a conception of life, it's the meaning of my life, and the meaning of my death." And he adds: "My conception of life is beyond everything."[4] For him, putting these two identities on the same level is like confusing "the sea with a swimming pool." French citizenship is the swimming pool, while Islam is the engulfing, all-encompassing sea, "beyond everything."

This way of setting the divine law above the law of men is characteristic of fundamentalists. Tariq Ramadan is aware of the fact, and intends us to be reassured: "My conception of life tells me that, wherever I am, I must respect the social norms."[5] He does not see this as "a contradiction, but as a clarification." When it comes to clarification, this added proviso only makes his conception of citizenship more opaque. The message is so ambiguous that one can make anything one wants of it. A reader who is generally well disposed towards him will retain the fact that Tariq Ramadan calls for respect for the law, particularly since, in his books, he emphasizes this aspect: "A Muslim, whether simply a resident or a citizen, must think of himself as bound by a moral and social contract to the country in which he is living. In other words, it is up to him to obey the law."[6] Someone more critical of Ramadan, or one of the faithful, will pay attention, above all, to the other half of his message, in which he urges Muslims to consider their religious affiliation as "beyond everything," all the more since, in his lectures, it is this other aspect that he emphasizes.

The ambiguity of such a stance comes to light in the cassette "Vivre en Occident" ["Living in the West"]. At the outset, he appears to be harping on the same theme as in his books: "As a resident of this country and a citizen, I respect the Constitution. It's an Islamic principle." But then a crucial clarification gives this statement of intention a radically different sense. He stipulates that the Constitution and the laws are to be obeyed once "everything in this country—in social, cultural, economic and legal terms—that is not contrary to Islamic principles . . . becomes Islamic."[7] This added provision is obviously essential. Up to this point, one might well have thought that the civic and the religious were compatible, without, as yet, being certain which side would win in case of conflict. Tariq Ramadan's reply is clear: a Muslim respects the country's laws, so long as they do not contradict Islamic principles. And on the same cassette he drives the point home: "Whatever in the culture in which we live is not in contradiction with Islam, we accept." Which eliminates the rest.

This view of things has practical consequences. In the name of this conception, Hani Ramadan urged young French Muslims not to serve in the French army if France was at war with Muslims, such as the Taliban, for example. Tariq Ramadan also advocated conscientious objection: "In cases in which two unjust principles clash, conscientious objection is the wise course and the one to be preferred. A Muslim citizen of an Occidental country must be mature in his analysis and determine what is at stake in his choice: alone, before God, with his conscience, and after having consulted the relevant legal authorities."[8] The footnote to this sentence refers to the debates between Islamic "scholars" concerning the participation of American Muslims in the war in Afghanistan. Ramadan simply notes that certain scholars authorized taking part, in the name of loyalty to one's country, while others refused to do so. The preacher encouraged Muslims to decide in all conscience: if they held that the war was a just one, then let them take part! If not, then let them refuse. He, himself, had his own opinion on the subject, and regretted the fact that the American Muslims did not denounce the war as illegitimate: "Citizens of the Muslim faith were obliged to prove their patriotism and their allegiance to the extent that even pausing to question the legitimacy of bombing Afghanistan was itself considered condemnable."

Integration equals assimilation

One aspect that most fascinates people about Tariq Ramadan is that he gives the impression of having at last found a third way between assimilation and withdrawal into communitarianism in a society that no longer wants to have to choose between the two alternatives. Until recently, integration seemed to represent a middle ground. Today, preachers such as Tariq Ramadan take advantage of the disappointment engendered by the failures of integration to shift the terms of the debate in such a way that "integration" becomes the equivalent of "assimilation."

In a lecture entitled "Notre identité face au contexte: assimilation, intégration ou contribution?" ["Our identity and its context: Assimilation, integration or participation?"] his proposal is as follows: "We agree to integration, but it is up to us to determine the contents." And what are these contents? "I accept the law, provided it does not force me to do something in contradiction with my religion."[9] In other words: "If, to be a good citizen, you must be a bad Muslim, the answer is no."[10] This declaration would not raise any problems if Tariq Ramadan stood for a modern, enlightened Islam. But we know this is not the case. As it is, his way of treating Islam as superior to everything, laws included, means that he is as dangerous a reactionary as is a fundamentalist Christian who considers the Bible as infinitely superior to the Declaration of the Rights of Man. Moreover, Ramadan comes close to treating the Declaration—at any rate the concept of citizenship that it implies—as an instrument in the hands of "secularists" and "Zionists" conspiring against Muslims:

> No declaration of the rights of man can, at any point, require of a person that he give up part of himself in order to become a citizen! You will notice, moreover, that this idea is the interpretation given by certain atheist, secularist, or Zionist ideologues who, it turns out, want to determine for themselves the nature of Muslim identity, a definition that it is up to us to contest.[11]

The conspiracy in question no doubt referred to the Islamic headscarf, without which Tariq Ramadan considers a Muslim woman to have sacrificed a part of herself: "If by integration is meant: 'Be a Muslim, but change your clothing,' then it's no."[12] This intransigence concerning one of the issues that divides archaic Islam from modern Islam is only a start, building up to a conception of citizenship according to which integrated Muslims are labelled "assimilated." In a conference on "Muslim identity," Tariq Ramadan alluded in thinly veiled terms to the rector of the Paris Mosque, whom he described as the very prototype of the assimilated Muslim. He warned against taking an open-minded approach, the equivalent of denying one's identity: "You are so open-minded that you are no longer anything at all; seeking assimilation, you no longer take pride in what you are, because you are afraid of being judged for what you are." He ended by explaining that "giving in on principles" is the sign of "fear" and "weakness." He is outspoken in his refusal to allow Islam to "become a form of relativism within relativism,"[13] in the name of what he calls "developing a clear-cut sense of our identity as Muslims" so as to avoid being "dissolved" in Occidental societies."[14]

Resist being dissolved in Western culture

This way of considering citizenship as simply "a geographical accident," while defending Muslim identity as a besieged fortress that Western influences threaten to overwhelm, is no doubt due, in part, to his family history. Just recall his claim to have had as many as six nationalities. In his eyes, a passport is nothing but a scrap of paper, in no way comparable to the radical Muslim identity that welded his family together. He himself described the Geneva Islamic Center as an institution designed to furnish Muslims living in Europe with the means to "preserve their identity and not enter into the process of assimilation."[15] The little boy who preferred, after a soccer match, to take a shower fully clothed in front of his team mates grew up within a clan that regarded the outside world as a permanent threat. Thinking back on his experience as a child brought up in exile, traumatized by the fear of being assimilated, one can understand why, despite appearances, Ramadan promulgates a hermetically sealed Islam that transforms his disciples into eternal exiles within their own countries.

Haunted by the fears inherited from his father and marked by his grandfather's obsessive concerns, Tariq Ramadan abhors the idea that young Muslims living in the West should succumb to cultural influences that might turn them away from fundamental Islamism. His grandfather wanted to "close the dance halls," "control the theater and the cinema," "screen the plays to be staged and sent on tour," and "control the broadcasting of popular songs by a strict selection process." Astounding as it may seem, his grandson—a century later and in the very heart of Europe—takes exactly the same position when he advocates "an alternative Islamic culture," designed as a substitute for non-Islamic influences.

To be sure, it is not in these terms that Ramadan will present things. As usual, he takes pains to set up a framework in which his proposals will appear to occupy the center ground. He begins, in particular, by reminding us that "scholars" categorically forbid music, film, and photography in the name of Islam. One might expect that a man who purports to be a reformer, helping Muslims live in harmony with their times, would seize the occasion to criticize such extremists. Not at all. On the contrary, he asks European Muslims to respect them and not treat them as "fundamentalists"![16] In convincing European Muslims that such a stance deserves respect, he succeeds in radicalizing them, so that he himself can then appear as a moderating influence, arguing for the acceptance of certain cultural traits, so long as they are not in opposition to Islamic moral standards. "There's no reason to reject everything that Victor Hugo has done," he is fond of repeating. With exemplary open-mindedness, Tariq Ramadan even criticizes Islamic libraries that have refused any work by the author of *Les Misérables*: "Everything of his has been thrown out, but why? Because we approach this society in a state of fear. We have lost confidence in our own principles. Islam has universal principles; we should be more confident."[17] Note that the acceptance of certain works considered to be part of "Occidental culture" is not based on qualities such as open-mindedness or tolerance, but is in the name of the overwhelming superiority of Islamic universal values—values that must be thoroughly digested before one reads non-Islamic writings without running the risk of contamination. And provided, of course, that they have been pre-selected. "French literature is one of the richest in the world. It is not to be rejected out of hand," he explained. And then, by way of precautionary instructions for use, he added: "One has to choose, to select; and the community must take part in the process."[18]

This last sentence sums up the communitarian concept of culture that, in spite of his denials, Ramadan defends. If selection is not an individual matter, but a collective obligation, then that means the community must organize the censorship of books, films, and music considered to be in conflict with Islamic morality—which comes down to having the clan superintend the cultural tastes and choices of youngsters born into Muslim families. Furthermore, rather than select, Ramadan would prefer to have an alternative culture, designed in such a way that children would not seek distractions elsewhere. A sort of cultural police disguised as an alternative culture. "We must find a solution for handling this free time, this need for distraction, by providing a noble Islamic culture . . . so that we can progress together towards a European Islamic culture."[19] For "noble," read "moral." But what does a culture designed to be moral look like? Ramadan does not really go into detail. He presses the community to develop "cartoons and games for Islamic children," but he himself cites only countermodels, disapproving, for instance, of a young child playing with a Power Ranger as a sign of "creeping colonialism." But what exactly does an Islamic toy look like? Tariq Ramadan is never clear on that. Except when he gives examples coming from countries that offer, in his eyes, a model to be imitated in terms of "Islamic culture." Then everything becomes clear. For women, he looks to Iran. For culture, he looks to the Sudan of Hassan al-Tourabi, a leader whose "imaginative cultural management" he admires.[20]

From cultural xenophobia to censorship

The worst aspect of this is not that Tariq Ramadan is a fundamentalist, but that he seeks to force his fundamentalist vision of culture on the Muslim community and even on society as a whole. His association, Présence Musulmane, advocates banning films, music and photography that conflict with Islamic morals: "The contents of artistic works, as well as their form (be it music, song, photography, cinema or drawing), must be in keeping with Islamic ethics and not give rise to attitudes that run counter to them."[21] For this reason, the association invites its members to pick and choose when it comes to European artistic production, and, above all, to avoid "sub-cultures" defined as follows: "Negative artistic productions that are immoral and indecent, mass evening gatherings, and dehumanizing concerts." Advice that applies "to oneself, one's family and one's entourage."

Once again, we come across the first three points of al-Banna's program: the individual, the family, and then society. Like al-Banna, Tariq Ramadan encourages Muslims to call for censorship in the name of respect for Muslim culture:

> As members and citizens of Western societies, Muslim men and women must have their say on art and culture. Muslims must question meanings, debate values, challenge institutions, and participate in the vast debate on human dignity and ethics. You are not the only ones to be put off by the weird innovations of "post-modern" artistic expression. With people of like faith and conscience, you must dare to say no, to express your determined resistance, so that the freedom of speech, which is our claim to dignity, does not become a pretext for the partisans of an "all-permissiveness" sunk in absurdities and tumult.[22]

To night clubs you shall not go

Anti-discrimination associations have been organizing campaigns against night-club bouncers harassing would-be customers because they look North African. Tariq Ramadan has a better way of avoiding the ordeal of discrimination. He prohibits young Muslims from going to night clubs! The preacher paints a particularly somber picture of Western societies, interested only in free time and leisure activities—something he is never far from equating with idleness and even decadence. The cult of the night symbolizes for him the worst aspect of this "sub-culture": "You are living in a society in which night-time provides a very special sort of entertainment . . . . The lights go dim, there's more racket and you lose your head."[23] The phenomenon is of concern to him. He reprimands the Muslims who go to discotheques: "I know it's true: even some of you, forgetting who you are, do go there and join in." In a tone of voice more paternal than ever, he warns them: it is out of the question to go to every non-Muslim evening party just to be more integrated. "We're not going to act like them, just to have them think we're part of the same culture."[24]

Ramadan not only warns against "the dark and shadowy distractions" of smoke-filled night clubs. His strict standards also ban listening to music late at night, even Islamic music performed at the close of Muslim meetings! He rejects anything and everything that could possibly make one "lose one's head" before turning in. "Before going to bed," he expounded to young Muslims, "one doesn't lose one's head in Islam; one opens one's heart." And then he went on to explain what he proposed instead. A schedule in which daily prayer replaced night-time music. "Celebrations are not occasions to lose track, but to achieve equanimity."

To rap you shall not listen

Tariq Ramadan makes no secret of his dislike of rap. "The philosophy of rap is not the philosophy of the heart."[25] There is, no doubt, much to be said on the subject of the sexism of certain male rappers, but that is not what Ramadan has in mind. The fact that rap is often sexually explicit music, raw and candid, undoubtedly shocks the sensitivity of a preacher who is such a bigot and moralist. But that is not the only thing that bothers him. Just what is it that he disapproves of in the music? First of all, the idolatry. True to a monotheistic religion built on its opposition to polytheism, he is disturbed to see that Muslim men and women can so adore an idol that they ask for his autograph. "For it is a serious matter, it is not the sort of culture we should have." But that is not all: the youngsters from the poor districts who find in rap a form of expiation and expression are usually not those whom the Islamists succeed in indoctrinating.

In his book *Qu'Allah bénisse la France* [*Let God Bless France*], the rapper Abd al-Malik recounts that he was, for many years, active in the Tabligh and the UOIF, where he never missed any of Tariq Ramadan's lectures—but that he then drifted away so as to enjoy greater liberty of faith and to create.[26] In the beginning a fervent follower, this independently minded artist began to feel hemmed in by a conception of religion that was so closed to cultural mixing. His discontent only intensified when he asked Tariq Ramadan how to reconcile his faith with his love of rap. One winter's night in 1998, he took advantage of the preacher's visit to Strasbourg to arrange a meeting. The conversation was cordial but disappointing. The artist did not understand when Tariq Ramadan urged him to restrict his creativity to

Islamic influences: "All the trends, genres, and styles in vogue today had their separate roots, but they fed into one another, all the more so in the multicultural West. The recommendations of our mentor might have been applicable in literature, in the choice of subject, even in vocal interpretation; but from a strictly musical point of view it made no sense." The artist was taken aback when Tariq Ramadan ended by suggesting that his malaise stemmed from the fact that his musical compositions were not in harmony with Islam: "These words made my blood run cold. Was it possible that he was right? And if so, was he insinuating that I should be attuned to his interpretation of Islam? Even when I was on the bottom of the heap, I had always jealously defended my freedom. I was asking for advice, not for an ideological tutor." Abd al-Malik has continued to be a musician, but he has come closer to a more spiritual Islam less given to lecturing—the Islam of the Sufis.

Rap communicates the rage of those faced with discrimination and forced to live in ghettoes, but the music transforms this rage into a form of culture. Ramadan wants to transform this rage into morality. He has nothing against music if it serves to transmit his message. On this score, Ramadan admits that "music is a language that can't be overlooked." The only singers that find favor in his eyes are those who devote their music to the service of religion and propagation of the faith, like Cat Stevens, now Yusuf Islam. But even in this case, it is not sufficient to make music and "add a touch of Islam." He wants songs that are entirely Islamic.

Certain films thou shalt not see

Fundamentalists never admit that they detest the liberty of thought inherent in artistic creation. They simply say that they want art to respect religion. Which means either reducing it to a tool of propaganda or adopting censorship. That is exactly what the American fundamentalists do when they campaign with cries of "blasphemy" against any film that they cannot suppress, such as Scorsese's *The Last Temptation of Christ*—the better to approve films that serve their propaganda objectives, such as Mel Gibson's *The Passion of the Christ*. Hani Ramadan adopts the same approach. He condemns, as symptomatic of "the decline of the West," films which "under the guise of eroticism and art" display sexual acts on the big screen, but stipulates: "That does not mean that Islam rejects the seventh art. On the contrary, cinema and theater have considerable cultural qualities, so long as these genres serve an ideal that protects moral values and human dignity."[27] We have seen how this statement is interpreted by Tariq Ramadan. He would, no doubt, approve of a play glorifying the Prophet that had been produced with Qaradawi's "seal of approval," but quite evidently not Voltaire's version.

As far as cinema is concerned, his favorite target—one that embodies the very acme of cinematographic decadence—is *Titanic*. "A film that Muslims have not seen," he said ironically, and even with a certain touch of humor. As good a way as any of getting across the idea that "true Muslims" should not have gone to see this typically Hollywood melodrama. He warns against any film that threatens to violate Islamic moral standards: "Make sure that, because you're fond of the movies, you don't go to see something disgraceful, something immoral."[28] And what does he propose? Not forbidding, but selecting: "Go to see things, but learn where the limits are . . . . Develop a culture of dignity and a sense of limits."[29] This is another piece of advice that comes strikingly close to al-Banna's program, with a dash of realism added. In an Islamic country, such a conception of art would clearly result in the banning of any film or song that did not conform to Islamic morality—a policy that would be indefensible in the West, where banning would serve only to alienate non-Muslims, as well as young Muslims. Ramadan is aware of the fact: "In a society where everything is permitted, if you forbid everything, you are going to lose your children," he explained to parents. He then went on to propose that the community organize itself in order to supervise and manage its youngsters' free-time activities.[30] He remembers the day his father authorized him to go and see *Twelve Angry Men*: "He said to me: that one you have to see! . . . I'll remember it all my life."[31] Which only goes to show how exceptional such authorizations were.

The four pillars of Muslim identity according to Ramadan

Apparently the five pillars of Islam that are to do with matters of faith are not enough for Ramadan, who added a further four pillars (all of them political) as non-negotiable constituents of Muslim identity:[32]

1. Faith: "living our spirituality and practicing our religion in full"
2. Comprehension: "learning our religion"
3. Education: "being able to inform and educate our children in the message"
4. Action: "being able to act in the name of our faith."

In appearance, this proposition seems harmless. It shocked none of those readers who saw him as a modern, secular Muslim. No doubt they would have been more intrigued had they also heard the cassette version of this presentation on Muslim identity, in which Tariq Ramadan stated: "If a society denies me one of these four features, I will resist it, I will fight it."[33] Enough to make one want to reread more closely these famous four pillars that are supposed to determine Muslim identity, and which are to be respected if a war against the Muslim community as a whole is to be avoided.

The first problem concerning this definition is that it eliminates any possibility of a Muslim living his faith in a private and individual fashion, for a good Muslim must commit himself in the name of Islam. This conception of Islam, which is, of necessity, collective, and thus communitarian, is not in itself shocking. It only becomes so in the hands of radical Muslims. All Islamists advocate a communitarian form of faith, which has the advantage of providing them with low-level recruits. In Algeria, the Islamic Salvation Front began by urging Muslims to pray collectively and not in their homes, even on days other than Friday; it subsequently began using these outside prayer meetings to deliver a far more political message. In Ramadan's case as well, "being able to act in the name of our faith" quickly becomes a political issue: "You cannot tell me that, in order to be a good Frenchman, I must remain a spiritual being who does not act in society."[34] Acting in society means acting politically. Harmless enough, except that it implies resisting a state that does not allow proselytizing—especially in school and in some public places, above all when the third pillar of Muslim identity stipulates that one must be able to "inform and educate our children in the message."

"Educating our children in the message"

Such a statement, coming from a preacher from the Muslim Brotherhood, a movement that has prospered by using Islamic education as a means of propaganda, has far-reaching consequences. It is about the idea that there are Muslim children and not simply children of Muslims, so that any interference in the education given to these children is taken as an infringement of their Muslim identity. This concern with educating one's children without any intrusion on the part of the Republic is not only the result of exile, it is also an obsession common to all fundamentalists. All of them dream of raising their children safe from the influence of the modern world; all of them, starting with the fundamentalists of the American religious Right, are determined to maintain segregation and the teaching of creationism in their private fundamentalist universities. Tariq Ramadan himself is not an advocate of a separate educational system for Muslims. Not that he looks down on the idea, but he fears that providing a uniquely Muslim education would not produce militants adept at Islamizing their milieu. As he explained on one of his cassettes: "An Islamic education cannot do without instruction in the Koran and the tradition of the Prophet (peace and blessings on his name), but neither can it do without instruction concerning the immediate environment in which we live and in which we must be active."[35] It is important to remember that Ramadan is an Islamist charged with *dawa* in Europe. If you lose sight of his objective, namely to train as many Muslims as possible—wherever they might be—as agents of Islam, it becomes impossible to understand why there is always such a huge difference between the extreme rigour of his Islam and the very open-minded way in which he goes about spreading it. He encourages Muslims to enter the state schools, where they will learn to know their milieu and to influence their comrades, rather than having them educated apart from society in private schools. That is why he has no trouble replying to reporters who ask him if he urges the faithful to boycott certain classes: "The situation is clear; they must attend because it's the law. It's not open to discussion, we're not going to begin tampering with school schedules," he declared in *Le Monde des Débats*.[36]

That does not mean that he will not do his utmost to limit the school's influence as far as possible. Nor will he allow the school program to take precedence over Muslim principles, in particular with regard to sports and biology. Muslim children are not to boycott biology classes; they are to assert their disagreement by questioning, criticizing and finally refusing to accept the theory of evolution on the basis of their "complementary" Islamic education—in this case thanks to the "complementary" courses, at which they learn that men are not descended from apes but were created by God. This is spelled out in a footnote to *Muslims in a Secular Society:* "School biology courses can include teachings that run counter to Islamic principles. Moreover, the same is true of history and philosophy courses. This does not mean that students should be excused from attending classes. It is preferable by far to provide these youngsters with supplementary instruction that teaches them Islam's replies to the problems that arise. That will be a true source of enrichment."[37] As far as enrichment is concerned, this recommendation is an outright invitation to propaganda and to the refusal of dialogue, all the more disturbing in that it is applicable not only to biology, but also to history, philosophy and physical education. It is made even more explicit in the published proceedings of the symposium "Muslims in French-speaking countries," edited under the direction of Tariq Ramadan in 2001. Among the strategies recommended by the steering committee that he headed, it is said that "education is a domain in which the tactics employed must be extremely rigorous." The French-speaking Muslims were urged to "keep watch over scholastic programs and prevent the transmission of values not in accord with our principles"; to "set up a framework in which the official program would be combined with Islamic education (whether admitted as such or not)"; and finally, to "gain a footing within the state schools by profiting from the students' free time to give complementary religious instruction."[38] Ramadan's supporters could, for instance, find material for their "complementary instruction" in the work published by Tawhid, *L'homme descent-il du singe? Un point de vue musulman sur la théorie de l'évolution* [*Is Man Descended from the Apes? A Muslim View of the Theory of Evolution*], which argues for creationism and denies evolution.

For his followers understand perfectly well what is meant by this directive, even if it is discreetly given in a footnote. It sometimes happens that, despite the precautions he takes, Tariq Ramadan"s instructions come to the attention of the public at large. It is this passage in particular that alerted the teachers of the college where he taught, in particular his biology colleagues. But he sidestepped the issue by arguing that the suspicion was misplaced (see Chapter 2). On occasion, he also avoids this (for him) awkward subject by simply lying outright. In December 2003, in the midst of a heated debate with Jean-François Kahn on the TV program *Cultures et dependences,* he could find no way out when Kahn asked him point blank whether he belonged to the group of Muslim theologians who accepted evolution theory. That day, as was often the case when on TV, Ramadan preferred to agree, rather than express his true convictions in front of the general public.

On his cassettes, not only does he advocate complementary instruction as an antidote to the theory of evolution, but Ramadan quite explicitly encourages girls not to take part in certain sports: "Women are forbidden to engage in sports in which their bodies are disclosed to men."[39] Is it any surprise, then, that young girls refuse to take part in some sports, in particular swimming? Ramadan himself takes it for granted. In his eyes, it is up to the secular institutions to be reformed or to develop Islamic activities. And, once again, he refers to his model, Iran, where Rafsanjani has organized Islamic sports for women! This conception of education is alarming when it comes from a preacher; but it is terrifying in the case of a schoolteacher. The time has come to take stock of the consequences of the growing influence of a preacher-professor like Tariq Ramadan over young Muslims.

In the testimony given to the Stasi Commission (a government-appointed commission that, in 2003, held extensive hearings on the status of secularism in the French state school system) and in the ensuing debate on the meaning of secularism, many teachers spoke of the increasing difficulties they were encountering when it came to studying the Holocaust or evolution.

100 percent in favor of secularism?

All French Islamists who have the slightest sense of strategy claim to respect the principle of secularism. Amar Lasfar, rector of the Lille Mosque and an activist in the Union of Islamic Organizations of France (the association that encourages young girls to go to school wearing the Islamic headscarf), made a point of affirming: "I am a thousand percent for secularism, because secularism means tolerance, and what I want is tolerance."[40] However Soheib Bencheikh, the mufti of Marseille, is not entirely convinced that these declarations from the staff of the UOIF are sincere: "They speak of dialogue only when they run into trouble with the laws of the Republic concerning secularism. I myself have heard Amar Lasfar say in a meeting of young people that 'Islam and secularism will never see eye to eye.'"[41] Another example is that of Yamin Makri of the Tawhid bookshop. When questioned by the press, he said he was someone who fought for secularism: "Secularism is today the best guarantee for protecting our community," he declared in 2001.[42] He gave this interview only a few days after the Union of Young Muslims, closely associated with the Tawhid bookshop, organized a meeting in honor of Hani Ramadan, the sworn enemy of "secular torturers." And what about that other leading light of the UOIF and the Tawhid bookshop? What does Tariq Ramadan have to say? The same thing, of course. He is, perhaps, not 1,000 percent in favor, like Lasfar; but he is at least 100 percent: "Five years ago I was only 99 percent in favor of the French version of secularism. Today, I think that Islam is totally compatible with the separation of Church and state."[43] Tariq Ramadan is not telling the truth. One year after this interview of January 2003, he was still not 100 percent in favor of secularism, since he declared: "The Islamic headscarf cannot as such be banned from school."[44]

Tariq Ramadan is also accomplished at lying by omission. What he forgets to say is that he is 100 percent in favor of his own interpretation of secularism. Let us look at what he was saying on his cassettes when he was only 99 percent in agreement with secularism—especially on the cassettes where the Muslims under his guidance are introduced to the concept of secularism. What are they told? That secularism is a remnant of colonialism, a model that they must get around in order to remain good Muslims! "The model of secularism that has made European societies what they are and that they have even forced on their colonies . . . well, as for us, we must select in that model what will allow us to remain faithful to our founding principles."[45] It is not a question of selecting from the religious principles those that can be made compatible with secularism, but the reverse. Moreover, Tariq Ramadan is adamant: Muslims must be actively engaged in the campaign to have secularism develop in such a way that it coincides with their fundamentalist vision of a political Islam: "The state cannot fail to pay attention when the people change, so we must change the people," he explained on his cassette "Islam and secularism."[46] On this score, he is even more radical than certain UOIF theologians; at any rate, more radical than the most moderate of them, Tareq Oubrou.

The Union of Islamic Organizations of France pays only the scantest attention to what Tareq Oubrou has to say, but it is more than willing for him to be its press spokesman, so as to give the impression of being moderate and respectful of secularism. Tareq Oubrou defends the idea of a "minority sharia" that is totally compatible with the secular principle. Unfortunately for civil peace, Tareq Oubrou enjoys far less success among French Islamists than does Tariq Ramadan, who is totally opposed to this proposal. The two men have often had occasion to present their differing points of view, in particular on the courses held in Lyon for the Young Muslims close to UOIF. One of these courses provided the material for a cassette entitled "Islam d'Europe: entre religion minoritaire et message universel" ["European Islam: Between minority religion and universal message"].[47] Listening to it, you realize to what extent Tareq Oubrou serves as a foil for Tariq Ramadan. Oubrou is a man of learning, well versed in the science of Islam, a true scholar. His language is on a par with the loftiness of his thought: full of jargon, highly specialized, practically incomprehensible. After several minutes of tedious verbosity, Tariq Ramadan had no difficulty in recapturing the audience's attention and making short work of Oubrou's proposal, even though the proposal in question was both theologically and politically reasonable, the idea being to think of the West as "a land of the secular," for which the sharia must be revised in accordance with its minority status. For Ramadan, Europe is not a "land of the secular" but, on the contrary, "a land to bear witness" (*dar el-shahada*)—in other words, a land suitable for proselytizing. He abhors the idea of a sharia that would grant certain rights to a minority. Politely but firmly, after having agreed with Oubrou as to the origins of the problem, he dismisses out of hand the political consequences that Oubrou draws, refusing to accept "rights granted to a minority that would be the rights of the dominated."[48] The minority status "is only a stage and we must go beyond," he explained, sending a thrill through the young audience in attendance.

Communitarian but not separatist

Tariq Ramadan denies advocating a communitarian Islam: "The concept of community that we defend is diametrically opposed to the communitarian idea."[49] Once again, he is playing with words. Just as he deliberately confuses "Salafism" with "literalism" so as not to be accused of Salafism, so he equates "communitarianism" with "separatism" so as not to be accused of communitarianism. However, Tariq Ramadan is, indeed, a communitarian, even if he is not a separatist. He always begins his preaching on Muslim identity by condemning the communitarian withdrawal of Muslims: "The Muslims will get what they deserve . . . basically it's up to them to make a move . . . unless they have decided to remain forever marginalized by society as passive victims."[50] Talking this way is guaranteed to shake up the Muslim community. No words are too brutal to decry the "ghetto mentality, the sloth, the infantilism, and the victimization that drag this community down."[51] His words communicate a renewed sense of dynamism, an incentive to pride and action. They quite naturally appeal to those who would see in him the one to galvanize a generation of children of immigrants into seizing hold of their citizenship. An impression that is often corroborated by youngsters he has trained when they talk to journalists. Abdelaziz Chaambi is there to explain that Tariq Ramadan helped the youngsters of Lyon break out of their communitarianism: "We came to realize that withdrawal into the community was a bad idea for everyone."[52] It is a fact that, a few years ago, the Union of Young Muslims was on the threshold of separatism. At that time, the association attracted only hardliners. Today, it is a dynamic organization, capable of attracting a far larger public, and less atypical. But is this good news?

One would be tempted to think so on reading, or skimming, a book such as *Muslims in a Secular Society*, in which Tariq Ramadan urges Muslims not to remain aloof from society, but to take part:

> The process of intellectual and physical ghettoization runs counter to the spirit of Islam. Living one's life in a community setting to strengthen oneself morally is one thing; living apart from the surrounding society is another. On the legal and political level, Muslim men and women must see themselves as individuals, exercising in all conscience their rights and fulfilling their duties as citizens; and this implies knowing the law, participating in the social, political and economic dynamics of the society in which they live, and playing their role to the full.[53]

One can only welcome the fact that Tariq Ramadan has given impetus to European Muslims, some of whom are victims of economic, social, and racial exclusion. But where is he taking them? Not on the road to secularism.

To judge Tariq Ramadan's impact on young Muslims only in terms of dynamics and initiative is to lose sight of a key element: his objective. It is essential to understand that, when he urges his followers to become active citizens, he does not see it as a process of exchange. It is made clear that Muslims should become citizens in order to act on their environment, but there is no question of this environment or their citizenship acting on them. Ramadan proposes that everything that is Islamic should be integrated, but he campaigns as hard as he can for the community to remain sealed off from everything that is not Islamic: "I am prepared to integrate what is good in the name of universal values, but I will not be dissolved, I will not cede to relativism." And in the next sentence: "My philosophy is all-encompassing."[54] Exchange is, then, a one-way street: Muslims are asked not to allow themselves to be dissolved in Western societies, but to seize hold of their citizenship the better to Islamize their environment. It is in these terms that the name of his association, Présence Musulmane, is to be understood. The objectives of the organization, as stated, are: "1) to protect our faith and 2) to bear witness to our religion."

Our contribution = Islamization

Hassan al-Banna used to refer to the Muslim Brotherhood as a citizens' movement:

> Whoever thinks that the Muslim Brotherhood is irritated or disgusted by the concept of nation or the idea of citizenship is wrong. Muslims are the people who have the most genuine relations with their respective countries; among those that serve their country they are the ones whose service is the most serious-minded and the most respectful. You can then understand how fully they assume their citizenship and what a powerful role they intend for their community.

He then added: "However, Muslims are different from others whose goal is simply citizenship, in that the basis of Muslim citizenship is their Islamic faith."[55] Tariq Ramadan thinks of citizenship in the same terms. It is just one means among others to propagate Islam, rather than a bond tying one truly to a country. It is in these terms that one should understand what he calls the Muslim "contribution" that he presents as a third way between integration and assimilation. He is quite explicit in the manner in which he explains this concept to his followers: "We must play an active role in all areas open to us where we can move towards more Islam."[56]

Tariq Ramadan is no hothead intent on "commandeering power." He does not want to organize a putsch in France or Switzerland. He is well aware that it is neither the time nor the place for *coups d'état*. His objective is the same as al-Banna's, but his methods, on the other hand, take account of the democratic Western context:

> Brothers and sisters should keep in mind that it isn't a question of when we are going to take power, that's not of interest to us. Our objective is to demonstrate to those in power that we are not mere instruments and that we have no intention of being treated as animals. And when those in power understand and take us into account, then we will be supportive.[57]

The very fact that Tariq Ramadan finds it necessary to clarify matters in this way for his audience proves that he is in contact with Muslims for whom the eventuality of taking power is not totally out of the question. As for him, he simply refuses to be troubled by this perspective: "It's not a question of power, it's a question of society . . . power is only a means."[58] Ramadan is not thereby giving up the objective of Islamization. He is simply sticking to his grandfather's method, namely seeking first social conquest and then political conquest. His plan is both more subtle and more ambitious than a *coup d'état*—and, above all, more realistic: "We must go from being a minority in terms of numbers to being an ethical majority."[59] If his speech came with subtitles in English, you might think it was Jerry Falwell speaking, the founder of the Moral Majority in the United States. Here is a leader one would rather see as a separatist—at least then he couldn't be an influence in American politics!

Tariq Ramadan would have us believe that his approach is progressive minded because he is not a terrorist. But the American Christians who do the most harm are not those who, in the name of God, kill abortion doctors, but those who, day after day, in the name of God and using legal means, roll back the laws guaranteeing individual liberties. Once the Protestant fundamentalists gave up the idea of living apart from "modern decadence," they became the most powerful lobby in America, second only to big oil. In Tariq Ramadan's case, the program consists of opting for a reformist stance, that is to say "build on the privileges we have won and change what stands in our way."[60] But what stands in the way of this fundamentalist Muslim? Exactly the same thing that stands in the way of the fundamentalist Protestants of the American Christian Right: everything that blocks the advent of a moralistic and theocratic society. For the fundamentalists of the American religious Right, this objective means giving priority to the fight against secularism, feminism, and homosexuality. For Tariq Ramadan, it entails giving priority to the fight against secularism, feminism and integration.

Apart from differences in language and emphasis, they stand shoulder to shoulder in regard to social programs. Just as they are both ready to use all the resources of democracy to consolidate their hold on the political sphere. The American religious Right operates by distributing voting instructions via its networks, urging that pro-choice candidates be eliminated in favor of pro-life ones. Ramadan himself would have us believe that he has no desire to become a lobby: "The essential question is to decide whether the Muslim communities in Europe or the United States should organize as pressure groups and turn towards political lobbying . . . . The net conclusion of our analysis is that the answer to this question is no."[61] However, the rest of the book takes exactly the opposite tack. Ramadan, in fact, makes a pretense of equating lobbying with separatism. He then denies intending to create a Muslim lobby by simply claiming that what he wants is a Muslim lobby that "acts for the common good of all." Once again, this objective would in no way be reprehensible if Tariq Ramadan stood for universal principles in the name of Islam, and not ultra-reactionary principles in the name of Islamism. As it is, his lobbying would be as harmful as that of the religious Right in the United States. He does not have the same kind of networks, but he does, nonetheless, give voting instructions, not in order to have Muslim candidates elected (the few Muslim candidates that do exist are often integrated and liberal) but to have those who serve Islamist interests elected: "It's not a question of choosing candidates that are members of "the community"; one can be Muslim and not be that honest."[62] As a result, he does not call for the election of candidates on the basis of their religion or their ties to the community, but on the basis of what they are prepared to do for the Muslim community as Tariq Ramadan understands it—that is, for Islamism.

No shortcuts

Does this mean that, in the end, Tariq Ramadan's ambition is as politically oriented as that of his grandfather? That is the question that an increasing number of journalists are asking. Often quizzed as to his intentions, he has taught his followers how to dodge embarrassing questions:

> Some will ask you point blank: What is your objective? Is it to Islamize Europe? You want everyone to become Muslim? Is that what you want? When some Muslims are questioned in this manner, their replies are not entirely clear. It is not clear. Does it mean remaining Muslim and bearing witness or does it mean arriving on the scene as a conqueror?[63]

Note that Tariq Ramadan has still not answered the question; he prefers giving examples of what not to say. He criticized the statements of certain British Islamist leaders, such as Sheikh Omar Bakri, as counterproductive. Bakri declared to the press that one day he would plant the Islamic flag at 10 Downing Street. "It was at 8 o'clock in the evening on BBC, and it terrified more than one viewer," Ramadan explained to his troops. Note that there is no question of criticizing the objective, only the method! Moreover, how could Tariq Ramadan object to wanting to fly the Islamic flag on high? This declaration by Omar Bakri, no doubt the most extreme jihadist Salafist in Europe, is but a repetition of the last point in the program of Ramadan's grandfather: "We intend, in the future, that the Islamic flag flutter on high in the wind once again in all those countries that have had the good fortune to harbor Islam at one time or another, countries in which the voice of the muezzins will reverberate in the *takbirs* and the *tahlils*." Omar Bakri has studied al-Banna. He was even a Muslim Brother in Syria. The real difference between a jihadist Salafist and a reformist Salafist like Tariq Ramadan is that the former is in more of a hurry than the latter. For Tariq Ramadan, given the European context, there is no question of going beyond the first three points—"the individual, the family and then society"—while the people have not changed. This difference of pace is essential to our understanding of why Bakri despises Tariq Ramadan's over-scrupulous side, and, vice versa, why Tariq Ramadan cannot abide those who, like Bakri, take shortcuts that risk endangering his gradualist approach. It upset his grandfather when certain Brothers thought they were advancing the cause by taking shortcuts. Tariq Ramadan is of the same opinion. He can appear exasperated by those who do not have the same keen sense of political rhythms. It is, in part, this difference in the way of timing the stages, rather than any disagreement on basics, that led to his falling out with the Union of Islamic Organizations of France at the time when the Council of the Muslim Faith was being set up. Which does not mean that Tariq Ramadan has given up on the idea of having the West progress towards "more Islam."

As far as Muslim countries are concerned, he is in favor of establishing law based on the sharia—something he dare not say openly in France. Aziz Mouride, a Moroccan journalist, attended several of his lectures in France and in Morocco. He was struck by Ramadan's way of applying two different standards: "I was astonished to hear him say things in Morocco that he would never dare say in Switzerland or in France. For example, for him the law must conform to the Koran whenever the text is explicit. Wine is explicitly forbidden in the Koran, therefore it should be forbidden by the law and that's an end to it."[64] Are we to conclude that that is what he dreams of for Europe? Nothing would indicate the contrary. In 2004, Tariq Ramadan took an active part in drawing up the list of Muslim candidates for the European elections, in collaboration with the Muslim Council of Britain, an association of radical British Muslims. It is rumored that he might, one day, be the standard bearer of a sort of Muslim European party. One day, perhaps, when the time is right. In the meantime, his priority is to train a generation of Western Muslims capable of putting into practice his hopes for the future.

Savior of the suburbs or false prophet?

In 2001, Dounia Bouzar—then with the Department of Supervision of Minors—published a book in which she presented Muslim preachers such as Tariq Ramadan as "a new kind of social worker" on whom one could count to enrol the young of the French suburbs and put them on the right track.[65] The title, *L'Islam des banlieues* [*Islam in the Suburbs*] was designed as a counterpoint to another work, *Les banlieues de l'Islam* [*Islam's Suburbs*], in which Gilles Kepel described how Islamist groups close to the Muslim Brothers or the Tabligh took advantage of the exclusion and racism from which the young suffered to Islamize the suburbs, with the result that a number of youngsters considered themselves more Muslim than French. Dounia Bouzar—who had already published a book entitled *L'une voilée, l'autre pas* [*One Wears the Veil, the Other Doesn't*] with one of Ramadan's students—set out to convince us of the opposite.[66] This was explained in the blurb: "Becoming religious, far from being 'a return to fundamental principles' turns out to be a factor that favors integration, opening the way for these youngsters to live in harmony both with their parents and with Western society." And she adds: "This is particularly true for young girls of North African descent; they can, from now on, assume their identity as resolutely modern Frenchwomen."

All one can say is that the activists of Ni Putes Ni Soumises (literally, Neither Whores nor Submissive[67]), defending the rights of the women in the suburbs, do not share this optimism. For Fadela Amara, the president of this association that campaigns against sexist violence, it is undeniable that the deterioration in relations between boys and girls in the suburban housing developments coincided with the arrival of Islamist preachers, such as Tariq and Hani Ramadan:

> In the 1990s, there appeared a fundamentalist Islamist movement, derived from the Muslim Brotherhood, with a very negative interpretation of the Koran and, as if by chance, a very negative interpretation of the status of women in the sacred texts. In France, in particular, these reactionaries, known as "basement imams," developed a political interpretation that fostered closed minds and male chauvinism."[68]

Silem, a Ni Putes Ni Soumises militant, confirmed the impact of this male chauvinism on the suburban housing estates: "In the 1980s, there were mixed marriages and sexuality was treated in far less intolerant terms. There was a sense of life. Today, there is nothing left in these neighborhoods: no sense of life, no love, nothing but prohibitions." Leïla Babès speaks even of "real social control" since the day the preachers began arriving and making a place for themselves on the estates.[69] How could sociologists have given the impression that Tariq Ramadan and those like him were "a new kind of social worker" on whom the government could rely to help the young Muslims to combine their faith with their citizenship?

The 1990s marked a real turning point in intellectual and political thinking about integration in France. Short of ideas as to how to reduce delinquency in the poorer neighborhoods, where violence was rife, a number of political figures—men and women, from the Left and the political Right—were ready to believe that the Muslim preachers could restore order and peace where they themselves had failed . . . even if it meant favoring fundamentalism. They were like Margaret Thatcher, who had shown herself keen to leave the responsibility for developing social links to the religious, even if that meant transforming England into a nerve center of Islamism. Just as in the suburbs of the Bronx, where charismatic Christian churches have replaced some shop fronts with churches, so certain cities have taken the risk of entrusting the maintenance of a viable social environment to preachers such as the Ramadan brothers. Even the representatives of the Socialist Party have given up the anti-racist struggle in favor of a policy of patronizing religious leaders. Nadia Amiri, a consultant for the French Ministry of Equal Opportunities, who has always fought both racism and fundamentalism, while at the same time being highly critical of the political parties, well remembers the change that came about in the 1990s: "All of a sudden it was enough to add the word 'Muslim' to the name of an association to benefit from a subsidy."[70] Ten years later, the results are alarming. In the short term, certain delinquents rediscovered "the straight and narrow path," thanks to an Islam that was drip fed into the suburbs like a dose of tranquillizer. But coming to grips with reality will be a painful experience. Many of the young no longer listen to the blaring of rap, loud enough to upset passers-by. They burn fewer cars . . . But Sohane, a young girl from Vitry-sur-Seine, was burnt alive because she was considered too "free."[71] Everywhere, in the wake of the Muslim Brotherhood, anger and revolt are transformed into a hatred—more silent, but more deadly; hatred against women, against France, against the West . . . And, contrary to what Tariq Ramadan would have those on the outside believe, he himself is largely responsible. For proof, just observe the groups that have developed under his influence. In practice, fascination with Tariq Ramadan almost always entails a turn towards a radical, intolerant Islam.

The Ramadan generation

The young Muslims that have come under Tariq Ramadan's influence–Abdelaziz Chaambi, Farid Abdelkrim, Amina Mensour, Siham Andalouci, Fouad Imarraine, Ali Rhani, Saïda Kada, etc–are immediately recognizable. They wear well-trimmed beards or the Islamic headscarf, but they appear open and affable, particularly with journalists. They refer to figures well known to the general public, and give the impression of being part of a process of evolution and change. But if one digs deeper, one finds they are radicals with steel-plated rhetoric. Farid Abdelkrim, one of the leaders of the Young Muslims of France, belongs to this "Ramadan generation." He has written a book, *Na'al*

Bou la France?! [*Cursed Be France?!*], which is a précis of the lectures given by his model. In terms that are sometimes difficult to understand, he invites young Muslims to take part in society, the better to influence the course of "Mother Democracy" by campaigning for the headscarf, against bikinis in the swimming pools and making fun of the film *Titanic*, as well as recommending Thierry Meyssan's *L'effroyable imposture*—a book that claimed 9/11 was an American plot—and glorifying al-Banna.[72] As for Abdelaziz Chaambi of the Union of Young Muslims, he warns us: "We are prepared to participate in politics and the economy, but without being bleached of our beliefs."[73]

It is certainly possible that some youngsters with strong characters will end up slipping out of Ramadan's hands, like the rapper Abd al-Malik (who refused to sacrifice his artistic and spiritual inspiration to the integrist Islam of the Muslim Brotherhood). On the Internet forums, such as oumma.com, where the pro-Ramadans surf, it is not unusual to hear messages from followers fed up with listening to him produce unctuous speeches for the outside world, while talking like a warrior chief, authoritarian and paternalist, for the benefit of those inside:

> It would be a good idea for Tariq Ramadan to quit the French public scene and leave us to manage for ourselves. It's true that he helped us during the first ten years to get rid of our complexes when speaking in public. I don't want to talk him down or start a polemic, but I find that Tariq is authoritarian and sometimes a bit too pleased with himself. I've been listening to his speeches and lectures for the last ten years and *maash'allah* [thanks be to God] he did help me acquire maturity in my approach to religion. However I have difficulty listening to his speeches nowadays; he always says the same thing and I've noticed that he always wants to be right and he's quick to be hard on his brothers, whereas on TV he seeks consensus.[74]

Despite these early signs of disaffection, Tariq Ramadan continues to fascinate an impressive number of the young who lack the maturity to be selective. He cultivates the image of a preacher for the disinherited, a sort of worker-priest, especially when he recounts how he took things in hand after one of his students, a certain Thierry, took an overdose. In the style of the charismatic sects, he cultivated the myth of a drug addict cured thanks to cassettes of the Koran and faith. In reality, he himself admits that he has little effect on young dropouts. He appeals, for the most part, to middle-class students and young graduates: "I'm good for the middle," he says jokingly[75]—a quip that is intended to absolve him of his fundamentalist impact. As if the middle classes, which have furnished the greater part of the suicide bombers over the last few years, were not capable of producing radicals. In fact, this confession is appalling; far from saving the young from drugs or delinquency through Islam, Tariq Ramadan introduces youngsters with a promising future to a form of Islamism that they would never have paid any attention to if it had come from a narrow-minded, grotesque Islamist. The moral of the story: he transforms youngsters—who have all that it takes to reconcile their faith, their origins, and their citizenship—into intolerant and communitarian-minded fundamentalists. Instead of encouraging these youngsters to succeed despite the racist obstacles in their path, he takes them down a dead-end street: a hardline Islam, source of tension, confrontation and professional handicaps in the future—such as for the women who give up being schoolteachers to wear the Islamic headscarf.

It is the same for boys who rush headlong into the *dawa*. The escape into Islam undoubtedly provides them with a renewed sense of their identity, but at the risk of turning them into veritable tyrants for their family and relatives—first, in regard to their sisters who become their wards. But also in relation to their parents, whom they start lecturing on Islam and citizenship, with a certain disdain for the older generation that sought to be "integrated." Wherever the Brothers' Islam takes hold, the Islam of their Fathers crumbles, and with it the peace-loving, popular tradition of Islamic culture. The result is that the Islamic identity to which they lay claim is no longer a source of enrichment and diversity for all, but a source of conflict and tension, even within the family. One day in Lyon, after I had given a lecture on secularism versus fundamentalism, in the course of which I had mentioned Tariq Ramadan's influence, a mother sought me out to talk of her son. A first-class athlete who earned an excellent living, he began swearing by Tariq Ramadan, and then suddenly locked himself up in an extremely intolerant form of Islam: "Since then, it's difficult for us to communicate. My son has always been an intellectual. Now he only reads books published by Tawhid. He used to enjoy rap, but he doesn't listen to it anymore. It's hard on me to see my son close up like this. I love him still, but I no longer recognize him."

Islamism, in particular Tariq Ramadan's brand of Islamism, operates like a sect. He cuts individuals off from their milieu, the better to manipulate them. That is what Father Christian Delorme came finally to understand. As a priest, he was known for his commitment to combating racial discrimination. For many years he was close to the Lyon Union of Young Muslims—which Dounia Bouzar, in all seriousness, presented as a dynamic association "working to introduce more spirituality into a secular society" [*sic*]. For a while, he considered the Lyon Union of Young Muslims to be the equivalent of the Jeunesse ouvrière chrétienne (Christian Youth Worker Movement). After having defended Tariq Ramadan against all those who had their doubts, he confesses today that he was naive regarding the influence this sort of preacher has on the young:

> I came to understand that they were dangerous when I saw that they cut the ties between the young and their families, explaining that their parents did not practice the true Islam; that they were not on the right path. I also understood that they wormed their way into institutions, taking advantage of secularism, using the rhetoric of secularism, but using it only as a means; for basically they were against integration, and the identity they sought was that of a community of Muslims, living autonomously in the Republic, like a potent countervailing power.[76]

He reached these conclusions on the basis of his experience in the field, where tensions mounted wherever Tariq Ramadan had a following: "In Lyon, where the Union of Young Muslims wields considerable influence, ghettoization is on the increase. Which is to be expected, since boys are set against girls, and Muslims against non-Muslims. On the contrary, in the suburbs that have resisted the Islamists, such as in Vaulx-en-Velin, the segregation is less evident. All the social workers say the same thing."[77]

Chapter 6

Not a Clash but a Confrontation Between Civilizations

For the last decade or so, Tariq Ramadan has been a permanent fixture at all the prestigious round tables on "the dialogue between civilizations" organized by international institutions, in particular in Europe and the Euro-Mediterranean region. For example, he was a member of the Advisory Committee on dialogue between people and cultures set up in 2003 by the European Commission at the request of Romano Prodi.[1] The professorship that he was to have taken up at Notre Dame University (in the United States) in autumn 2004 was to have been devoted to the study of "religion, conflict, and peacebuilding." No doubt Tariq Ramadan is a great connoisseur of religions and conflicts, but one might wonder what he could draw on to teach peace between civilizations . . . For, contrary to what many observers have thought on reading his works, Tariq Ramadan shares some aspects of *The Clash of Civilizations,* a book he recommends to his followers, but one to be read from the Muslim perspective. The preacher agrees with Samuel Huntington that "the challenges of the future are civilization challenges."[2] This favorable opinion might come as a surprise, seeing that Huntington's book has, above all, been used by the Pentagon hawks as proof that the West should wake up or it will lose the civilization war to Islam. All observers who were even slightly anti-racist or who believed in peaceful international relations stepped in to condemn such a Manichean view. But Tariq Ramadan has nothing against Manichean ways of looking at things. He has taken it for granted that a war of civilizations will take place between Islam and the West, and he agrees with Huntington: "He [Huntington] has understood that Islam will be a bastion of resistance against Western hegemony."[3] On second thoughts, it appears naive to have assumed, even for a moment, that Tariq Ramadan would be hostile to this vision of the Western world threatened by the awakening of the *Muslim* world . . . Those who think they have found in him a champion of resistance to globalization and to the clash of civilizations are in for a further rude awakening. For, by way of alternative, Tariq Ramadan proposes nothing less than the globalization of Islam as the outcome of *The Confrontation of Civilizations,* the title of one of his books![4]

Islam and the West

Tariq Ramadan has often set his European or Anglo-Saxon interlocutors at ease by insisting that he warns Muslims against the temptation of defining their identity in opposition to the West and Western values. In reality, what he means is that, for him, Islamic civilization is so superior to Western civilization that he finds it unbearable that Islam should envisage defining itself in terms of a reaction to the West, instead of relying on its own principles and its own values. He does, in effect, warn his followers against the temptation of "demonizing" the West: "Even if the whole world were to caricature Islam, God has not granted us the right to caricature the other side, nor to ridicule their history or the stands they take."[5] Rather than "the other side," it would be more accurate to say "our adversaries." For if Ramadan makes a point of not caricaturing the various values that the West (according to him) represent, it is simply in order to reject them one by one.

Several of his lectures are devoted to the theme of "Islam and the West." In many regards, his perspective is close to that of the author of *The Clash of Civilizations,* beginning with the unshakeable belief that at stake is civilization itself, and that there exist very different civilizations. "A civilization takes the form of a system of values, a system of principles which all derive from particular traits."[6] So what, according to Tariq Ramadan, are the "traits" that supposedly define the West? He speaks of a triptych—"individualism, rationalism and modernism"—that make of the West a civilization turned towards secularism, individual liberty and progress. On the face of it, this description is not intended as negative, but simply descriptive: "As yet, nothing in what I have said points to a negative characteristic."[7] However, these traits soon turn out to be excesses that are to be combated; for Ramadan then lapses into an uninhibited apocalyptic description of the decadence of the West, on a level with the tirades of fundamentalist Christians. Dominique Avron, an assistant professor of history at the University of Montpellier-III, analyzed the situation with great perspicacity in an article for *Nunc*: "Tariq Ramadan hesitates between the image of a West in the throes of disillusion and a decadent West, even though he claims that he is unwilling to go as far as Serge Latouche, who published variations on Spengler's theme of the decline of the West."[8] But in fact Tariq Ramadan does quite frequently cite Latouche, who is also his friend, in his lectures. The specter of decadence is out and abroad. And for him, that is good news: the West's decadence foretells the renewal of Islam. Which will take place with the help of all men of good will, including Westerners. For Tariq Ramadan is not sectarian. He defends a dualistic view of the world, but he is ready to make common cause with anyone prepared to fight alongside him. To the extent that his "clash" is not really the clash of Islam with the West, but that of fundamentalism with secularism.

Secularism + individual liberties = moral permissiveness

First accusation against the West: excessive secularization. After having defined secularization objectively as "a process whereby the public sphere is freed of the influence and authority of religion," he warns against what he describes as "the negation of religion" that results when secularization is pushed too far: "Excessiveness has turned something positive into something negative. We have freed ourselves from religion, and finally, by taking it too far, have come to deny the reality of religion in the education we give to our children and the people."[9] This view is common to many of the supporters of an "open secularism," but it is quite a different matter coming from a preacher who is such a fundamentalist and so politically-minded, and in whose eyes the ideal society is one marked by "reference to God and his revelation."[10] He berates, as well, "the promotion of the individual that culminates in the Universal Declaration of the Rights of Man." This same extremism has led to a form of individualism that he equates with selfishness: "The process that has granted autonomy to individuals has, when overdone, produced individualism." Or again, "promoting the individual is a good thing, but lapsing into individualism is dangerous." Here we have an adroit way of condemning individual liberties and the right to free choice. Permissiveness and individualism are also the accusations that Christian fundamentalists launch against the right to abortion, denounced as egoism. Ramadan displays the same bitterness. It is not expressed in a wholesale condemnation of freedom of choice that would be counterproductive (although he is adamant in defending freedom of choice when it comes to the wearing of the Islamic headscarf); rather, he tends to present individualism in caricatural terms as libertarian excess: "Liberty, which means the freedom to make one's own choices, has taken on such importance that, when pushed to the extreme, it results in people losing their bearings. It becomes moral permissiveness."[11]

Modernism = decadence

"Who can question the validity of modernity?" Tariq Ramadan declared in the introduction to his book on the *Confrontation of Civilizations.*[12] It sounds reassuring. Until one discovers that it is, in effect, a confession—for it is the very question that Ramadan himself has dared to introduce. As always, he has recourse to a slight shift of meaning, whereby the rejection of modernity will turn out to be a middle-of-the-road solution. Here he makes a point of distinguishing between "modernity" and "modernism" so as to berate Western modernism as excessive and to propose in its place a counter-model: Islamic modernity. Whereas modernity simply means living in one's epoch and immediate environment, modernism means advocating a progressivism that implies liberty and a secularism considered to be incompatible with Islamic modernity. Jacques Jomier, a Dominican priest and expert on Islam, summed up the preacher's position in one cogent sentence: "It is not a question for him of modernizing Islam, but of Islamizing modernity."[13] Ramadan is willing to be modern, provided that he can use the advantages of modernity to combat modernism, which he equates with Westernization.

He urges Muslims to distinguish carefully between "modernity" and "the Western way of interpreting modernity,"[14] while stipulating: "We will never be modernist to the point of saying 'be done with principles,' so essential are principles to set us on the right path."[15] In another lecture on "Islam and the West" he insisted: "We can live modernity, while remaining faithful to our revelation."[16] The declaration does not appear to say much, unless one considers what it is that Tariq Ramadan includes in the expression "remaining faithful to our revelation." According to him, modernity and progress must come to a halt when they contravene the principles set down in the seventh century, and all attempts to adapt them entail an excess of progressivism and modernism that betrays a Westernized conception of the world. One understands better what he's getting at when listening to his diatribe against "the way Westerners live their modernity." What does he give as examples to avoid? The break-up of families, the fact of accepting homosexuals as priests, and even androgyny, which, according to him, is on the rise . . . He criticizes, in particular, those who think that the Catholic Church should keep up with the times by denying Sodom and Gomorrah, "which brand homosexuality a curse."[17] He also condemns as excesses typical of "modernism" the cult of leisure and the taste for distraction, by which one becomes "the slave of one's own freedom, the slave of one's moral relativism, the slave of one's own pleasures."[18] An indication of just how fundamentalist his conception of "Islamic modernity" really is. However, a dose of anti-imperialist and anti-capitalist rhetoric is enough for him to maintain ties with people on the Left: "By dint of giving preference to rationality, efficiency and productivity in the name of progress, our societies are on the brink of disaster," he explains in his book *The Confrontation of Civilizations.*[19] An anti-globalist reader might well take this as an attack on ruthless capitalism. Yet it is not productivity at all costs that Ramadan criticizes, but the evolution of the family: "Islamic principles are in total contradiction to the process of which we have just spoken [the evolution of family patterns]. If modernity is to be achieved at this price, it is obvious that the Koran and the Sunna refuse point blank the realization of this kind of modernism." Note that it is not only "modernism," but "modernization" that is in itself a problem.

Not only is Tariq Ramadan anti-modernist, but he is anti-progressive as well. He is against any form of progress that is contrary to tradition and religion: "It is the autonomy that comes with progress that uproots the individual, confusing him by opening up all the possible choices that liberty provides, leaving him with a future that has no memory of the past."[20] Furthermore, he tells us: "Progress that is without roots is progress that knows no limits; for it is roots that give it direction." And he has only to conclude with a citation from Albert Jacquard in order to explain how it is that philosophers—moreover Christian philosophers—have shown that "progress has reached the point where we have progress without conscience, and without conscience we are left without landmarks."[21] This rhetoric is one of the classics, also used by Christian fundamentalists campaigning in the name of ethics against abortion, euthanasia, and scientific discoveries that challenge Judeo-Christian morality. Tariq Ramadan, who often uses the term "ethics," also advocates a form of progress that takes place within the framework of the sacred. He contrasts the "progress without conscience" typical of the West, with "the progress guided by revelation" that characterized the splendor of Muslim civilization: "We cannot conceive of progress that runs counter to revelation, only a progress that is guided by revelation."[22] He even speaks of "Islamic progress." As a matter of principle, he refuses to conceive of Islamic progress as a mere refusal of progress as it is exists in the West. In concrete terms, his notion of "progress guided by revelation" turns out to be the antithesis of Western modernism. Which does not mean that Tariq Ramadan is not modern in the sense of refusing all the advantages of modernity. One can be a fundamentalist and still be in the vanguard of progress, especially if one makes use of technology to combat modernism.

As a preacher bent on proselytizing, Ramadan needs computers, the Internet, and satellites to spread his faith. He cannot afford to do without these assets, but claims that he refuses the ideology that comes with them. In other words, he recommends being selective, so that exchange is consistently in one direction only: towards Islamization and never towards Westernization. "Computers are not of interest to us; they are capable of having us lose our sense of morality and our ethical sense because of all the invitations to moral perdition that accompany them."[23] On the other hand, he has nothing against harnessing technology to the cause of the *dawa*: "Computers that can spread our message more effectively, that can make our work more productive, that can increase our capacity to edify people—of course they are of interest to us." Everyone will have understood what is meant by "edify"—the spreading of Islam's message through cyberspace.

Ramadan is not a separatist when it comes to methods, since he wants to succeed in propelling the world towards "more Islam"; but this modernity in terms of method should not be confused with the end objectives, which are clearly archaic. And yet . . . At certain moments in the course of his talk on "Islam and the West" he comes close to agreeing with his friend Serge Latouche, who distrusts even the instruments of modernity, such as computers or television. It is best expressed in Ramadan's own words:

> Serge Latouche said one thing that had a great effect on me and that I haven't stopped thinking about to find a solution. He said: "Dear Tariq, you're a dreamer . . . ." When, for instance, I said to him: "You have to select instruments and make use of them," he replied: "It's not entirely true, I don't entirely agree with you, because in the instrument itself there's already an ideology." And that, that made me stop and think, really.

Ramadan is unsure whether or not he can use TV as a propaganda tool without risking being contaminated by it: "One could use TV to be educational, and Latouche replied: 'You're dreaming. With television, given the way it's been set up, there's something about it that communicates the ideology of those who invented it. And when we're up against that, when we watch international television or television by satellite, what's to be done?'"[24]

The Taliban found the solution: they forbade it. As for the Iranian mullahs, they wage war against dissident Internet sites and satellites capable of influencing Iranians from the outside. Even though he claims to be anti-modernist, Tariq Ramadan is close to being simply anti-modernity. He says he is seeking a way to adapt these tools to the reform that he proposes. But in the end his opinion leaves no room for doubt: "Even if you are not in Europe, these means of communication render you submissive to Western ways of thinking."[25] It's what he calls "colonialism via information."

The rejection of globalization as a form of Westernization

For Tariq Ramadan, globalization is a front for a vast initiative to spread Western colonialism: "Globalization is another name for Westernization."[26] He then presents the ongoing colonialism as imperialism on several levels: judicial and political, but also economic, technical, informational and cultural. Each of the conclusions he comes to could well be shared by a militant antiglobalist, sincerely devoted to resisting hegemony and the forces of standardization at work in the world, but only if one puts aside the fact that Ramadan's criticisms are based not on a refusal of hegemony—which he approves of when it is Islamic hegemony—but on hatred for the rationalist, progressive and modernist project that Western influence represents.

Ramadan begins by condemning political and legislative colonization—a process that is still under way, since the term includes any "influence" exercised by a Western country on a Muslim nation. Even today, several decades after decolonization, Tariq Ramadan considers that colonization continues to exist, so long as the constitutions and the laws of Muslim countries have not been entirely purged of any Western influence. "If I [the colonizer] depart from you, but leave in your keeping the rules and regulations of my everyday life, I am still in your house."[27] Ramadan not only complains of the judicial confusion created by the former presence of Western regimes in certain countries. As a way of eliminating this colonial past, he rejects any provisions that recall in any manner whatsoever a "Western" conception of law. "Some Muslim countries today are turning to the French, Swiss and German constitutions to find inspiration for their own laws."[28] Which he finds shocking.

If tomorrow Morocco or Algeria were to adopt measures granting a greater degree of secularization, in particular with regard to their family codes, Ramadan would surely consider it a symptom of a "Western conception of the law" and therefore a form of colonization. In his eyes, every judicial step towards modernity represents colonial intrusion. When Jacques Neirynck asked him whether Tunisia and Turkey could serve as "models for a future Islam," he replied "absolutely not" and added: "The laws that are applied in those countries are remnants of the colonial epoch."[29] Disingenuousness has here given way to the rewriting of history. During the colonial period, the occupying nations rarely modified the habits of the occupied countries. They maintained most traditional provisions in the name of that cultural differentialism so dear to Ramadan. The secularization that the preacher condemns is the result not of colonization, but of the decisions taken by the governments of countries that became independent, such as that of Bourgiba in Tunisia. Turkish secularization is even less the result of colonization, in that it has never been colonized! At the head of the Ottoman Empire for several centuries, Turkey has always been a *colonizing* country, rather than a *colonized* country. However, the fact that Atatürk decreed secularization makes him, in Ramadan's eyes, a henchman in the service of the West. And this "colonization" will last as long as all the Muslim constitutions have not been purged of secularism, rationalism and any reference to the Declaration of the Rights of Man in favor of what, if not the sharia?

Western influence = colonization

Ramadan constantly shifts from a legitimate condemnation of political colonialism to the denunciation of any sort of cultural "influence" as a form of colonization. This shift results in an essentialist and even xenophobic conception of cultural exchange. It is here that his repeated calls for "an alternative Islamic culture" reveal their fundamentalism. Moreover, he often evokes his resistance to "cultural colonization" as a pillar of the Salafist reformist tradition from Afghani's time up to al-Banna. Yesterday the aim was to resist Christian missionaries; today he cites television as the peak of "cultural colonization": "It's cultural colonization that's the worst thing, and today it reaches into our living rooms with television."[30] Then come McDonald's, Coca-Cola, and Hollywood films: "Hollywood, it's not a film production center, it's an industry and an industry that conveys an ideology."[31] And, once again, he gives the example of *Titanic*, which he makes fun of in an anti-capitalist vein, reminding us that the film grossed more than Mauritania's total GDP. "The money spent on producing this film," he wrote, "is the equivalent of one year's GDP for Mauritania. It upsets me when I go to Yemen and

I see the schoolbooks of totally destitute children decorated with photos of DiCaprio! It's not healthy. Do I have the right to say so without being considered a barbarian Islamist?"[32] Ramadan would in no way resemble a "barbarian Islamist" if he were content to denounce the globalization of culture as a Hollywood-like machine eliminating diversity. Unfortunately, we know that this is only, so to speak, the tip of the iceberg of his discourse, since, in his cassettes on Islamic culture, he warns against certain films—not just in the name of resistance to globalization, but in the name of morality, the decline of which he regards as part of a Western process endangering Islamic values. On the subject of the Spice Girls, he even speaks of a "cultural invasion" akin to idolatry.[33] To his way of thinking, it is not a question of preserving cultural diversity, but of closing down the cultural frontiers so as to keep the Muslim world—including the Muslim community in Europe—sealed off from all Western influences that are not in conformity with Islamic principles!

Takeover bid for Averroës

Tariq Ramadan plays on the neo-colonial complex so as to rewrite history without being disavowed. Muslim colonization and the active participation of Arab countries in the slave trade are never brought up; it is the West that is made to bear the full burden of guilt. Another subject that Ramadan harps on continually is the neglect of Islam's contribution to the Renaissance. He is right to remind us that Andalusia was a region of extraordinary intellectual vitality, where Arab intellectuals played an active role in developing what is now our common cultural heritage. But why accept the idea of mixing only when it goes in one direction? And why do these influences not lead him to conclude that the myth of the Occident is just about as absurd and racist as the myth of the Orient, seeing as the two myths encompass the same thinkers and the same traditions of thought in entities that are neither separate nor clearly defined?

Take the case of Averroës. Here we have an Arab philosopher, born in Spain, to whom all the rationalists said to be "Western" lay claim. Yet this claim infuriates Tariq Ramadan, who denounces it as "a colonial intellectual takeover bid for Averroës."[34] He refuses to consider him a rationalist, but rather as someone who made use of reason to remain faithful to his fundamental principles. Yet he has just explained to us that Averroës was a thinker who had taken part in the Renaissance, which was characterized by the emancipation of art and philosophy from religious doctrine . . . And, above all, he forgets to remind us that Averroës was persecuted for his ideas by the Islamic fundamentalists of his time!

This way of rehabilitating the contribution of Arab thinkers to Western traditions, while at the same time refusing to recognize that they were rationalists persecuted by the fundamentalists, proves to what extent Ramadan manipulates history to serve his political ends. The essential thing is to exercise control over the critical perspective, in the name of multiculturalism, so as to distinguish correctly between exchange and colonization. Ramadan sets himself up as the one to judge what is to be regarded as resistance and what is to be seen as collaboration vis-à-vis "Westernization," always to be equated with colonization: "Since not everything is bad in the other camp, and not everything is good, the intelligent thing is to determine what to resist and what to accept."[35] He is not awkward to the point of denying that Muslim societies are faced with huge problems. "It's a black picture, no doubt about it," he conceded on the subject of the degree of poverty, the rapid population growth, and the illiteracy characteristic of the countries in question. But what does he propose as a solution? Nothing in any way reminiscent of the West. He is opposed, for instance, to family planning—a Western conspiracy to force Southern countries to produce fewer children. Exactly the line taken by the Vatican to incite the nations of the Organization of the Islamic Conference to vote against the family-planning programs proposed by the UN!

Economic "colonization"

Another aspect of Ramadan's exposition aims to show that the economy has become "a truly worldwide form of colonialism." Here again, it is not a question of condemning the exploitation of the South by the North as a form of domination—but rather as a form of Westernization. Ramadan is right to condemn the misuse made of international institutions such as the World Bank and the IMF. He remarks that the process, which began after the Second World War, coincided with the decline of political colonialism, as if this were a substitute, or at least a successor, to colonialism. It is unquestionably the case that these institutions, alongside the constraints due to debt, do create a situation whereby the North dictates the policies of nations of the South. But are we to equate political colonialism—established by an army of occupation—with a balance of power that is economic in nature?

If it is a question of resisting domination, then equating the two is counterproductive: it denies the violence of a military occupation and does not really help us understand how to resist the new forms of domination: unilateral globalization and subservience by debt. Never mind, since what counts for Ramadan is to link, by whatever means, economic imperialism and the extension of human rights: "Human rights are the pretext for economic policies that cannot be presented as such."[36] Once again, this opinion may well be shared by all those who are fed up seeing the American government drape itself in the cloak of humanitarianism every time it acts to defend its financial and oil interests, particularly in Iraq. But Tariq Ramadan has more than Iraq in mind. As it happens, his alternative economic model is none other than that of Hassan al-Tourabi's Sudan. And it is frankly embarrassing to see Tariq Ramadan attempt to head off any criticism of that country's failure to respect human rights on the grounds that Sudan has challenged the dominant economic model.

Sudan as model

The preacher has repeated several times that he condemns the "absence of political liberties" in Sudan.[37] However, Jean-Yves Chaperon, a reporter for Luxembourg's RTL radio and television network, remembers having encountered Tariq Ramadan, "who was well disposed towards Tourabi and his regime" in 1993, on the occasion of the high mass organized by the "Pope of Islamism" in Khartoum.[38] On his return, Ramadan gave several interviews saying how much of a "moderate" Tourabi was.[39] And why would he be critical of his host, seeing as how Tourabi had nothing but words of praise for him! In truth, even if Ramadan has, on occasion, expressed his reservations concerning the lack of public freedom in Sudan, these criticisms have been few and far between, compared to the number of times he has come to the defense of Tourabi and his policies. He has explained, in particular, that the countries "that take a moderate and open-minded view of the West are, as concerns respect for human rights in the political sphere, in a worse situation and less respectful of the elementary rights of man" than Sudan.[40] According to him, if Sudan is on the blacklist of international institutions, it is not because of its violations of human rights, but because it is a threat to American interests: "American propaganda sets the tone and people talk nonsense about this country."[41] Ramadan cites as a model of resistance to globalization the fact that Sudan opted out of the international monetary system in order to develop its own alternative economic model. In general, he looks on economic development as a Western mystification designed to reinforce Western domination, whereas "religion is a factor of true development."[42] The Muslims should thus create "an alternative economy," independent of the world's economic machinery. "What Muslims of any country have to understand is that they have to develop financial independence and political independence."[43] But how is it going to be possible to develop a separatist Islamic economy in a world in which the economy is global? While approving of Sudan quitting the international monetary system, Tariq Ramadan argues for a return to an economy based on raw materials and micro-credit. In fact, what he is advocating is self-sufficiency, in line with his "anti-mixture" phobia in international relations. Here again, he is at cross purposes with the anti-globalists. Tariq Ramadan does not want to block globalization so as to replace it with some "other globalization," but to put an end to all exchanges. That is, he advocates not to restore a certain balance in North–South relations, but to allow Muslim countries once again to institute economies that conform to Islamic rules.

Such a world would not be totally negative, just as not all is totally negative in Sudan. In the name of respecting divine revelation, long-term projects might well see the light of day. There would be less pollution and more agriculture. Unfortunately, it would not represent negotiated progress towards collective well-being, but rather a step backwards, dictated by a totalitarian religious purism. Loans would not be turned down because of the risk of debt accumulation, but because the Koran forbids them, as Tariq Ramadan explains: "The revealed word of the Koran is explicit: he who engages in speculation or loans money for interest is at war with the Transcendent."[44] Al-Banna also proposed an economic reform based on three priorities: agrarian reform, the banning of usury, and the elimination of income tax (to be replaced by the law on the giving of alms). It should be understood that this alternative economy is a regressive process, inseparable from social and political regression. In "Islam and the West" Ramadan offers us a foretaste: "There exists not one society in majority Muslim, nor one Muslim region, that has not made it abundantly clear that a social and political project cannot afford to dispense with Muslim principles."[45]

Resistance will arise from the "Islamic revival"

Tariq Ramadan agrees with Samuel Huntington: "He makes it clear that Muslim civilization is in the process of creating within itself forces of resistance, forces that will resist Westernization."[46] He concurs with Huntington's analysis, which considers Islam to be a possible alternative: "It's a side thesis, but at the same time a capital one that he introduces."[47] Adopting Huntington's binary approach to the issues of civilization, he insists that "the reaffirmation of our identity in religious as well as cultural terms" is "one of the elements that will enable us to redefine North–South relations." More to the point, it is via this reaffirmation that resistance will develop: "The affirmation of Muslim principles can produce resistance to the dominant structures."[48] It is what he calls the "possible alternative offered by the 'Islamic revival.'" He took pleasure in announcing as an "extremely heartening development" the fact that the Islamism inaugurated by his grandfather was gaining ground: "For the last fifty years, although no one foresaw it, there has not been a single society in majority Muslim, nor a single minority Muslim community, that has not been living the revival of its faith."[49] This revival, and the menace it represents for Western interests, is enough to explain, according to him, the demonization of Islamism: "There's no doubt that it is on that account today that demonization and 'diabolization' have become so widespread in the West." Thus resistance to fundamentalism is a "demonization" designed to protect Western interests.

The alternative to the Western model, the revival model that Tariq Ramadan dreams of, bears a striking resemblance to the American "awakenings," the name given to the four turning points in American history, when the evangelists travelled throughout the country to rekindle the faith of their fellow citizens. Tariq Ramadan takes after them. He is a preacher seeking conversions. Moreover, he compares conversion to being "born again," the term used by the fundamentalists to indicate that the rediscovery of faith is like a second birth. Like the most mystic of Christians, he sometimes tells the story of a brother who experienced revelation after a session of spiritualism in which the Koran appeared in a vision, reducing the audience to tears. His concern with proselytizing is such that he pleads for the converted to be "integrated" into the Muslim community.[50] He makes no secret of his determination to make of the West not his battlefield (*dar el-harb*) but his "land of witnessing": *dar el-shahada*. Yet it is worth noting that translation of *dar el-shahada* as "land of witnessing" is in itself a euphemism, for *shahada* is the term used for conversion to Islam. The words "recall" or "witnessing" are, in reality, employed so as to avoid use of another word that is far more accurate, but that provokes hostility: the word "proselytize." Not only has it negative connotations; it is, in theory, contrary to Islam. But Ramadan, despite his denials, is incapable of abdicating. "As for *dawa*, I don't translate it as 'preaching,' for to Christians . . . preaching is proselytizing, and we know we don't have the right to proselytize. We bear witness; we transmit the message and Allah transforms people's hearts."[51] Let us not be fooled. This circumspection with regard to terminology is nothing but a show. Ramadan is a tireless preacher, someone entirely devoted to converting as many people as possible to his vision of Islam. This obsessive proselytizer counts openly on Europe's "spiritual crisis," which he refers to as "the axis of the future," to make of Islam a source of attraction.[52] All his energy, all the effort he puts into fine-tuning his rhetoric and teaching Muslims how to talk to journalists—his network building and infiltration—they are his very life: "We bear the responsibility to remind men of the presence of God, and to act in such a way that our presence among them and with them will consist in itself of a reminder of the Creator, of spirituality and of ethics."[53] It is his most deeply rooted jihad: enlarge, unify and reinforce the *umma,* such as the Muslim Brothers conceived of it: "Fraternity is a jihad. I am on a jihad for fraternity."[54]

The sense of being on a jihad explains why Tariq Ramadan never stays put and never remains at the head of an organization for long. His role is not to supervise an association in one country, but to labor in the field throughout the Occident, so as to give birth to small groups that will together enlarge the *umma.* What Ramadan is aiming at is not national political reform, but a world cultural revolution. One thing he has understood: revolutions are no longer made by mass movements. Thanks to the development of computer networks and the media, a handful of militants who are determined and intelligent, if they occupy strategic posts throughout the planet, can change the face of the world: "Things don't change any more because of the numbers involved, that's over with . . . . You don't need a hundred per city, only ten!," he explained to his troops.[55] In other words, things are easier than they were during the time of Hassan al-Banna, who had stockpiled a thousand rifles to change the course of Egypt's history. For Ramadan's world, cultural revolution draws less on Maoism than on the reformist Salafists who, he claims, had "understood before their time" the degree to which cultural issues came before political ones.[56] Like al-Banna, Tariq Ramadan has a detailed plan in mind, made up of successive stages: "Everything that is international is of interest to us; everything that is national, as well; but our priority is the local."[57] Which does not prevent him from dreaming of an Islamist International, consisting of a multitude of cells concentrating on local issues . . . "Thousands of small-scale initiatives will add up to something big," he promised.[58]

The preacher has effectively played a major role in the rise of Islamism at the local, national and international levels. Wherever he goes, his lectures breathe new life into activist groups, setting them on the right course and giving them a new dynamism, so that soon they will be taking over public debate. In Brussels, for instance, here is how he addressed his followers at a conference given in 1995: "I'll make a little pact with you and the organizers of this conference. Every one of you knows the situation in Brussels. Can we agree that, in one year from now (*insh'allah*), we will meet here again to see what you have been able to do in the meantime?"[59] The preacher kept on insisting. No question of letting the evening go by without producing something concrete: "Create fraternal ties among you, create learning centers for yourselves, create a dynamics in Brussels." He explained to his followers that this was necessary in order for his message to be credible in the eyes of journalists and not give the impression he was isolated: "Your silence will cast doubt on my intentions . . . . Your surrender will cast doubt on what our brothers are saying . . . . Wake up!" And he added: "It is time to speak. It is time to talk Islam!"

Unification is our strength

One of Ramadan's objectives is to globalize the Islamic awakening: "One of the challenges faced by the resistance concerns what I call the phenomenon of transnationality, the transnational reference to Islam. In all countries, the United States as well, the Islamic fervor within Muslim communities is phenomenal." One sole drawback: "These phenomena are not necessarily coordinated. Our greatest problem is that we do not communicate enough with the others."[60] Ramadan sees himself in this role of coordinator. He has been working for years to get the groups in touch with one another, to have them mobilize together. This objective explains why he warns against perpetuating the traditions that belong to the different Muslim cultures. It is not simply a question of protecting Islam from criticism by shifting the blame onto traditional customs; it is also a way of breaking down the cultural barriers between Muslims to facilitate their coming together in one single Islamist International, even if this means standardization and thus the sacrifice of the rich diversity of the Muslim world. It is one of the ironies of his anti-globalization: to defeat globalization, he is prepared to replace one form of globalization—Western—with another, Muslim, standardization. Fiammetta Venner has an expression that sums up this way of trying, at all costs, to weaken Muslim cultural diversity for the sake of a simplified, unified Islam: "Tariq Ramadan, he's Islam's McDonald's."[61] Even if he offers a warning not to "confuse the oneness of our identity with cultural standardization," that is exactly what he is doing when he encourages Muslims to disregard geographical boundaries and consider themselves as Brothers in a single Islam, rid of its historical, local evolution: "And are not the questions that we ask of ourselves as French Muslims the same as those asked in Indonesia? Is it the right thing to do to keep dividing up the world geographically?"[62]

The desire to globalize Islam is not without consequence: it explains why a European leader like Tariq Ramadan refuses explicitly to condemn stoning—out of fear of offending Nigeria, even if it thereby suggests that European Muslims are still debating whether or not they should stone someone to death for adultery! In addition to weakening local cultures, the standardization sought by Ramadan always involves further radicalization of Muslims. After having awakened them, and connected them to the network, the preacher spends his time and energy having them lose all critical sense vis-à-vis the Islamists, and—the flip side—having them learn to scorn liberal Muslims. All this in the name of Islamic fraternity! Woe betide anyone who treats a brother or a sister "dressed according to the sunna . . . as an extremist!"[63] On the basis of a verse of the Koran, he strikes terror into any Muslim who would take it into his head to suspect another Muslim of being a fundamentalist: "Speaking ill of one's brother is like eating one's own flesh. Do you intend to eat the flesh of your brother once he is dead?," he asked in dramatic tones of his dumbfounded audience. And what does he give as an example of criticism to be avoided? The rumors circulating that suggest Secours Islamique, or Islamic Relief, is an Islamist organization that seeks to Islamize rather than just help. But according to Tariq Ramadan, a Muslim who believes such rumors is a traitor to his community. "It has been said: the Secours Islamique, there are questions about it. But have you checked into it? Have you done your research? If you don't know, keep it for yourself!"[64] And what does he cite as the division that represents the supreme sin against the community? The attack by the Muslims of the Northern Alliance under Commander Massoud on the Taliban!

Ramadan had people believe that he was close to Commander Massoud during the war against the Soviets. However, he was forthright in his condemnation of the Northern Alliance once it went to war with the Taliban. On December 11, 1994, during a conference given for the Association des étudiants islamiques de France (Association of Islamic Students of France), a founding member of which was Hassan al-Tourabi, he expressed anger at the idea of Massoud's Northern Alliance besieging Kabul:

> Many of you were pleased and happy to see that, in the name of "There is no God but God," the Afghan people rose up against their Russian oppressors. They fought against oppression and defended themselves like true freedom fighters. But just look at what a disaster it is today. Have you seen what is happening? The defense of selfish interests has won out over the thought of God, and they have taken to killing each other. At the very moment that I am speaking to you, not one hour goes by without a rocket falling on Kabul. Muslims suffering terrible violence at the hands of other Muslims. . . . Is that not forgetting the very essence of our faith?[65]

Ramadan does not defend the same Islam as the Taliban, but he never has really harsh words for these fundamentalists that he defines, at worst, as adherents to a particularly traditionalist, even reactionary, interpretation of Islam, especially as regards women; yet he asks European Muslims to respect the sincerity of their ways.[66] After this he drops his skepticism, granting them a form of absolution in his haste to condemn foreign influences: "We are well aware that the great powers know how to exploit sincerity for their own ends. Today, behind the Taliban, there is the Pakistani secret service, there is Saudi Arabia, and, behind them all, there is the United States, which considers this ultra-closed society an obstacle to its geostrategic plans for the region."[67] He is far more severe with regard to Saudi Wahhabism, which he finds catastrophic; but here again, his criticism serves essentially as a means of attacking American influence. In fact, Ramadan is never as hard on the fundamentalists as he is on their enemies. In general, the ban on speaking ill of other Muslims means only not speaking ill of the Muslim Brotherhood, and in particular of him, who must be protected against the critics. On the other hand, as we have seen, he reserves the right to "eat the flesh" of certain Muslims, such as the modernist Muslims that he makes a habit of referring to as false Muslims (when it is not "Islamophobes"). The call for fraternity is designed to stymie all criticism of fundamentalists. And the expected result is the radicalization of all Muslims who fall under his influence.

The merest doubt about 9/11

Tariq Ramadan has often claimed to be an outstanding agent of peace: "On several occasions I have had the opportunity of speaking with government authorities, and they were well informed in regard to the Islam that I advocate—an open-minded Islam that participates in society in a positive way," he declared to Agence France-Presse at the time he was banned from entering France. He does advocate "an open-minded Islam"—but only for the benefit of the outside world. And even then . . .

Whenever he is asked—in particular by the press—he is, of course, quick to condemn terrorism. As almost all Islamists do—when asked. They will tell you they condemn terrorism, but approve of "resistance." If one listens closely, these are exactly the terms used by Tariq Ramadan. On October 3, 2001, he published an opinion piece in *Le Monde* which began with these words: "The condemnation of the attacks on the United States must be unanimous."[68] A nice start. Unfortunately, this severity did not last long. In the following sentences, Tariq Ramadan insinuated that there was no proof that bin Laden or any Muslims had been behind 9/11: "Is it possible, in the midst of this outpouring of unquestioned affirmations, to express the slightest doubt? For, after all, there's reason to be upset if one compares the incredible sophistication of the methods used to prepare and pull off such an act—and the series of blunders committed afterwards that pointed to the bin Laden connection." And he added: "The real question still needs to be asked: who stands to profit by these attacks? No 'Arab' or 'Islamic' cause will derive any advantage." The rest of the article is designed to show that the American government undoubtedly profited from these attacks, seizing the opportunity to curtail public liberties and launch a crusade against the Muslim world. Which led him to call on Muslims and non-Muslims to "resist" such an eventuality "together."

It is about the only time that Tariq Ramadan has taken pen in hand to condemn terrorism. His declaration would be moving—and even the second part of his analysis would be acceptable—if it did not serve to imply that the American government stood to gain from the 9/11 attacks! That leaves a sour aftertaste, coming as it does from an Islamist leader who claims to be an agent of peace.

His lack of enthusiasm in condemning Muslim extremism also emerged in another interview he gave to the French news weekly *Le Point* the month after the attacks of March 11, 2004 in Madrid. This time it was as an expert on Islam and the West that Tariq Ramadan was interviewed, and he declared in professorial tones: "You will find no support worth mentioning, whether in the French suburbs or in Muslim countries, for the interventions in New York, Bali or Madrid. One must not confuse the resistance in Iraq or Palestine with pro-bin Laden operations."[69] Tariq Ramadan is really a past master in the art of euphemisms. Thus, the attacks by Hamas, or those launched by Saddam Hussein's partisans, including those that have killed civilians (Israelis and Iraqis!), are elevated to the rank of "resistance," not to be confused with "pro-bin Laden operations." Even more serious, the pro-bin Laden operations are no longer referred to as "attacks" but as mere "interventions." The term came as a shock to more than one attentive reader. It was all the more revealing since Tariq Ramadan always chooses his words with great care. A member of his thesis jury was shocked at his way of phrasing things. In *Aux sources du renouveau musulman* [*On the Origins of the Muslim Renaissance*], the preacher spoke of the murder of Anwar Sadat by a Muslim Brother as an "execution" and not an "assassination." One of the distinguished professors on the jury picked up on it, but the word remained unchanged.

The mildness with which Tariq Ramadan condemns terrorism when he is speaking outside the Muslim community affords us a glimpse of what he says within it. In his lectures, the objective is not to warn against this plague, but rather to reprimand those who oppose the extremists—in particular the media, which he accuses of caricaturing Islamism, insinuating at the same time that these campaigns are related to the influence of intellectuals bent on defending Israeli interests. Only a few days after 9/11, the preacher gave a lecture in Vénissieux organized by the Union of Young Muslims. Was he going to take advantage of the occasion to make the young of this particularly radical association aware of their responsibilities? A *Lyon Mag* journalist who attended the conference reported the following: "Whereas the young Muslims spoke of nothing else but the attacks, Tariq never said a word about them throughout his lecture. He waited until the very last minute to mention the tragedy, insisting that there was no evidence implicating bin Laden. And he added, in front of several hundred young Muslims, that if any state had an interest in launching the attack, it was Israel."[70]

Pro-Hamas

Manifestly, the idea of a Zionist conspiracy is a most handy way of cleansing the blood that stains the hands of the Muslim Brotherhood in Algeria and elsewhere. At other times, the attitude of Israel serves to justify recourse to murder, including the murder of children and civilians. In an interview given to the magazine *Panorama* of Milan, cited in the *Courrier International* edition of September 16 to 22, 2004, regarding an eight-year-old child, killed because she would be a soldier when she grew up, Tariq Ramadan declared: "In itself it's morally condemnable, but understandable given the context," since "the international community has delivered the Palestinians into the hands of their oppressors." In general, he stands by the positions taken by Hamas, whose *fatwa* authorizing suicide attacks comes from Yusuf al-Qaradawi. He makes a point of presenting the Islamist terrorist movement as a model of legitimate resistance. In *Questioning Islam*, flanked by Alain Gresh, he vigorously defended the military branch representing the Muslim Brothers in Palestine: "All those who have been there can testify to the fact that the labels 'obtuse fundamentalists' and 'extremists' that they have foisted on Hamas in no way correspond to reality; the majority of the leaders are in favor of dialogue and have never spoken of 'driving the Jews into the sea.'"[71] Despite which, they have taken to blowing them up from time to time . . . Tariq Ramadan added a few lines afterwards: "I have spoken of the illegitimacy of attacking civilians, but have the hypocrisy and the cynicism of the American government—and the Arab government as well—left the Palestinians any choice?"

Tariq Ramadan was a latecomer as a pro-Palestinian supporter. In Geneva, where there was a very active pro-Palestinian network, no one remembered having seen him. "It was never his cause," one of the activists of the movement confided to me, preferring to remain anonymous. In fact, his position on Palestine only emerged when Hamas began to play a role in the conflict. Like the Hamas that he defends, he was critical both of Yasser Arafat and of the peace process. As for the rest, most of what we know of his position on Palestine comes from the snatches of conversation that figure in his book of interviews with Alain Gresh. There he explains that, since advocating the destruction of Israel was not tenable, he had come round to the solution of a single state governed by Jews, Christians, and Muslims:

> In the end, a single state will have to be established . . . . This state should grant everyone—Jew and Christian, Muslim and humanist—an equal status as citizen and the right for his religion to be respected both in daily life and in the holy places. It is difficult to define the exact nature of this state. We have to proceed by stages, beginning by analyzing the existing structures, both Israeli and Palestinian, and studying in detail the reality of the discriminations written into the law. In the end, with the increase in the Israeli, Arab, and non-Jewish population we will have to question, in Claude Klein's phrase, "the Jewish character of the state of Israel."[72]

Appearances notwithstanding, this proposal for a single state, in which everyone would be accepted, bears no resemblance whatsoever to the secular, but at the same time utopian, proposal made by the PLO in the 1970s. Ramadan proposes not destroying the state of Israel, but replacing it with a single state, whose Jewish nature would soon be . . . "questioned." That is to say, called into question. And how? By stages? But of course—by stages, as always. The first stage: proclamation of a state in which Jews, Christians, and Muslims are declared equal. A splendid idea, which would, in effect, provide a way of ending the discrimination from which Palestinians and Arab Israelis suffer. The problem is that, with Ramadan, this egalitarian state is only a first step. He has already admitted as much. With the increase in the population that is "Arab and non-Jewish"—meaning Muslim—it will be necessary to take stock of the situation and redefine the nature of this state. "Difficult to define the exact nature of this state," he tells us. Difficult, at any rate, to express it publicly before reaching that stage. The Muslim Brotherhood is already dreaming of restoring the caliphate, in which Jews and Christians would be classed as *dhimmis*.[73] There is no reason to believe that Ramadan does not share this dream.

Anti-Semitic?

Does that mean he is anti-Semitic? Not in the European sense. Ramadan is faithful to the Koran. The Jews, who can be allies of the Muslims, are "protected" and fully accepted. "They are in right guidance," says the Koran.[74] Ramadan agrees. He has nothing against Jews—if they lend him their support. The others, however, immediately become his worst enemies. In the Koran, the Jews who refuse to support Islam are doubly cursed, described as "lost souls" that God has transformed into apes and swine, "obstinate in their rebellion," deserving nothing but hatred: "Amongst them we have stirred up enmity and hatred until the Day of Resurrection."[75] The ambiguity of the Koran, torn between two extremes in its treatment of the Jews, is also that of Ramadan, always ready to denounce attacks on Jews, especially religious Jews, but at the same time imagining a Jewish conspiracy around every corner. In 2002, Ramadan and his followers condemned the acts of violence perpetrated against Jewish places of worship. It is the least one could expect on the part of a monotheist, hoping that inter-religion dialogue will lead all monotheists to make common cause against atheistic materialism. In this regard, Ramadan has never been a Judeophobe. He is quite ready to sign petitions for peace between Palestinians and Israelis, along with other intellectuals. But none of this really indicates whether he is anti-Semitic. Whenever one tries to get to the bottom of his feelings about Jews as a people, he emphasizes the fact of having come to the defense of Jews as members of the Jewish faith. As if the absence of Judeophobia signified absence of anti-Semitism. This ambiguity has its advantages. In particular, it divides the Left, split between those who think that Ramadan is anti-Semitic and those who believe the accusation to be unfounded—an opportunity for the preacher to see who are his real collaborators and who are more reticent.

Solidarity with Algerians . . . but Islamist Algerians

Has Tariq Ramadan even once stopped to think compassionately of all those intellectuals, artists, men, women, and children murdered in the name of Allah in Algeria? No. In the glossary that was published as an annex to the French edition of *Etre musulman européen* [*To Be a European Muslim*], after the *Nouvel Observateur* ended up refusing it, here is all he has to say about the Islamic Salvation Front:

> The leaders of the political wing of the Front are a mixed bag. Voices are raised that are constructive and reasonable, but they vie with others that are far more reactionary, more aggressive, and more obtuse. Early on, the Islamic Salvation Front piled blunder on blunder and made political mistake after political mistake, and its responsibility for the present state of Algeria is considerable. One must, however, remember that the electoral process was cut short, and no error of a political nature can justify the terrifying repression unleashed against them.[76]

This sentence is the ultimate in political cant, fit to be recorded in the annals of Islamist rhetoric. It would be a laughing matter if the result were not to play down the fact of so many deaths. Every word is weighed, and weighed again, but the net effect is finally quite clear. Tariq Ramadan reproaches the Islamic Salvation Front above all for having committed "blunders," in other words for not having respected the rhythm that was part of Hassan al-Banna's method of establishing an Islamic regime without encountering resistance—"blunders" that could not justify the "terrible repression" of which they were the victims. This double standard is appalling, coming as it does from a man who was in contact with the Front's leaders. He does, in fact, say that he pointed out to them how wrong they were to use every means to prevent women from working . . . Did he really not have anything more to say to them? It would appear not.

From the same glossary, this is what he had to say about the Armed Islamic Groups (GIA): "The Armed Groups are to be condemned outright. Yet, at the same time, it is clear that these groups are infiltrated. Perhaps one day we will know more about the double game played by certain high-ups in the military who stuff their pockets while the bodies of so many Algerians are drained of their blood." But who is draining these bodies of their blood? Who is massacring entire villages? The army? That is what Islamists like Tariq Ramadan and his brother are insinuating. It is possible that the Algerian army did try to infiltrate some GIA cells to arrest or even liquidate the jihadists, in particular when Zeitouni was in command of the GIA—a leader so bloodthirsty that he succeeded in creating havoc within the organization itself. It is probable that the security forces tried to stir up rivalries within the GIA to put an end to their deadly hold on Algeria. But is it enough to assert that the Islamists were manipulated by the army for them to be forgiven the blood on their hands? This revisionism, combined with conspiracy paranoia, is unfortunately not that uncommon among the militant anti-colonialists, bent at all costs on casting the Islamists in the role of victims. It is even more chilling when it comes from one of the descendants of Hassan al-Banna, trained in the school of Qutb, and in contact with the "oppressed" in question.

Once again, if Tariq Ramadan is willing to talk in these terms publicly, imagine what he teaches within the movement! In his lectures, each time he takes up the question of Algeria, Ramadan laments the death of the Islamists, but not the democrats' dead. "It's not only intellectuals that have been killed in Algeria, intellectuals who think in Western terms; the entire political class of committed Muslim intellectuals has been decimated."[77] In other words, Tariq Ramadan treats as equivalent the radical militants ready to kill to take power and the men and women fighting to maintain freedom who have been assassinated simply because they dared denounce the Islamists' violence. Sorry, he does not treat them as equivalent . . . He considers it abominable that Islamists have gone to their death because they wanted to establish an Islamic dictatorship, but remains coldly indifferent to the murders and threats of death that have been visited on those Algerian intellectuals who have resisted Islamism. Moreover, he refuses to consider as "intellectuals" Algerian women such as Khalida Messaoudi who have opposed Islamism: "One day it will come out that she has been subsidized, aided and supported by the regime in power."[78] Tariq Ramadan was hostile to Messaoudi not because she accepted support from the Algerian government for her campaign in defense of Algerian women; he was hostile to her because she fought against the Islamists of the Islamic Salvation Front.

When speaking within the movement, Ramadan denounces the "smear campaign" aimed at Ibn Taymiyya, the man that all the Islamists look up to, including the extremists; the man whom Ramadan recommends and whom he defends as having "a method and an approach intellectually well founded."[79] Taymiyya's approach is so well founded that it is invoked by the Islamists who have gone in for murder, in particular the GIA members who assassinated seven Trappist monks in Tibéhirine in 1996. To be sure, Tariq Ramadan does not approve of this sort of thing, but it is the death of Islamist fighters that he regrets the most: "The assassination of the monks is an abhorrence that we condemn in the same way and with the same intensity that we condemn the murder of all those intellectuals of whom nothing is said and who are killed because of their faith."[80] The statement just goes to show how quickly the condemnation of the GIA is passed over. It serves as a pretext for immediately lamenting the loss of the militants of the Islamic Salvation Front and the GIA, whom Ramadan treats as "intellectuals," in order the better to denigrate those intellectuals "of whom the press does speak" and who have been killed because they resisted the Islamists. Ramadan speaks of these murders, in particular the murder of the monks, as being "a dishonor for the GIA," but he adds that the assassinations only go to prove "the inability of the Algerian government to ensure internal security."[81] But ensure internal security against whom?

If he really disapproved of the GIA, Ramadan would not be a friend of the only man to have dared declare in writing that the Tibéhirine massacre was justified in terms of the Koran: Yahya Michot. In 1997, this Belgian convert to Islam came to prominence for having dug out a *fatwa* of Ibn Taymiyya, dating from 1417, that proved the murder was justified on religious grounds. His booklet—*Le statut des moines* [*Rules Pertaining to Monks*]—was published under the name of Nasreddin Lebatelier, but Michot finally admitted to being the author. It is said there that, in cases of conflict, the killing of monks is permitted if they are in contact with other men (for they could keep Muslims from pursuing their goals). On the other hand, it is illicit if the monks are within walls. The GIA assassins thus acted in perfect conformity with Ibn Taymiyya, since they murdered all the monks, except for one who had taken refuge in his cell. This led Michot to conclude that the monks should have heeded the order to leave the country issued by the GIA in 1993: "The drama could, no doubt, have been avoided with a bit of common sense, if the monks had agreed to 'take a bit of a vacation in France.'"[82] In brief, the man is far from respectable. Few non-jihadist reformers have agreed to be seen with him since. Tariq Ramadan, however, is still one of his friends. In March 2002, the preacher even wrote a preface to his latest book, a book published by Jeunesse sans Frontières, the Islamist association of Montpellier for which Tariq Ramadan is an esteemed figure. Admittedly, the book does not deal with Tibéhirine. It is entitled *Musulman en Europa* [*Muslim in Europe*], but Ramadan's moral support was an eloquent message for all the young Muslims who followed this affair. All the more so, in that Michot indicated in his bibliography that he had translated Ibn Taymiyya's *fatwa*. One might have expected that Ramadan would express some reservations over the positions taken by the author. Not at all. Ramadan recommended Yahya Michot as "a brother and a friend." He had nothing but praise for him, presenting him as "one of the few Muslim thinkers who know how appealing a generous sense of humor can be." Er . . . But Ramadan does take care to leave himself a way out by adding the following sentence, meaningless in itself, but which he can always cite if necessary: "Many a time we were in disagreement, often we were at odds." But over what? The youngsters who read the book will never know. And as a result, they adopt as a model this "brother" recommended by Ramadan—this brother so humorous and so apropos. In the book, Michot describes Ibn Taymiyya as "our principal guide" and "one of the great Muslim scholars."[83] He frequently cites Khomeini, refers to the modern *jahiliyya* (the pre-Islamic decadence), goes back over the Crusades once again to exonerate the Muslims of any guilt for the crimes committed in the name of Islam : "I would say straight out, even if it may appear shocking, that we Muslims can afford to kill a lot, to liquidate and massacre a lot, before reaching the degree of inhumanity that was the standard in the past for the ancestors of those who today accuse Islam of being a religion of violence."[84] What a splendid model for European Muslim youth! And what a calling card for someone who claims to be an uncompromising agent of peace.

The bait

Unlike his brother, Tariq Ramadan does not have to call openly for a jihad to radicalize the Muslims that listen to him. His "open-minded" Islam is far more efficacious. His approach, seemingly moderate, succeeds in attracting the more or less modern Muslims that he will gradually initiate into radicalism, and then fundamentalism, the environment that produces future terrorists. How? By pretending to advocate a form of fraternity and tolerance that has the effect, above all, of making any moderate Muslim feel guilty in comparison to the extremists. Once their vigilance has been dismantled, he has only to put those he has thus outfitted in touch with the Brothers' network. A youngster lured by the "modern" language of Tariq Ramadan will begin by ceasing to look on fundamentalists with a critical eye. He will be convinced, from then on, that those who are hostile to the Islamists are Islamophobes. Having studied al-Banna's thought and his method, he will, from this point on, belong to a fraternity that stretches from the Union of Islamic Organizations of France to Hamas, via the Islamic Salvation Front and the GIA. He will absorb all that Tariq Ramadan has written, even the books he has prefaced. The girls will have as their model Zaynab al-Ghazali and the boys will eat up Yahya Michot. The religious authority will be Yusuf al-Qaradawi, the Muslim Brothers' theologian that Ramadan recommends, the man who approves of suicide attacks. Ramadan also recommends Mawlawi, the head of one of the principal Lebanese terrorist organizations. "Mawlawi is right to emphasize that, according to the majority of the ulemas, Muslims are bound by the decisions and the acts of an unjust leader or a dictator 'so long as he does not commit a sin or act contrary to the teachings of Islam.'"[85] Even if Ramadan talks of using "legal means," remember that it is in the name of these legal means that Qutb yesterday and Mawlawi today call for a jihad against "apostate" tyrants. Given his influence, does it come as a surprise that Tariq Ramadan's name appears in the dossiers held on certain terrorists? Or that Djamel Beghal, the Lyon Islamist arrested for terrorist activities, had listened to his lectures without ever being dissuaded from waging a jihad? Does it come as a shock to learn that Malika, the wife of one of the two assassins of Massoud was a Ramadan fan—or that she approved of her husband's act?[86] Does it come as surprise, finally, that Tariq Ramadan continues to be the star performer of the most hardline Muslim Brothers—in Algeria, in Yemen, in Syria—despite a press that still sometimes insists on presenting him as a reformer and a pacifier? The answer is simply that the press is mistaken: Tariq Ramadan is not an agent of peace but an agent of radicalization—all the more to be feared in that he is so difficult to pin down.

Chapter 7

The West as the Land of "Collaborations"

Tariq Ramadan knows full well that the future of Islam is to be played out not in the Orient but in the Occident. While Islamism has its work cut out for it in the Maghreb and the Machrek (the Middle East), because of government repression and the mobilization of civil society, the West, with its human rights provisions, offers a sanctuary from which to launch campaigns to swell the ranks and prepare for revenge. Ever since the failure in Algeria, this strategy has been the top priority of the Muslim Brotherhood. The fact that Yusuf al-Qaradawi turned down the official role of Supreme Guide, explaining that he would be more useful in Europe, speaks volumes for the fraternity's hope of initiating the Islamist awakening in Europe. As leader of the international branch of the Muslim Brotherhood, Saïd Ramadan was the first to believe in this strategy. Of all his heirs, Tariq Ramadan is the most gifted. In the past fifteen years he has proved a remarkably effective agent in the service of this idea. He has ensured Islamic renewal by the *dawa*, while at the same time weakening the forces opposed to Islamism thanks to the contacts he has established with other religious leaders, with academia and, above all, with the anti-globalist, secular Left.

The *dawa* not only functions by means of conversion or by radicalizing Western Muslims. In Tariq Ramadan's own words, it is a question of establishing "spheres of collaboration" with non-Muslims. The term is his. On his cassettes, he openly encourages his followers to form alliances: "I want you to understand that we are not alone in daring to challenge this Westernization that is without soul and without conscience . . . . The future hinges on being intelligent enough to grasp a dual approach: locate the spheres of resistance and develop the spheres of collaboration . . . . We cannot remain one against the many."[1] One would, at first, think that Ramadan is calling on Muslims to become the allies of non-Muslims vis-à-vis globalization. Except that we know what Ramadan means by resisting Westernization: not some "other" globalization, but a *Confrontation of Civilizations* that will result in the triumph of Islam. Here is how it is explained on his cassettes:

> Look, I'm going to turn Huntington's proposal around. What did Huntington say? He said that the Occidental powers should seek out in the Muslim countries those who defend the West's ideology. That's to say, seek out the Muslims known as "secular" or the Muslims known as "liberal." You know: the Muslims without Islam! . . . Well as for us, those with whom we're going to cooperate, it's exactly the opposite. We're going to locate in the West—and collaborate with—all those who defend rights, justice, and human dignity. We're going to develop these bridges; we're going to be there in the center of academic and social dialogue. For there are lots of people who have negative opinions about Islam because they don't know it, but who will be ready once they do know it—once they are talked to in the right way—ready to defend, along with us, the rights of Muslims and more and more . . . . Believe me, this phenomenon is already under way. So we are against a philosophy of conflict, but we are for a philosophy of resistance within collaboration.[2]

The word "collaboration" is not without significance. For those who might have been tempted to think that this common resistance implied an exchange, Ramadan set the record straight: "Some people think that the opposite of conflict is marriage. No. The opposite of conflict, it's intelligent resistance and collaboration concerning what is just and honest; it's not a form of submission—we resist, and we collaborate on the intellectual level."[3] In other words, you must separate the sheep from the goats. Ramadan knows that he needs the Westerners, and even certain atheists, to conduct his jihad against "Westernization" and atheistic materialism—but he has no intention of losing his soul in the process. It's clearly a question of a temporary alliance, until the great day dawns. On that day, the Left, and the non-Muslims in general, will, in any case, be so few in number that they will be no match for the Islamists bent on establishing an ideal society based on the sharia. Meanwhile, following what happened in Iran, Ramadan has understood that there is a vast store of potential allies, either conniving or naive, ready to support him if he knows how to handle them tactfully. Herein lies the reason for his double talk, conceived as a way of establishing political bridges.

The strategic advantages of double talk

Wafa al-Banna was certainly right to entrust her son, Tariq, with the job of preaching to the outside world. Never has an actor been better suited to his role. In the course of the last fifteen years, during which he has practiced speaking both to ultra-radical Islamist audiences and to ultra-skeptical audiences of secular activists, he has become a virtuoso of rhetorical and semantic undermining—an art that he has taught his followers, to whom he has explained the necessity of having "a strategy of communication" so as to establish "spheres of collaboration": "There are, in fact, an enormous number of people who are ready—intellectuals, thinkers, people with social obligations—people who would be ready to be partners in our resistance on one condition: that we develop our ability to communicate."[4] In order to be more effective, he has urged Muslims to know their various audiences and adapt accordingly: "You must attune your speech in accordance with the ear that is listening to you. It's essential, but to attune your speech to the ear that is listening, you must also know that ear's disposition."[5] With his usual shrewdness, he speaks of this adaptation process as "developing a form of discourse that clarifies so that we can communicate with our interlocutors."[6] Never mind "clarifying": this is more like duplicity, used in an attempt to deflect any suspicion.

Tariq Ramadan edited—and for the most part wrote himself—a little treatise on "understanding, terminology and language" for the benefit of French-speaking Muslims. The first objective, we are told, is to "adopt a form of discourse that is faithful to our principles" while at the same time being "understood." One passage stipulates: "Being faithful to our principles is the priority."[7] Published by Tawhid, this brochure constituted the proceeding of the International Symposium of French-speaking Muslims, held in Abidjan on August 4–6, 2000. Ramadan directed a workshop on the semantic modifications of the terms "rights, rationality, democracy and community." For each term, the booklet explains how the word is understood by Westerners and what problems it poses for Muslims, and proposes a "conceptual formulation" that amounts to a redefinition capable of confusing listeners.

Here we find all the preacher's semantic tricks. The word "rationality," for example, is not the equivalent of a critical attitude born of the Enlightenment, but "an intellectual process leading to the rediscovery of faith." Just one example among many. In fact, for every key word that Ramadan knows will be sprung on him, he has developed a second definition—of which all those who have attended his courses or read his most confidential books are apprised. This makes it possible for him to speak in an apparently inoffensive manner, while remaining resolutely "on" his eminently Islamist message, and without openly lying—at least to his way of thinking. If one adds that Ramadan has redefined the word "secularism" as simply a context in which freedom of religious faith is guaranteed, and not as the separation between the religious and the political; that by "citizenship" he means a "geographical region" and not a country to which one is bound; and that he claims to be a reformer, while forgetting to specify that he is in favor of a fundamentalist reform—then you can see why so many people are wrong about him. On the outside, Ramadan appears as a rationalist reformer, advocating civic participation on the part of Muslims, and thus their acceptance of the laws of the Republic. Within the movement, his followers know full well that Ramadan is a fundamentalist preacher who counts on them to make use of their status as citizens to bend the laws "towards more Islam." And it is those on the inside that have got it right. They have at their disposal the "translation manual" that enables them to read between the lines of Ramadan's official discourse, which is designed to appeal to an outside audience.

Once again, the reliance on a doublespeak, internal and external, is not confined to Islamists alone. It is a tactic used by all sects and by all movements that wish to conceal their objectives. But Ramadan is a champion at this game, even modulating his tone of voice to fit the public he is addressing. On his audiocassettes, when speaking to a Muslim audience, his tone of voice is that of a full-fledged preacher, even scary at times. Almost all his sentences are laced with quotations from the Koran, and he never pronounces the name of the Prophet without adding the ritual benediction: "Peace and blessings on his name" in Arabic. When speaking at a public meeting or on TV, Ramadan keeps a low profile, speaks in a slightly timid, academic voice, hardly ever cites the Koran and, above all, carefully avoids mentioning the name of the Prophet, so as not to have to recite the obligatory benediction.

In fifteen years, the "heir presumptive" has become an expert at defusing semantic landmines. All his expressions, all his euphemisms are carefully thought through and judiciously calculated, so as to overcome resistance and convert the skeptical. The rest of his strategy comes down to a shrewdly conceived program of infiltration, by which he convinces those on the Right as well as those on the Left; the most anti-religious as well as the most religious; Tony Blair as well as the anti-globalists . . . And all to the one end that he will never admit: advance of the *dawa*—Islamization as the Muslim Brotherhood conceives it.

Doublespeak on trial

Some people have been on to Ramadan's doublespeak for a while. Arab and/or Muslim journalists and intellectuals, for example, are not fooled. They are too well aware of his method to be taken in, and are impervious to accusations of "Islamophobia." Antoine Sfeir is one of them. Editor of the *Cahiers de l'Orient*, not only is he an expert on Islam with a perfect mastery of the subject, but he is also a Lebanese intellectual esteemed both in France and abroad. A Christian—one who is both Arab and pro-Palestinian—he is an ambassador of the Orient respected for his culture, his discernment, and his typically Levantine manners. He is one of the very first journalists to have warned of Tariq Ramadan's "double discourse." His vigilance was matched by that of *Lyon Mag*, an independent investigative journal based in Lyon that was well situated to observe the devastation sown by the preacher. In October 2001, one month after the 9/11 attacks, the journal braved the taboo and asked the question that everyone had tried to duck: "Should we be afraid of the Islamist networks in Lyon?"[8] The result of the inquiry was devastating for Ramadan, whose ambiguities stood revealed. It was the first article that had really served to unmask him. It was also the first time that the preacher decided to go to court. But *Lyon*

Mag did not back down. In January 2002, the editorial staff decided to substantiate their allegations by interviewing Antoine Sfeir, who confirmed what they had thought. Sfeir spoke of "a skilful orator," "a persuasive fundamentalist," "a specialist in doublespeak." He did not class Ramadan among the violent, but by no means minimized the danger he represented:

> I consider the non-violent to be the most dangerous, precisely because they appear inoffensive. The terrorists are hunted down. The non-violent appear reassuring. Sometimes they even succeed in putting an end to delinquency in certain neighborhoods. And this delights the police, who don't themselves have enough authority to impose order. To me, it's the Islamists that are most frightening. . . . All these movements that are actively opposed to integration, it's a real time bomb.

The analysis could not be more accurate. It is therefore all the more embarrassing. And this time, for once, Ramadan could hardly accuse Antoine Sfeir of racism without making a fool of himself. And there was no question of intimidating Sfeir by leaving insulting messages on his answering machine or putting pressure on his superiors. So he went to court a second time. The two cases, the lawsuit against *Lyon Mag* and the suit against Sfeir, were combined into one. The verdict was tough on Ramadan. In the decision handed down on May 22, 2003, the Appeals Court of Lyon agreed that Sfeir was right to declare that the language employed by preachers such as Tariq Ramadan "can influence young Muslims and can serve as a factor inciting them to join up with those engaged in violent acts."

Embarassing. But Ramadan found a way of softening the blow. He had people believe that he won against Sfeir by deliberately mixing up the two cases, the one concerning the editor of the *Cahiers de l'Orient* and the other concerning *Lyon Mag*. He did this so that he could claim on TV that he had won his lawsuits against all those who had accused him of resorting to a double language. On the TV show *Campus*, for example, on December 4, 2003, he was targeted by Guillaume Durand: "You lost the lawsuit against Antoine Sfeir . . . " But Ramadan persevered . . . and lied: "No, I won my suit against Antoine Sfeir." The *Cahiers de l'Orient* editor couldn't get over it: "I knew he was adept at doublespeak; now I know he's a horrendous liar as well."

Conclusion

When I began this inquiry, I had, as you can imagine, certain preconceptions about Tariq Ramadan. Having read a number of his books, I expected to be analyzing a form of discourse that was deceptive in its complexity but not necessarily duplicitous. I was convinced that the portrait I would gain would be not of a progressive anti-globalist, but of a bigot and a moralist—though not especially of a fundamentalist. I thought I would come across the Muslim Brotherhood, or at least their influence; but I still believed Ramadan when he claimed he was an independent thinker. I do not believe him any longer.

The months spent dissecting his evolution, his discourse, and his impact have convinced me that he is a pure product of al-Banna's ideology, without doubt one of its most dangerous emissaries, and certainly the most effective. The opacity of his objectives is not due to the complexity of his language: it is a rhetorical Trojan horse, skilfully put together so as to confuse and finally to overcome resistance. Thanks to a double-sided sales pitch that conveys one meaning on the "inside" and another on the "outside," he lives up to all his promises: he disarms those who are wary of Islamism, establishes "spheres of collaboration," discredits the liberal Muslims and radicalizes the others. It is quite possible that some tendencies within the Brotherhood are not wholly in accord with the strategy employed by al-Banna's grandson, but the others are quite right to trust him. What he is in the process of accomplishing, following in the footsteps of Saïd Ramadan, could well result in the realization of his father's dream and that of al-Banna before him. Like his father, Tariq has understood that the future of Islamism is to be played out in the West. He is better equipped than his father to penetrate democracy, to take advantage of freedom of speech to exploit the naiveté of the West and make it his area of operations: for dawa, for *shahada*—and for revenge. Surprising though it may seem, it is this dream that motivates Tariq Ramadan, descendant of the founder of the Muslim Brotherhood, who fills in for us, lecture after lecture, the outlines of an ideal society made up of Muslim individuals faithful to their origins, traditional Muslim families, and a Muslim "social arena."

But Ramadan is not without his own particular way of advancing towards this ideal. While remaining scrupulously faithful to the strategy mapped out by his grandfather, a strategy of advance stage by stage, he adapts it to his context. He aims not at a national takeover of power in Egypt, but at a transnational cultural revolution. That is why he never stays put; why he is constantly jetting from one airport to the next, either to sap the forces opposed to Islamism or to galvanize the Muslims—ever in search of conversions, obsessed with the idea of coordinating this "Islamic revival." His father and his grandfather alone changed the course of history. Tariq Ramadan has inherited their energy. He is perfectly capable, on his own, of hastening the coming of obscurantism.

Do we have here a providential man we can expect to modernize Islam and encourage dialogue between civilizations? The answer is no. And it is high time we put an end to our naiveté lest we become his accomplices.

Notes

Chapter one

1 Quoted by Xavier Ternisien in his portrayal of Tariq Ramadan in *La France des mosquées* [*France and its Mosques*], Paris, Albin Michel, 2002, pp. 206–22.

2 TV program videotaped in November 1997 by the Belgian broadcaster RTBF.

3 "L'intellectuel musulman fait peur! [The Muslim intellectual is frightening!]," *Le Journal du Mardi*, no. 155, March 9, 2004. Interview with Laurent Arnauts and Malika Es-Saïdi.

4 *Homme*, January 2004. *Homme* is the premier Moroccan men's magazine.

5 Laura Secor, "The reformer," *Boston Globe*, November 30, 2003.

6 Alain Gresh and Tariq Ramadan, *L'Islam en questions* [*Questioning Islam*], a debate organized and presented by Françoise Germain-Robin, Sindbad, 2002, pp. 33–34. Babel/Sindbad collection directed by Farouk Mardam-Bey (1st ed. 2000).

7 The Muslim Brotherhood's creed, ratified by the third congress of the Muslim Brotherhood in March 1935, in Olivier Carré and Michel Seurat, *Les Frères Musulmans (1928–1982)*, Paris, L'Harmattan, 2001 (1st ed., Gallimard, 1983).

8 Gresh and T. Ramadan, *L'Islam en questions*, p. 35.

9 *Ibid.*, p. 37.

10 Tariq Ramadan cassette, "Courants de la pensée musulmane contemporaine [Trends in Muslim contemporary thought]," parts 2 and 3 on "Hassan al-Banna," Tawhid.

11 The glossary in question had been commissioned by a *Nouvel Observateur* journalist but was refused because of its extremely partisan contents. Tariq Ramadan published it as an annex to *Etre musulman européen*, but not without protesting against this "bizarre way of proceeding" and against "this censorship." Tariq Ramadan, *Etre musulman européen: etude des sources islamiques à la lumières du contexte européen* [*To Be a European Muslim: A Study of Islamic Sources in the Light of the European Context*], Lyon, Tawhid, 1999, tr. from English by Claude Dabbak, p. 418.

12 Ingy Al-Qadi and Yolande Youssef, *Al-Ahram Hebdo*, June 14, 2000.

13 Thameem Ushama, *Hassan al-Banna, Vision et mission* [*Hassan al-Banna: His Vision and His Mission*], Percetakan Zafar Sdn. Bhd, Kuala Lumpur, 1995, p. 31.

14 Tariq Ramadan, *Aux sources du renouveau musulman. D'al-Afghani à Hassan al-Banna, un siècle de réformisme islamique* [*On the Origins of the Muslim Renaissance: From al-Afghani to Hassan al-Banna; a century of Islamic reformism*], Lyon, Tawhid, 2002, p. 203 (1st ed. Bayard, 1998).

15 Sura XLII, "Consultation," 36–38, *The Meaning of the Holy Koran*, ed. Abdullah Yusuf Ali, new ed., rev. tr., Beltsville (Md.), USA, 1989 [1409].

16 *Salaf* in Arabic means the "devout ancestors." It is important not to confuse literalist Salafism with the reformist Salafism (not literalist but still fundamentalist) of Tariq Ramadan, who is fundamentalist but not literalist. See also Chapter 3.

17 T. Ramadan, *Etre musulman européen*, p. 418.

18 Interview with Ali Mérad, March 8, 2004.

19 T. Ramadan, *Aux sources du renouveau musulman*, p. 22, note 6.

20 Interview with Mohamed Sifaoui, June 2004.

21 The second jury, presided over by Philippe Borgeaud, was made up of Bruno Etienne (IEP, Aix-en-Provence), Reinhard Schulze (Berne), Richard Friedli (Fribourg), and Sylvia Naef (Geneva).

22 Contrary to tradition, no copy of the thesis is available in the library. Only the Bayard edition exists with, in the form of an epigraph, the statement by the Dean of the Faculty of Letters, June 30, 1998.

23 Carré and Seurat, *Les Frères Musulmans*, p.11.

24 Quoted by Tariq Ramadan, *Aux sources du renouveau musulman*, p. 11.

25 Hassan al-Banna, *Epître aux jeunes* [*Letter to the Young*].

26 This and the quotes that follow are all taken from Hassan al-Banna, "Les cinquante demandes du programs des Frères Musulmans (1936) [The fifty demands of the Muslim Brotherhood program of 1936]," *Islam de France*, no. 8, October 2000.

27 Interview with Michel Renard, January 12, 2004.

28 T. Ramadan, "Courants de la pensée musulmane contemporaine: Hassan al-Banna."

29 *Ibid.*

30 Carré and Seurat, *Les Frères Musulmans*, p. 18.

31 In *Hassan al-Banna. Vision et Mission*, Thameem Ushama, a Brotherhood historian, took offense at the idea that the "enemies" of the Brotherhood had used this episode to discredit them, but does not deny the facts.

32 Hassan al-Banna, *Al-qawl al-fasl* [*Last Words*], 1948, and *Al-Bayân* [*Declaration*], 1948, two posthumous brochures quoted in R. Sa'îd, *Hassan...*, p. 149. Commented in Carré and Seurat, *Le Fréres Musulmans*, p. 32.

33 Ramadan, *Aux sources du renouveau musulman*, p. 200.

34 *Ibid.*, p. 218.

35 Given as the model to be imitated by Tariq Ramadan in his cassette devoted to Hassan al-Banna and in *Aux sources du renouveau musulman*.

36 T. Ramadan, *Aux sources du renouveau musulman*, p. 281, note 3.

37 al-Banna, *Epître aux jeunes*.

38 T. Ramadan, "Courants de la pensée musulmane contemporaine."

39 Gresh and T. Ramadan, *L'Islam en questions*, p. 25.

40 Carré and Seurat, *Les Frères Musulmans*, p. 37.

41 T. Ramadan, "Courants de la pensée musulmane contemporaine."

42 Carré and Seurat, *Les Frères Musulmans*, p. 23.

43 Zaynab al-Ghazali, *Des jours de ma vie* [*Some Days from My Life*], Beirut, Al-Bouraq, 1996, preface by Tariq Ramadan.

44 *Ibid.*, pp. 57–58.

45 *Ibid.*, p. 58.

46 T. Ramadan, *Aux sources du renouveau musulman*, p. 182.

47 Interview with Jean-Yves Chaperon, March 15, 2004.

48 See the book of interviews with Has-

san al-Tourabi edited by Alain Chevalérias: *Islam: avenir du monde* [*Islam: The Future of the World*], Paris, J. C. Lattès, 1997.

49 Serge Raffy, "Le vrai visage de Tariq Ramadan [The true face of Tariq Ramadan]," *Le Nouvel Observateur*, January 29–February 4, 2004.

50 Interview with Antoine Sfeir, December 29, 2003.

51 Interview with Richard Labévière, May 15, 2004.

52 T. Ramadan, *Aux sources du renouveau musulman*, p. 29.

53 Gresh and T. Ramadan, *L'Islam en questions*, p. 34.

54 Carré and Seurat, *Les Frères Musulmans*, p. 44.

55 T. Ramadan, *Aux sources du renouveau musulman*, p. 356.

56 *Ibid.*, p. 22.

57 Gresh and T. Ramadan, *L'Islam en questions*, p. 34.

58 T. Ramadan, *Aux sources du renouveau musulman*, p. 356.

59 *Dictionnaire mondial de l'Islamisme* [*World Dictionary of Islamism*], ed. by *Les Cahiers de l'Orient*, Paris, Plon, 2002, p. 188.

60 T. Ramadan, "Courants de pensées musulmane contemporaine."

61 Gresh and T. Ramadan, *L'Islam en questions*, p. 76.

62 T. Ramadan, "Courants de la pensée musulmans contemporaine: Hassan al-Banna."

63 *Ibid.*

64 "L'intellectuel musulman fait peur! [The Muslim intellectual is frightening!]," *Le Journal du Mardi*, no. 155, March 9, 2004. Interview with Laurent Arnauts and Malika Es-Saïdi.

65 Richard Labévière, *Les dollars de la terreur* [*The Terror Dollars*], Paris, Grasset, 1999, pp. 136–37.

66 Declaration dating from 15 January 1954, quoted by a biographer of Hassan al-Banna, Thameem Ushama in *Hassan al-Banna, Vision et mission*, p. 95.

67 Sayyid Qutb, "Social . . . ," quoted by Carré and Seurat, *Les Frères Musulmans*, p. 86.

68 Qutb's book and its context are admirably analyzed in Gilles Kepel, *Le Prophète et Pharaon* [*The Prophet and Pharaoh*], Paris, Seuil, 1993 (1st ed. 1984).

69 Quoted by Kepel, *Le Prophète et Pharaon.*

70 *Ibid.*, p. 213.

71 T. Ramadan, *Aux sources du renouveau musulman*, p. 416.

72 al-Ghazali, *Des jours de ma vie*, p. 33.

73 T. Ramadan, Preface to al-Ghazali, *Des jours de ma vie*, p. 11.

74 al-Ghazali, *Des jours de ma vie.*

75 *Ibid.*, p. 117.

76 She wrote: "He gave me a sallow smile and said, 'That means that you really are conspiring against Nasser and his regime. That's clear from your own words, pilgrim Zanab,' and I said, 'Islam knows nothing of conspiracy, but looks evil in the face and enlightens people as to the two roads between which they must choose: God's path, the road of righteousness; or the devil's path, the road of evil.'" *Ibid.*, p. 118.

77 T. Ramadan, Preface to al-Ghazali, *Des jours de ma vie*, p. 11.

78 Gilles Kepel, *A l'ouest d'Allah* [*West of Allah*], Paris, Points Seuil, 1994, p. 198.

79 T. Ramadan, *Etre musulman européen*, pp. 11–13.

80 Telephone interview with Mohammed Seddiqi, December 18, 2003.

Chapter two

1 Alain Gresh and Tariq Ramadan, *L'Islam en questions* [*Questioning Islam*], a debate organized and presented by Françoise Germain-Robin, Sindbad, 2002, p. 19.

2 Tariq Ramadan, *Islam, le face-à-face des civilisations. Quel projet pour quelle modernité?* [*Islam: The Confrontation of Civilizations. What Sort of Plan for What Sort of Modernity?*], Lyon, Tawhid, 2001, p. 6.

3 Gresh and T. Ramadan, *L'Islam en questions*, p. 25.

4 T. Ramadan, *Islam, le face-à-face des civilisations*, p. 6.

5 *Ibid.*, p. 7.

6 *Ibid.*, p. 9.

7 *Ibid.*, p. 7.

8 Cited in *Dictionnaire mondial de l'Islamisme* [*World Dictionary of Islamism*], ed. by *Les Cahiers de l'Orient*, Paris, Plon, 2002, p. 61.

9 Saïd Ramadan, *La sharia. Le droit islamique, son envergure et son équité* [*The Sharia: Islamic Law. Its Scope and Equity*], Paris, Al-Qalam, 1997.

10 T. Ramadan, *Islam, le face-à-face des civilisations*, p. 8.

11 Saïd Ramadan, *Islamic Law: Its Scope and Equity*, London, Macmillan, 1961.

12 *Ibid.*, pp. 9–18. French edition.

13 Quoted from the statutes of the Center.

14 Among the other sponsors listed prominently by the Center: Haïdar Bammate, Professor Muhammad Hamidullah, Abdul Hassan Ali al-Nadawi, Maulana Ahmad Zafar al-Ansari.

15 Saïd Ramadan, *Islam. Doctrine et mode de vie* [*Islam: Its Doctrine and Its Way of Life*], brochure no. 3 of the Geneva Islamic Center, published by Tawhid (Lyon, 1993), pp. 12–13.

16 Interview with Jacques Pitteloud.

17 Cited in the *Dictionnaire mondial de l'Islamisme*, p. 193.

18 Under the patronage of Riad al-Droubie, Ja'far Sheikh Idris, and T. Hassan.

19 Gresh and T. Ramadan, *L'Islam en questions*, p. 14.

20 Which was no problem. In Islam men are encouraged to spread the faith by taking women of the two other monotheistic faiths as wives.

21 Saïd Ramadan, *La Sharia*, p. 6.

22 Tariq Ramadan cassette, "Les grands péchés [The major sins]," recorded in Réunion, August 1999, QA 4, Tawhid.

23 T. Ramadan, *Islam, le face-à-face des civilisations*, p. 11.

24 *Ibid.*, p. 5

25 Serge Raffy, "Le vrai visage de Tariq Ramadan [Tariq Ramadan's true face]," *Le Nouvel Observateur*, January 29–February 4, 2004.

26 Gresh and T. Ramadan, *L'Islam en questions*, p. 24.

27 *Ibid.*, p. 24.

28 *Ibid.*, pp. 17–19.

29 Ghandour Abdel-Rahman, *Le jihad humanitaire, enquête sur les ONG islamiques* [*The Humanitarian Jihad: A Report on the Islamic NGOs*], Paris, Flammarion, 2002.

30 T. Ramadan, "Les grands péchés."

31 Quoted in Caroline Fourest and Fiammetta Venner, *Tirs Croisés. La laïcité à l'épreuve des intégrismes juif, chrétien et musulman* [*Crossfire. Secularism on the Edge of Jewish, Christian and Muslim Political Fundamentalism*], Paris, Calmann-Levy, 2003.

32 *Les musulmans francophones. Compréhension, la terminologie, le discours* [*French-speaking Muslims: Understanding, Terminology, Language*], Lyon, Tawhid, 2001.

33 Interview in *Yasmina*, no. 10, July 2003.

34 *Critères pour une organisation musulmane en France* [*Criteria for Muslim Organizations in France*], UOIF brochure. No date, but distributed during the UOIF annual meetings in 2002, 2003, and 2004.

35 Some are simply local offices; others are national associations named according to their sectors of activity: Muslim Women's League, Young French Muslims, French Muslim Students, Avicienne (an association of Muslim doctors), Les Imams de France (an association that trains imams), or mutual assistance associations, such as the Committee for Palestinian Charity and Relief. Two transnational organizations round off this list: the European Council for Fatwa and Research and the European Social Sciences Institute (a training center for imams).

36 Conseil européen de la fatwa et de la recherche, *Recueil de fatwas* [*Compendium of Fatwas*], series no. 1, preface and presentation by Tariq Ramadan, Lyon, Tawhid, 2002.

37 This *fatwa* can be consulted on the Hamas website.

38 The 11th session, held in Stockholm in July 2003, did in fact declare that kamikaze attacks were in every respect lawful. "The 'martyr operations' carried out by the Palestinian groups to resist the Zionist occupation in no way come under the heading of forbidden terrorism, even if it turns out that some of the victims are civilians." One of the justifications given by the European branch of the UOIF is that, in any case, "the so-called 'civilians' are 'soldiers' of the army of the sons of Zion" and as such these "so-called [Israeli] 'civilians' continue to be invaders and oppressors, both evil and tyrannical." Which gives an idea of the role played by the European Council for Fatwa in radicalizing Western Muslims. See "Qaradhawi favorable aux operations suicide lors d'une conference islamique en Suède," MEMR.I [Institut de recherché médiatique du Moyen-Orient], special issue no. 542, July 25, 2003.

39 www.aljazeera.net, June 17, 2004.

40 Cited in Raffy, "Le vrai visage de Tariq Ramadan."

41 Cited in *Le Monde*, February 12, 2003.

42 Christophe Ayad and Olivier Bertrand, "Predicateur tous terrain [An all-purpose preacher]," *Libération*, February 5, 2004.

43 *Ibid.*

44 *Le Courrier*, January 7, 1995.

45 "Les musulmans de Suisse étaient français [The Swiss Muslims turned out to be French]," *L'Hebdo*, December 22, 1994.

46 *Ibid.*

47 *Ibid.*

48 *Ibid.*

49 *Ibid.*

50 Tariq Ramadan cassette, "La vie conjugale en Islam [Married life in Islam]," recorded in Mauritius, Tawhid.

51 Tariq Ramadan cassette, "L'Islam. Le face-à-face des civilizations? [Islam: The confrontation of civilizations?]," interassociation training seminar, Brussels, Mediacom.

52 See the *Dictionnaire mondial de l'Islamisme*, p. 425.

53 *Ibid.*, p. 424.

54 Hani Ramadan, *Islam et la dérive de l'Occident* [*Islam and Western Deviance*], Paris, Maison d'Ennour, 2001, p. 57.

55 Hani Ramadan, *Aspects du monothéisme musulman* [*Some Aspects of Muslim Monotheism*], Lyon, Tawhid, 1998, p. 98.

56 Hani Ramadan, "L'impasse de l'homosexualité [Homosexuality: A dead end]," interview with Yann Gessler, *Le Nouvelliste*, January 25, 2003.

57 Hani Ramadan, *La Femme en Islam* [*Women in Islam*], Lyon, Tawhid, 1998.

58 *Ibid.*, p. 53.

59 Cited in the *Dictionnaire mondial de l'Islamisme*, p. 423.

60 Published in 2001 by the Geneva Islamic Center.

61 *La Tribune de Genève*, December 21, 1992.

62 Manuel Grandjean, "*Le Courrier* n'accordera plus de tribune à Hani Ramadan [*Le Courrier* will no longer publish contributions by Hani Ramadan]," *Le Courrier*, September 30, 2002.

63 *Le Courrier*, November 13, 2002.

64 T. Ramadan, "L'intellectuel musulman fait peur! [The Muslim intellectual is frightening!]," *Le Journal du Mardi*, no. 155, March 9, 2004. Interview with Laurent Arnauts and Malika Es-Saïdi.

65 Hani Ramadan, "L'impasse de l'homosexualité."

66 Opinion piece published in *Le Temps*, April 9, 2001.

67 Statement published in *La Tribune de Genève*, September 12, 2001.

68 *Le Progrès*, October 4, 2001.

69 Souffrant, the head of the Syrian Muslim Brotherhood finally canceled at the last minute, but the two brothers gave their introduction.

70 *Hebdo de Lausanne*, May 7, 1998.

71 Alain Gresh and Tariq Ramadan, *L'Islam en questions*, p. 49.

72 "Lettre ouverte à M. Hervé Loichemol," *La Tribune de Genève*, October 7, 1993.

73 Tariq Ramadan, *Les musulmans dans la laïcité* [*Muslims in a Secular Society*], Lyon, Tawhid, 1994, note 60, p. 175.

74 Cited in *L'Hebdo*, July 3, 1996.

75 Tariq Ramadan, "Critique des (nouveaux) intellectuals communautaires [Critique of the (new) communitarian intellectuals]," published October 3, 2003 on www.oumma.com.

76 *Libération*, November 25, 2003.

77 Tariq Ramadan, "Un pacte citoyen pour le culte musulman [A citizen's pact for the Muslim Faith]," opinion piece, *Le Monde*, August 12, 2003.

78 "Message aux Musulmans de France," LNMF (Ligue nationale des musulmans de France), cassette recorded in Rosny, 2003.

79 Richard Labévière, "Les réseaux européens des Islamistes algériens," *Les Cahiers de l'Orient*, 2nd trimester 2001, no. 62, pp. 133–49.

80 In accordance with the usual protective double discourse, "Mostafa Hamza,"

the pseudonym used in the staff's editorials, would have us believe that he had never met Saïd Ramadan in person. "I have never known Sheikh Saïd Ramadan personally, I regret it," one can read in *The Cause*. This admission is somewhat surprising, given that the editors of the *The Cause* also lived in exile in Geneva, were most admiring of Saïd Ramadan, and prayed in the same holy places. This statement can be interpreted in two ways: either it is a way of honoring the founder of the Center, while at the same time protecting his heirs from being questioned, or else Mourad Dhina and Moustapha Brahimi were actually in contact with his two sons, Hani and Tariq, and thus never knew the patriarch himself. *The Cause*, vol. 3, no. 25, August 12–19, 1995.

81 Labévière, "Les réseaux européens des Islamistes algériens."

82 *La Cause*, vol. 2, no. 17, March 3, 1995.

83 *La Cause*, vol. 2, no. 21, June 16–22, 1995.

84 *La Cause*, vol. 3, no. 29, October 7–13, 1995. *The Cause* has not been published since 1996.

85 T. Ramadan cassette, "Islam. Le face-à-face des civilisations?"

86 *Nouveau Quotidien*, November 29,1995.

87 On December 5, 1995, the committee organized an evening event at the University of Geneva in support of Tariq Ramadan, attended by 250 people.

88 Several well-known figures signed: Roger Garaudy, but also Albert Jacquard, Father Pierre, His Grace Gaillot, Michel Lelong, François Burgat, Christian Grobet, Jocelyne Cesari, Jean Ziegler, and Erica Deuber-Pauli.

89 *La Liberté*, Geneva-Vaud edition, December 10, 1995.

90 *Le Journal de Genève*, June 29, 1996.

91 Cited in *Le Progrès*, "Hani Ramadan. Le prêche habile d'un Islamiste laïque [Hani Ramadan: The skilful preaching of a "secular Islamist"]," October 4, 2001.

92 "Mille musulmans en colère devant l'ONU [A thousand angry Muslims on the steps of the UN building]," *Tribune de Genève*, October 7–8, 2000.

93 *Ibid.*

94 Memorandum issued by the National Police Headquarters based on information provided by the UCIE (Unidad central de informacion exterior), July 3, 2000.

95 *Le Courrier*, November 25, 2003.

96 Sylvain Besson, "Sur la piste des chefs d'Al-Qaïda [On the trail of the Al-Qaeda leaders]," *Le Temps*, December 4, 2003.

97 *Dictionnaire mondial de l'Islamisme*, p. 456.

98 *Le Courrier*, November 25, 2003.

99 Sylvain Besson, "La société Al-Taqwa, au coeur de l'Islamisme radical [Al-Taqwa at the center of radical Islamism]," *Le Temps*, December 23, 2003.

100 Sylvain Besson, "La vie secrète de Youssef Nada, ambassadeur de l'ombre des Frères Musulmans [The secret life of Youssef Nada, the Muslim Brotherhood's shadow ambassador]," *Le Temps*, November 20, 2002.

101 Cited in the *Dictionnaire mondial de l'Islamisme*, p. 454.

102 Interview with Richard Labévière, May 15, 2004.

103 Richard Labévière, *Les dollars de la terreur* [*The Terror Dollars*], Paris, Grasset, 1999, p. 148.

104 Pierre Péan, *L'extrémiste François Genoud. De Hitler à Carlos* [*François Genoud, the Extremist: From Hitler to Carlos*], Paris, Fayard, 1996.

105 Telephone interview with Ahmed Hubert.

106 Cited by Labévière, *Les dollars de la terreur*, p. 149.

107 Interview with Yann Gessler, *Le Nouvelliste*, January 25, 2003.

108 *Le Courrier*, November 25, 2003.

109 "Le vrai danger vient des Frères musulmans [The real danger comes from the Muslim Brotherhood]," *La Croix*, April 6, 2004.

110 Statement published in *La Tribune de Genève*, July 16, 2003.

111 He served as general editor for several volumes of this encyclopedia, which is a reference tool for fundamentalists, in particular Mary Martin and Scott Appleby (eds), *Fundamentalism and Society: Remaking Politics, Economics, and the Military*, Chicago, University of Chicago Press, 1997.

112 *Lyon Mag*, no. 134, March 2004.

113 *Ibid.*

114 Scott Appleby, "Job description for the next pope," *Foreign Policy*, 13–19 February 2004, available at www.foreignpolicy.com

115 Toby Helm, *Daily Telegraph*, September 12, 2005.

116 The following articles on Tariq Ramadan's doublespeak are worth consulting: Dominique Avon, "Une réponse à 'l'Islam réformiste' de Tariq Ramadan," *Nunc*, no. 4, October 2003; Jacques Jomier, "L'Islam et sa présence en Occident suivant les perspectives d'un Frère musulman," *Esprit et Vie*, February 17, 2000; Michel Audetat, "Les habits neufs du fondamentalisme," *L'Hébdo*, December 4, 2003; Cynthia Fleury and Emmanuel Lemieux, "L'entrisme de Tariq Ramadan," *Libération*, November 19, 2003.

Chapter three

1 Tariq Ramadan, *Etre musulman européen: etude des sources islamiques à la lumières du contexte européen* [*To Be a European Muslim: A Study of Islamic Sources in the Light of the European Context*], Lyon, Tawhid, 1999, tr. from English by Claude Dabbak, p. 452. This book is a translation of the English original, *To Be a European Muslim*, published by the Islamic Foundation of Leicester in 1999.

2 Tariq Ramadan, *Les musulmans d'Occident et l'avenir de l'Islam* [*Western Muslims and the Future of Islam*], Arles, Actes Sud-Sindbad, 2003, pp. 55–56.

3 T. Ramadan, *Etre musulman européen*, p. 397.

4 *Ibid.*, p. 397.

5 Tariq Ramadan, *Les musulmans d'Occident et l'avenir de l'Islam*, p. 56. The same statement occurs in *Etre musulman européen*, but with a slight difference. In 1999 the reference is to "Europe"; in 2003 it is a question of the "Occident." The later work, *Les musulmans d'Occident*, was greeted as representing a certain evolution in Ramadan's thinking. But an evolution in what direction? In 1999 it is Europe that is the target, in 2003 the Occident as a whole...

6 T. Ramadan, *Les musulmans d'Occident*, p. 56.

7 Leïla Babès, "L'identité européenne d'après Tariq Ramadan [Tariq Ramadan's concept of European identity]," *Islam de France*, no. 8, October 2000, p. 16.

8 Tariq Ramadan cassette, "Islam et Occident. Références et valeurs [Islam and the West: References and values]," part 2, lecture recorded in Abidjan, QA 15, Tawhid.

9 T. Ramadan, *Etre musulman européen*, pp. 389–403.

10 Alain Gresh and Tariq Ramadan, *L'Islam en questions* [*Questioning Islam*], a debate organized and presented by Françoise Germain-Robin, Sindbad, 2002, p. 36.

11 Cited by Martine Nouaille, "Tariq Ramadan, personnalité influente et controversée [Tariq Ramadan: An influential and controversial figure]," AFP, November 15, 2003.

12 This symposium was organized by the ADICR (Association du dialogue interculturel et interreligieux) on the topic "Religion and democracy."

13 Tariq Ramadan cassette, "Islam et le fondamentalisme religieux [Islam and religious fundamentalism]," QA 11, Tawhid.

14 Sura IV, "Women," 24. *The Meaning of the Holy Koran*, ed. Abdullah Yusuf Ali, new ed., rev. tr., Beltsville (Md.), USA, 1989, p. 190.

15 According to the statistics provided by the Minister of Health, 3,600 little girls undergo circumcision every day in Egypt; only 15 percent of the operations take place in clinics or hospitals.

16 Tariq Ramadan cassette, "La femme musulmane. Réalités et espoir [The Muslim woman: Realities and hopes]," part 2, recorded in Senegal in 1998, QA 20, Tawhid.

17 Cited in Azadeh Kian-Thiébaut, "L'Islam, les femmes et la citoyenneté" in "Islam et démocratie," *Pouvoirs*, no. 104, January 2003.

18 Sura IV, "Women," 38, *Meaning of the Holy Koran*, p. 195.

19 Tariq Ramadan cassette, "Islam, modernité et modernisme [Islam, modernity and modernism]," TAW 07, Tawhid.

20 Tariq Ramadan cassette, "Le renouveau islamique [The Islamic revival]," QA 23, Tawhid.

21 *Le Monde des Débats*, January 2, 2002. Sophie Gherardi and Jean-Luc Pouthier, Interview with Alain Boyer and Tariq Ramadan.

22 Babès, "L'identité européenne d'après Tariq Ramadan," p. 9.

23 Tariq Ramadan, *Peut-on vivre avec l'Islam?* [*Can One Live with Islam?*], an exchange between Tariq Ramadan and Jacques Neirynck, Lausanne, Favre, 2004 [1999], p. 121.

24 As recounted by Sakina Bakha, "Tariq Ramadan, cheval de Troie de l'Islamisme [Tariq Ramadan: Islamism's Trojan Horse]," address given on the occasion of the symposium organized by the journal *POUR*, April 2000.

25 T. Ramadan, *Peut-on vivre avec l'Islam?*, p. 146.

26 *Ibid.*, p. 148.

27 Sura IV, "Women," 34, *Meaning of the Holy Koran*, p. 195–96.

28 Youssef al-Qaradhawi, "Ce qu'on doit faire quand la femme se montre fière ou rebelle [What must be done when a wife is too proud and rebellious]," *Le licite et l'illicite* [*The Lawful and the Unlawful*], Paris, Al-Qalam, 2002 [1992], p. 207.

29 Tariq Ramadan cassette, "La vie conjugale en Islam [Married life in Islam]," recorded in Mauritius, Tawhid.

30 T. Ramadan, *Etre musulman européen*, p. 166.

31 On the program *A 100 minutes pour convaincre.*

32 On this subject, see Juliette Minces, *Le Coran et les femmes,* Paris, Hachette, 1996, p. 116.

33 *Libération,* November 25, 2003.

34 *Des filles comme les autres* [*Just Ordinary Girls*], a book of interviews with Lila and Alma Lévy, Paris, La Découverte, 2004.

35 T. Ramadan, *Peut-on vivre avec l'Islam?,* p. 131.

36 Tariq Ramadan cassette, "L'identité musulmane. Construire notre discourse [The Muslim identity: Developing our discourse," Abidjan, July 1999, QA 28, Tawhid.

37 T. Ramadan, *Les musulmans d'Occident,* p. 113.

38 Tariq Ramadan cassette, "Islam et politique, entre confusion et separation [Islam and politics, between confusion and separation]," QA 48, Tawhid.

39 *Ibid.*

40 T. Ramadan, "Islam et le fondamentalisme religieux."

41 "La démocratie est une donnée constante chez les Musulmans [Muslims have always stood for democracy]," interview in an Ivory Cost newspaper published on Tariq Ramadan's website.

42 T. Ramadan, "Islam et le fondamentalisme religieux."

43 "La démocratie est une donnée constante chez les Musulmans."

44 T. Ramadan, "L'Islam et le fondamentalisme religieux."

45 *Ibid.*

46 *Ibid.*

47 T. Ramadan, "Islam, modernité et modernisme."

48 Tariq Ramadan cassette, "Vivre en Occident. Les cinq fondements de notre presence [Living in the West: The five grounds for our presence]," part 1, QA 39, Tawhid.

49 T. Ramadan, "Islam et Occident. Références et valeurs."

Chapter four

1 *Yasmina,* no. 10, July 2003, interview with Nadia Khouri-Dagher.

2 But then he adds: "Since it is disgraceful for a wife to cut off her hair or shave her head, let her cover her head." 1 Corinthians 11.

3 St. Paul specifies, in fact: "For a man ought not to cover his head, since he is the image and glory of God, but woman is the glory of man. For man was not made from woman, but woman from man. Neither was man created for woman, but woman for man. That is why a wife ought to have a symbol of authority on her head." 1 Corinthians 11.

4 "The women should keep silent in the churches. For they are not permitted to speak, but should be in submission, as the Law also says. If there is anything they desire to learn, let them ask their husbands at home. For it is shameful for a woman to speak in church." 1 Corinthians 14.

5 The context in which the verses recommending the wearing of the veil were written, and their unwarranted interpretation, are brilliantly analyzed in Leïla Babès, "La voile comme doxa [The veil as doxa]," *MSR,* July–September 2002. See also Leïla Babès and Tareq Oubrou, *Loi d'Allah, lois des hommes. Liberté égalité et femmes en Islam* [*Allah's Law and Man's Law: Liber-*

ty, Equality and Women in Islam], Paris, Albin Michel, 2002.

6 Sura XXXIII, "The Leagues," 59, *The Meaning of the Holy Koran*, ed. Abdullah Yusuf Ali, new ed., rev. tr., Beltsville (Md.), USA, 1989, p. 1077.

7 Sura XXIV, "Light," 31, *The Meaning of the Holy Koran*, pp. 873–74.

8 Youssef al-Qaradhawi, "Que doit faire une femme pour rester en dehors de l'exhibitionisme [What a woman must do to avoid exhibitionism]," *Le licite et l'illicite en Islam* [*The Lawful and the Unlawful*], Paris, Al-Qalam, 2002 [1992], p. 171.

9 Cited by Azadeh Kian-Thiébaut, "Islam, les femmes et la citoyenneté," in "Islam et démocratie," *Pouvoirs*, no. 104, January 2003.

10 Tariq Ramadan cassette, "La femme musulmane face à son devoir d'engagement [The Muslim woman and her duty to participate]," part 2, recorded in Abidjan (Ivory Coast), QA 22, Tawhid.

11 Babès, "Le voile comme doxa."

12 Soheib Bencheikh, *Marianne et le prophète* [*Marianne and the Prophet*], Paris, Grasset, 1998, p. 145.

13 Tariq Ramadan cassette, "La femme musulmane. Réalités et espoir [The Muslim woman. Realities and hopes]," part 1, QA 19, Tawhid.

14 *Ibid.*

15 *Ibid.*

16 Tariq Ramadan cassette, "Relations hommes-femmes [Relations between men and women]," QA 5, Tawhid.

17 Hassan al-Banna, "Les cinquante demandes du programs des Frères Musulmans (1936) [The fifty demands of the Muslim Brotherhood program of 1936]," *Islam de France*, no. 8, October 2000.

18 T. Ramadan, "La femme musulmane face à son devoir d'engagement'.

19 Tariq Ramadan cassette, 'Vivre en Occident. Les cinq fondements de notre presence [Living in the West. The Five Grounds for our Presence]," part 1, QA 39, Tawhid.

20 T. Ramadan, "La femme musulmane face à son devoir d'engagement."

21 *Ibid.*

22 *Ibid.*

23 Interview with Jacqueline Costa-Lascaux, February 2004.

24 Asma Lamrabet, *Musulmane tout simplement* [*A Muslim Woman, No More, No Less*], Lyon, Tawhid, 2002.

25 "We are confronted by oppressive powers that are prepared to exceed the limits of humanity. It is thus necessary that we also prepare women for our defense." Sayyid Mawdudi, *Come Let Us Change This World*, Markazi, Maktaba Islami, Delhi, 1975, pp. 112–13. (Translated back from the French.)

26 *Ibid.*

27 L'Union feminine pour le respect et l'aide à la maternité [Feminine Union for Respecting and Supporting Maternity], an anti-abortion French association, explains that "a true feminism must respect our femininity and our maternal vocation." Extract from an information bulletin of the UFRAM, undated but probably 1991, private archives.

28 Tariq Ramadan, *Les musulmans d'Occident et l'avenir de l'Islam* [*Western Muslims and the Future of Islam*], Arles, Actes Sud-Sindbad, 2003, p. 244.

29 Tariq Ramadan cassette, "Le renouveau islamique [The Islamic revival]," QA 23, Tawhid.

30 T. Ramadan, "La femme musulmane. Réalités et espoir."

31 "Feminist movements conceive of the relations between men and women in terms of strength. We think of them in terms of complementarity." *Bulletin du CNFE*, March 1986.

32 A Bangladeshi woman doctor, condemned for apostasy by the Islamists on account of her stand in favor of feminism and secularism.

33 Tariq Ramadan, *Peut-on vivre avec l'Islam?* [*Can One Live with Islam?*], an exchange between Tariq Ramadan and Jacques Neirynck, Lausanne, Favre, 2004 [1999], p. 126.

34 T. Ramadan, "Relations hommes-femmes."

35 *Ibid.*

36 T. Ramadan, "La femme musulmane face à son devoir d'engagement."

37 *Ibid.*

38 Conseil européen de la fatwa et de la recherche, *Recueil de fatwas* [*Compendium of Fatwas*], series no. 1, preface by Tariq Ramadan, Lyon, Tawhid, 2002, p. 137.

39 T. Ramadan, "Le renouveau islamique."

40 *Ibid.*

41 T. Ramadan, "La femme musulmane face à son devoir d'engagement."

42 *Ibid.*

43 T. Ramadan, "La femme musulmane. Réalités et espoir."

44 Given, as an example of the open-mindedness of the Muslim Brotherhood in regard to women, by Tariq Ramadan, *Aux sources du renouveau musulman. D'al-Afghani à Hassan al-Banna, un siècle de réformisme islamique* [*On the Origins of the Muslim Renaissance: From al-Afghani to Hassan al-Banna; a Century of Islamic Reformism*], Lyon, Tawhid, note, p. 331.

45 T. Ramadan, "La femme musulmane. Réalités et espoir."

46 *Ibid.*

47 *Ibid.*

48 T. Ramadan, "La femme musulmane face à son devoir d'engagement."

49 Cited by Claudie Lesselier in "De la Vierge Marie à Jeanne d'Arc. L'extrême droite frontiste et catholique et le femmes (1984–90)," in Claudie Lesselier and Fiammetta Venner (eds), *L'extrême droite et les femmes* [*Women and the Radical Right*], Villeurbanne, Golias, 1997.

50 T. Ramadan, "La femme musulmane face à son devoir d'engagement."

51 See US Department of State, "Saudi Arabia country report on human rights practices for 1998," published February 26, 1999.

52 David Hirst, "Educated for indolence: Thousands of Saudi women get university degrees, few get jobs," *Guardian*, August 3, 1999.

53 T. Ramadan, "La femme musulmane face à son devoir d'engagement."

54 al-Banna, "Les cinquante demandes du program des Frères musulmans."

55 T. Ramadan, "La femme musulmane face à son devoir d'engagement."

56 T. Ramadan, *Peut-on vivre avec l'Islam?*, p. 126.

57 T. Ramadan, "La femme musulmane. Réalités et espoir."

58 T. Ramadan, "La femme musulmane face à son devoir d'engagement."

59 T. Ramadan cassette, "Islam, modernité et modernisme [Islam, modernity and modernism]," TAW 07, Tawhid.

60 T. Ramadan, "La femme musulmane

face à son devoir d'engagement."

61 Tariq Ramadan cassette, "La vie conjugale en Islam [Married life in Islam]," recorded in Mauritius, Tawhid.

62 Here is the statement made in 1987 by French National Front leader Jean-Marie Le Pen at the first congress of the Cercle national des femmes d'Europe: "When women work, the tragic result is the break-up of the family . . . and the handing over of the mother's role in the education of her children to the crèche or the school, with disastrous consequences that contribute to delinquency and drugs," *Bulletin du CNFE*, no. 20, December 1987–January 1988, cited by François Laroche, "Maréchal, nous voilà! Le Cercle national des femmes d'Europe," in *L'extrême droite et les femmes.*

63 Dom Gérard, *Itinéraires*, March 1988.

64 T. Ramadan, "La vie conjugale en Islam."

65 *Ibid.*

66 *Ibid.*

67 T. Ramadan, "La femme musulmane face à son devoir d'engagement."

68 *Ibid.*

69 T. Ramadan, "La vie conjugale en Islam."

70 *Ibid.*

71 1 Corinthians 11. This passage is often quoted in the journals and bulletins of French traditionalists.

72 Tariq Ramadan cassette, "L'homme musulman aujourd'hui. Spiritualité, équilibre affectif et sexuel, rôle familial et social [Today's Muslim man: Spirituality, emotional and sexual balance, family and social role]," lecture recorded in Roubaix (France), QA 37, Tawhid.

73 Alain Gresh and Tariq Ramadan, *L'Islam en questions* [*Questioning Islam*], a debate organized and presented by Françoise Germain-Robin, Sindbad, 2002, p. 280.

74 T. Ramadan, "La femme musulmane. Réalité et espoir."

75 Conseil européen de la fatwa et de la recherche, *Recueil de fatwas* [*Compendium of Fatwas*], series no. 1, preface by Tariq Ramadan, Lyon, Tawhid, 2002, p. 156.

76 Gilles Kepel, *Le Prophète et le Pharaon* [*The Prophet and Pharaoh*], Paris, Seuil, 1993, p. 201.

77 M. Boudejenoun, *Le marriage en Islam. Modalités et finalités,* Paris, Maison d'Ennour, 2001, p. 80.

78 T. Ramadan, "La vie conjugale en Islam."

79 Tariq Ramadan cassette, "La conception islamique de la sexualité. Innocence, responsabilité et maîtrise [The Islamic conception of sexuality: Innocence, responsibility and mastery]," recorded in Mauritius, QA 38, Tawhid.

80 *Ibid.*

81 *Transfac,* December 1995.

82 T. Ramadan, "La conception islamique de la sexualité. Innocence, responsabilité et maîtrise."

83 Yousouf Ibram, "Le conseil européen de la fatwa. Rôle et objectifs [The European Council for Fatwa. Its role and objectives]," lecture, HC 19, Tawhid.

84 Conseil européen de la fatwa, *Recueil de fatwas*, p. 126.

85 T. Ramadan, *Peut-on vivre avec Islam?*, p. 138.

86 T. Ramadan, "La conception islamique de la sexualité."

87 *Ibid.*

88 T. Ramadan, *Peut-on vivre avec Islam?*, p. 152.

89 T. Ramadan, "La conception islamique de la sexualité."

90 *Ibid.*

91 T. Ramadan, *Peut-on vivre avec l'Islam?*, p. 152.

92 Qaradhawi, *Le licite et l'illicite en Islam*, p. 91.

93 T. Ramadan, "Islam, modernité et modernisme."

94 Cited by Qaradhawi, *Le licite et l'illicite en Islam*, p. 199. Use of the term "homosexuality" comes as a surprise, since the word only appeared in the nineteenth century.

95 T. Ramadan, "La conception islamique de la sexualité."

96 *Ibid.*

97 Tariq Ramadan cassette, "Les grands péchés [The major sins]," recorded in Réunion, August 1999, QA 4, Tawhid.

98 T. Ramadan, "L'homme musulman aujourd'hui."

99 "Wa in kânat 'alâra' – si tannûrin," 'Aînî, IX, p. 484.

100 T. Ramadan, "La femme musulmane. Réalités et espoir."

101 T. Ramadan, "Relations hommes-femmes."

102 *Ibid.*

103 *Ibid.*

104 Tariq Ramadan cassette, "Islam et société. La conception de l'homme en Islam [Islam and society: The conception of man in Islam]," lecture recorded in the Ivory Coast, QA 27, Tawhid.

105 T. Ramadan, "La femme musulmane. Réalités et espoir."

106 T. Ramadan, "L'homme musulman aujourd'hui."

107 *Ibid.*

108 *Ibid.*

109 *Ibid.*

110 T. Ramadan, "Les grands péchés."

Chapter five

1 Tariq Ramadan, *Les musulmans d'Occident et l'avenir de l'Islam* [*Western Muslims and the Future of Islam*], Arles, Actes Sud-Sindbad, 2003, p. 17.

2 Tariq Ramadan, *Les musulmans dans la laïcité* [*Muslims in a Secular Society*], Lyon, Tawhid, 1994, note 4, page 36.

3 Tariq Ramadan cassette, "Notre identité face au contexte: Assimilation, integration ou contribution? [Our identity and its context: Assimilation, integration or contribution?]," recorded in France, QA 44, Tawhid.

4 *Ibid.*

5 *Ibid.*

6 T. Ramadan, *Les musulmans dans la laïcité*, pp. 30–31.

7 Tariq Ramadan cassette, "Vivre en Occident [Living in the West]," part 2.

8 T. Ramadan, *Les musulmans d'Occident et l'avenir de l'Islam*, p. 173.

9 T. Ramadan, "Notre identité face au contexte: Assimilation, integration ou contribution?"

10 Tariq Ramadan cassette, "L'identité musulmane. Construire notre discours [The Muslim identity: Developing our discourse]," Abidjan, July 1999, QA 28, Tawhid.

11 *Ibid.*

12 T. Ramadan, "Notre identité face au contexte. Assimilation, integration ou contribution?"

13 Cassette "Islam d'Europe: entre reli-

gion minoritaire et message universel [European Islam: Between minority religion and universal message]," debate organized in Lyon between Tariq Ramadan and Tareq Oubrou, HC O24, Tawhid.

14 Tariq Ramadan cassette, "Islam et laïcité. Compréhension et dialogue [Islam and secularism: Understanding and dialogue]," part 2, recorded in Senegal in 1998, QA 18, Tawhid.

15 T. Ramadan, *Les musulmans dans la laïcité,* p. 152, note 50.

16 Tariq Ramadan cassette, "Pour une culture islamique alternative [For an alternative Islamic culture]," QA 33, Tawhid.

17 T. Ramadan, "Vivre en Occident."

18 T. Ramadan, "Pour une culture islamique alternative."

19 *Ibid.*

20 Tariq Ramadan cassette, "Rapports Nord-Sud."

21 "Paroles et musique," *Présence Musulmane,* bulletin no. 6, April 1999.

22 Tariq Ramadan, "Une culture islamique européenne," *Présence Musulmane,* bulletin no. 6, 1999.

23 T. Ramadan, "Pour une culture islamique alternative."

24 *Ibid.*

25 *Ibid.*

26 Abd al-Malik, *Qu'Allah bénisse la France,* Paris, Albin Michel, 2004, p. 134–36.

27 Hani Ramadan, *L'Islam et la dérive de de l'Occident,* Ennour, 2001, p. 71, note 52.

28 T. Ramadan, "Vivre en Occident."

29 T. Ramadan, "Pour une culture islamique alternative."

30 Tariq Ramadan cassette, "La femme musulmane face à son devoir d'engagement [The Muslim woman and her duty to participate]," recorded in Abidjan (Ivory Coast), QA 22, Tawhid.

31 T. Ramadan, "Pour une culture islamique alternative."

32 T. Ramadan, "Notre identité face au contexte. Assimilation, integration ou contribution?"

33 T. Ramadan, "L'identité musulmane. Construire notre discours."

34 T. Ramadan, "Notre identité face au contexte. Assimilation, integration ou contribution?"

35 Tariq Ramadan cassette, "Islam et Occident. Références et valeurs [Islam and the West: References and values]," part 2, lecture recorded in Abidjan, QA 15, Tawhid.

36 *Le Monde des Débats,* January 2, 2002.

37 This footnote has already been cited, but Tariq Ramadan complained that his opponents had not cited it in full. I have therefore given the quote *in extenso. Les musulmans dans la laïcité,* note 60, page 175.

38 Colloque International des Musulmans de l'Espace Francophone, *Les musulmans francophone. Compréhension, la terminologie, le discours,* Tawhid, 2001, p. 101.

39 T. Ramadan, "La femme musulmane face à son devoir d'engagement."

40 Cited by Josette Alia and Carole Barjo, in *Le Nouvel Observateur,* November 20, 2003.

41 Cited in *Le Nouvel Observateur,* September 4, 2003.

42 *Le Progrés,* October 20, 2001.

43 *Le Monde,* January 18, 2003.

44 *Le Monde des Débats,* January 2, 2002.

45 T. Ramadan, "Islam et laïcité. Compréhension et dialogue."

46 *Ibid.*

47 "Islam d'Europe: entre religion minoritaire et message universel."

48 *Ibid.*

49 Tariq Ramadan cassette, "Etre musulman européen [To be a European Muslim]," QA 4, Tawhid.

50 T. Ramadan, *Les musulmans d'Occident et l'avenir de l'Islam*, pp. 21–22.

51 Tariq Ramadan cassette, "Vivre en Occident. Les cinq fondements de notre presence [Living in the West: The Five Grounds for our Presence]," part 1, QA 39, Tawhid.

52 Cited in Christophe Ayad and Olivier Bertrand, "Predicateur tous terrain [An All-purpose Preacher]," *Libération*, February 5, 2004.

53 Tariq Ramadan, *Les musulmans dans la laïcité*, 2nd revised ed., Lyon, Tawhid, p. 35.

54 "Islam d'Europe: entre religion minoritaire et message universel."

55 Hassan al-Banna, *Epîtres aux jeunes* [*Letter to the Young*].

56 Tariq Ramadan cassette, "Islam et laïcité. Compréhension et dialogue [Islam and secularism: Understanding and dialogue]," part 2, recorded in Senegal in 1998, QA 18, Tawhid.

57 Tariq Ramadan cassette, "Le renouveau islamique [The Islamic revival]," QA 23, Tawhid.

58 *Ibid.*

59 T. Ramadan, "Islam d'Europe: entre religion minoritaire et message universel [European Islam: Between minority religion and universal message]," debate organized in Lyon between Tariq Ramadan and Tarek Oubrou, HC O24, Tawhid.

60 T. Ramadan, "Islam et laïcité. Compréhension et dialogue."

61 T. Ramadan, *Les musulmans d'Occident et l'avenir de l'Islam*, p. 285.

62 *Ibid.* pp. 287–88.

63 T. Ramadan, "Vivre en Occident."

64 Interview with Aziz Mouride, February 26, 2004.

65 Dounia Bouzar, *L'Islam des banlieues. Les prédicateurs musulmans: nouveaux travailleurs sociaux?*, Paris, Syros, 2001.

66 *L'une voilée, l'autre pas* [*One Wears the Veil, the Other Doesn't*], Paris, Albin Michel, 2003, served as a media springboard for Saïda Kada, a young Islamist trained by the Muslim Sisters of Lyon.

67 This French association was founded in 2001 to defend the rights of women, particularly those of North African descent, living in working-class neighborhoods, who were victims both of racism and also of virulent sexism based on tradition or religion.

68 Fadela Amara, *Ni putes ni soumises*, interviews with Sylvia Zappi, Paris, La Découverte, 2003, pp. 73–75.

69 *L'Humanité*, February 20, 2003.

70 Interview with Nadia Amiri, January 31, 2004.

71 This crime led, in February 2003, to the Marche des femmes contre les ghettos et pour l'égalité [Women's March Against Ghettoes and For Equality], which, in turn, gave birth to the movement Ni Putes Ni Soumises.

72 Farid Abdelkrim, *Na'al Bou la France?!*, preface by Ahmed al-Micherfi, La Courneuve, GEDIS, 2002.

73 Cited by *Le Monde*, February 12, 2003.

74 Internet message (February 2004, since removed) on www.oumma.com

75 *Le Monde*, November 17, 2003.

76 Interview in *Le Progrès*, October 16, 2001.

77 Interview with Christian Delorme, March 5, 2004.

Chapter six

1 The High-Level Advisory Group on the Dialogue between Peoples and Cultures, presided over by Assia Alaoui Bensalah and Jean Daniel, was assigned to submit a report concerning the Euro-Mediterranean Area. The other members were Ms. Fatima Mernissi, Ms. Simone Susskind-Weinberger, Ms. Tullia Zevi and Messrs Malek Chebel, Juan Diez Nicolas, Umberto Eco, Shmuel N. Eisenstadt, George Joffé, Ahmed Kamal Aboulmagd, Bichara Khader, Adnan Wafic Kassar, Pedrag Matvejevic, Rostane Mehdi, Tariq Ramadan, Faruk Sen, and Faouzi Skali.

2 Tariq Ramadan cassette, "Islam et Occident. Références et valeurs [Islam and the West: References and values]," part 2, lecture recorded in Abidjan, QA 15, Tawhid.

3 *Ibid.*

4 Tariq Ramadan, *Islam, le face-à-face des civilisations. Quel projet pour quelle modernité?* [*Islam: The Confrontation of Civilizations. What Sort of Plan for What sort of Modernity*?], Lyon, Tawhid, 2001.

5 Tariq Ramadan cassette, "Le renouveau islamique [The Islamic revival]," QA 23, Tawhid.

6 T. Ramadan, "Islam et Occident. Références et valeurs."

7 *Ibid.*

8 Dominique Avron, "Une réponse à 'l'Islam réformiste' de Tariq Ramadan [A reply to Tariq Ramadan's 'reformist Islam,'" *Nunc*, no. 4, October 2003.

9 T. Ramadan, "Islam et Occident. Référence et valeurs."

10 *Ibid.*

11 *Ibid.*

12 T. Ramadan, *Islam, le face-à-face des civilizations*, p. 25.

13 Jacques Jomier, "L'Islam et sa présence en Occident suivant les perspectives d'un Frère musulman [Islam's presence in the West from a Muslim Brother's perspective]," *Esprit et Vie*, 17 February 2000, p. 74.

14 T. Ramadan, "Islam et Occident. Références et valeurs."

15 Tariq Ramadan cassette, "Islam, modernité et modernisme [Islam, modernity and modernism]," TAW 07, Tawhid.

16 T. Ramadan, "Islam et Occident. Références et valeurs."

17 T. Ramadan, "Islam, modernité et modernisme."

18 *Ibid.*

19 T. Ramadan, *Islam, le face-à-face des civilisations. Quel projet pour quelle modernité*, pp. 25–26.

20 T. Ramadan, "Islam et Occident. Références et valeurs."

21 *Ibid.*

22 *Ibid.*

23 T. Ramadan, "Le renouveau islamique."

24 T. Ramadan, "Islam et Occident. Références et valeurs."

25 Tariq Ramadan cassette, "Rapports Nord-Sud."

26 T. Ramadan, "Islam et Occident. Références et valeurs."

27 *Ibid.*

28 *Ibid.*

29 Tariq Ramadan, *Peut-on vivre avec l'Islam?* [*Can One Live with Islam?*], an exchange between Tariq Ramadan and Jacques Neirynck, Lausanne, Favre, 2004, p. 124.

30 Tariq Ramadan cassette, "L'identité musulmane. Construire notre discours [The Muslim identity: Developing our discourse]," Abidjan, July 1999, QA 28, Tawhid.

31 T. Ramadan, "Rapports Nord-Sud."

32 Cited in François Dufay, "L'Islam en France. La fausse prophétie des Islamologues," *Le Point,* no. 1516, 5 October 2001.

33 T. Ramadan, "Islam et Occident. Références et valeurs."

34 Tariq Ramadan cassette, "Islam et laïcité. Compréhension et dialogue [Islam and secularism: Understanding and dialogue]," part 2, recorded in Senegal in 1998, QA 18, Tawhid.

35 T. Ramadan, "Islam et Occident. Références et valeurs."

36 T. Ramadan, "Rapports Nord-Sud."

37 In his cassette "Rapports Nord-Sud" he mentions in passing "the totalitarian deviations of a regime that does not allow for much freedom" before launching into a detailed defense of the government.

38 Interview with Jean-Yves Chaperon, March 15, 2004.

39 Interview with Luiza Toscane in *Islam. Un autre nationalisme,* Paris, L'Harmattan, 1995, p. 205.

40 T. Ramadan, "Rapports Nord-Sud."

41 T. Ramadan, *Peut-on vivre avec l'Islam?,* p. 205.

42 T. Ramadan, *Islam, le face-à-face des civilisations.*

43 T. Ramadan, "Islam et Occident. Références et valeurs."

44 Tariq Ramadan, "Les musulmans et la mondialisation [Muslims and globalization]," *Pouvoirs,* no. 104, 2003, pp. 101–02.

45 T. Ramadan, "Islam et Occident. Références et valeurs."

46 *Ibid.*

47 T. Ramadan, "Le renouveau islamique."

48 T. Ramadan, "Rapports Nord-Sud."

49 T. Ramadan, "Islam et Occident. Références et valeurs."

50 Tariq Ramadan cassette, "La question de la conversion. Nos responsabilités communes [The Question of conversions: Our common responsibility]," QA 12, Tawhid.

51 T. Ramadan, "L'identité musulmane. Construire notre discours."

52 T. Ramadan, "La question de la conversion. Nos responsabilités communes."

53 Tariq Ramadan, *Dar Ash-Shahada. L'Occident espace de témoignage* [*Dar Ash-Shahada. The West, a Land for Bearing Witness*], Lyon, Tawhid, 2002, p. 65.

54 T. Ramadan, "L'identité musulman. Construire notre discours."

55 Tariq Ramadan, "Message aux musulmans de France," cassette edited by the Ligue Nationale des Musulmans de France (2003).

56 T. Ramadan, "Le renouveau islamique."

57 T. Ramadan, "Message aux musulmans de France."

58 T. Ramadan, "Le renouveau islamique."

59 Tariq Ramadan cassette, "L'Islam. Le

face-à-face des civilisations? [Islam: The confrontation of civilizations?]," interassociation training seminar, Brussels, Mediacom.

60 T. Ramadan, "Islam et Occident. Références et valeurs."

61 This phrase was featured on the cover of *Charlie Hebdo*, no. 603, January 7, 2004, after Tariq Ramadan had taken part in the European Social Forum.

62 Cassette "Islam d'Europe: Entre religion minoritaire et message universel [European Islam: Between minority religion and universal message]," debate organized in Lyon between Tariq Ramadan and Tareq Oubrou, HC O24, Tawhid.

63 Tariq Ramadan cassette, "Les dangers de la parole. Suspicion, médisance, calomnie [The dangers of speech: Suspicion, slander, calumny]," recorded in Lyon in 1997, QA 51, Tawhid.

64 Tariq Ramadan cassette, "Les grands péchés [The major sins]," recorded in Réunion, August 1999, QA 4, Tawhid.

65 This conference was a great success; it was published in *L'Islam et les musulmans. Grandeur et decadence*, Lebanon, Al-Bouraq, 2000 [1995]. See page 67 of later edition.

66 Tariq Ramadan cassette, "La femme musulmane face à son devoir d'engagement [The Muslim woman and her duty to participate]," part 2, recorded in Abidjan (Ivory Coast), QA 22, Tawhid.

67 *Ibid.*

68 "Condamner et resister ensemble," *Le Monde*, October 3, 2001.

69 *Le Point*, April 22, 2004.

70 "Faut-il avoir peur des réseaux Islamistes à Lyon? [Should we be afraid of the Islamist networks in Lyon?]," investigative report by Lionel Favrot, Jérôme Berthaut, Mathieu Sarfati, Thomas Nardone, and Fariq Hamza, *Lyon Mag*, October 2001.

71 Alain Gresh and Tariq Ramadan, *L'Islam en questions* [*Questioning Islam*], a debate organized and presented by Françoise Germain-Robin, Sindbad, 2002, pp. 123–26.

72 *Ibid.*, pp. 89–90.

73 The "protected" status provided by Islam for those of other monotheistic religions. Even if it can be considered as tolerant for the times, their status was part of a hierarchical system that transformed non-Muslims into subcitizens, and thus falls short of the idea of equality.

74 Sura III, 20, *The Meaning of the Holy Koran*, ed. Abdullah Yusuf Ali, new ed., rev. tr., Beltsville (Md.), USA, 1989, p. 131.

75 Sura V, 60–64, *ibid.*, pp. 267–69.

76 Tariq Ramadan, *Etre musulman européen: etude des sources islamiques à la lumières du contexte européen* [*To Be a European Muslim: A Study of Islamic Sources in the Light of the European Context*], Lyon, Tawhid, 1999, p. 418.

77 Tariq Ramadan and Alain Gresh cassette "Y a-t-il un peril Islamiste? [Is there an Islamist menace?]," TAW 09, Tawhid.

78 *Ibid.*

79 T. Ramadan, "Islam et laïcité. Compréhension et dialogue," part 2.

80 T. Ramadan, "Islam, modernité et modernisme."

81 T. Ramadan, *Peut-on vivre avec Islam?*, p. 28.

82 Ibn Taymiyya, *Le statut des moines*, French translation (referring to the Tibéhirine affair) by Nasreddin Lebate-

lier [Yahya Michot], Beirut, El-Safina, 1997 [1417].

83 Yahya Michot, *Musulman en Europe* [*Muslim in Europe*], preface by Tariq Ramadan, Paris, Jeunesse sans Frontière, 2002, p. 2.

84 *Ibid.*, p. 107. In his defense, Michot argues that he is drawing a sort of absurd line of thought, for, of course, a Muslim cannot kill because the Koran forbids it.

85 Tariq Ramadan, *Les musulmans d'Occident et l'avenir de l'Islam* [*Western Muslims and the Future of Islam*], Arles, Actes Sud-Sindbad, 2003, p. 165.

86 See Marie-Rose Armesto, *Son mari a tué Massoud*, Paris, Ballard, 2002.

Chapter seven

1 Tariq Ramadan cassette, "Islam et Occident. Références et valeurs [Islam and the West: References and values]," part 2, lecture recorded in Abidjan, QA 15, Tawhid.

2 *Ibid.*

3 *Ibid.*

4 *Ibid.*

5 *Ibid.*

6 *Ibid.*

7 Colloque International des Musulmans de l'Espace Francophone, *Les musulmans francophones. Compréhension, la terminologie, le discours* [*French-speaking Muslims. Understanding, Terminology and Language*], Tawhid, 2001.

8 "Faut-il avoir peur des réseaux Islamistes à Lyon? [Should we be afraid of the Islamist networks in Lyon?]," investigative report by Lionel Favrot, Jérôme Berthaut, Mathieu Sarfati, Thomas Nardone, and Fariq Hamza, *Lyon Mag*, October 2001.

Index